Bowl, 'Bama, Bowl

BOWL, 'BAMA, BOWL

A Crimson Tide Football Tradition

by
AL BROWNING

Rutledge Hill Press
Nashville, Tennessee

To Sissie,
who believed

In memory of Thomas E. McMillan

Copyright © 1977, 1981, 1987, 1992 by Al Browning

Published in Nashville, Tennessee, by Rutledge Hill Press, Inc., 513 Third Avenue South, Nashville, Tennessee, 37210.

Photographs courtesy of the University of Alabama, *The Birmingham News,* and the *Tuscaloosa News.*

Previous editions of *Bowl 'Bama, Bowl* published by The Strode Publishers, Huntsville, Alabama, in 1977 and 1981.

Library of Congress Cataloging-in-Publication Data

Browning, Al.
   Bowl, 'Bama, bowl : a crimson tide football tradition / by Al
Browning. —4th ed.
     p.   cm.
   ISBN 1-55853-195-5 : $14.95
   1. Alabama Crimson Tide (Football team)—History. 2. University
of Alabama—Football—History. I. Title.
   GV958.A4B76 1992
   796.332'63'0975184—dc20   92-22823
                                                     CIP

Manufactured in the United States of America
   1 2 3 4 5 6 7 8—97 96 95 94 93 92

Contents

Foreword

Followers of University of Alabama football fortunes have come to expect a bowl game as part of the regular Crimson Tide schedule.

A bowl game is a reward for a successful season, and Alabama has certainly had its share, and more, of successful seasons. As a result of that success, along with exciting teams and coaches and great fan support, Alabama now goes with bowls better than Rice Krispies. The Alabama bowl record is impressive. Only once since 1959 has Alabama played a season without making a bowl appearance.

Without a doubt, the Alabama bowl record has been well-chronicled. But until now, those histories have been concerned more with statistics than with people. Al Browning now provides us with the stories about people who make the Alabama bowl story so colorful, including just the right amount of statistics and other data to make the story complete. This is a book for Alabama football fans, certainly, but it is also excellent reading for football fans in general.

Writing a foreword for this book is difficult, because it should indicate the highlights of the story. In the case of this work, every page is a highlight.

Kirk McNair
Editor
Bama Inside The Crimson Tide Magazine.

Preface

Forty-four bowl games. That is quite a number. Now, finally, the University of Alabama bowl story. It is a long-needed factual and colorful account of each of the games played by the Crimson Tide.

This book may settle some arguments—or perhaps start some—but the glory of Alabama in bowl games is required reading for its many alumni and friends who have enjoyed the games in the stands and on radio and television.

The college football bowl game is truly an American tradition and means so much to so many people. The history and records of one bowl game conjure up memories of one of the more important events in the history of a university. But forty-four bowl games, as in the number Alabama has played, is an outstanding record. *Bowl, 'Bama, Bowl* is a tribute to the great players and excellent coaches who have made the Crimson Tide tradition possible.

The enjoyment and thrills of a bowl game trip have become an important part of the college scene. From the university president to the youngest student manager, bowl games have meant something special to Alabama loyals.

This book is a very valuable addition to any library, for it tells the story of the favorable attention bowl appearances have gained for the University of Alabama and college football nationwide.

—Jeff Coleman

(Jeff Coleman, former director of alumni affairs at the University of Alabama, has attended every Crimson Tide football bowl game except the most recent one.)

Introduction

It started with roses.

It is a blockbuster tradition, from birth to present.

The road could be called Bowl Boulevard, and Alabama knows the curves, hills, and slippery spots along the way better than any other college football program. Its surface has been painted a shade of red, in Crimson Tide style, as well as in record fashion. No other program has played in or won as many post-season games.

Forty-four times Alabama has made the trip down Bowl Boulevard, including a national record twenty-five consecutive times after regular seasons from 1959 through 1983. There are solid gold memories that will be cherished long after the Crimson Tide plays its last game.

A final game? Well, almost everything ends at some juncture, but it is difficult to imagine an end to the storied history of Crimson-clad Alabama engaging in fall-time warfare and almost as hard to imagine a Christmas arriving without Crimson-clad fans talking, thinking, and boasting about another bowl appearance.

"Where are you going on your vacation this year?" one Alabama fan was overheard asking another Crimson Tide loyal in 1972.

"Oh, I guess I'll either go to Miami, New Orleans, or Dallas," the fan answered.

"My gosh, what are you planning to do, get some sun, drink whisky, or eat steak?" the questioner continued.

"I'm going to watch football," the traveler answered. "Whichever bowl Alabama goes to, I'll be there."

Similar stories abound, and each reflects brashness among Alabama followers. But the Crimson Tide record speaks for itself. Christmas comes once a year. So does an Alabama bowl invitation.

Paul "Bear" Bryant, probably the greatest college football coach of all time, guided Alabama to bowl games from 1959 through

1982. He died a month after winning his last bowl game, the 1982 Liberty Bowl, shortly after he retired as coach.

Bryant loved Alabama. He also loved the thrill of the hunt, the big game, postseason style.

"We're playing a great football team," Bryant said before Alabama opened the 1971 regular season against Southern California. "It's a big game for us, the first of twelve big ones this year. That's right, I said twelve. Alabama teams play twelve games every year."

Eleven during the regular season and No. 12 in a bowl.

Three months before Alabama was to open the 1977 regular season, Bryant leaned back in his chair in his spacious Memorial Coliseum office and explained his confident remark in 1971. He also talked about the importance of bowls to the Alabama football program and reflected on memories he has had as a Crimson Tide player and coach.

"I knew we had a team capable of earning a bowl invitation in 1971," Bryant said, "so I said so. Of course, being good enough to merit an invitation is one of our goals every year.

"Bowls are part of our tradition at Alabama and they are certainly good for our program. They give the school great exposure, they help our recruiting, and they bring in money. We paid for our stadium with bowl money and we have built many buildings on the Alabama campus with money we received for our bowl appearances.

"The players love to play in bowls and the university people favor them, so I'm for them, too."

Bryant got excited when the postseason arrived. He was accused, maybe rightfully so, of manipulating in the matchmaking process. He got Alabama in a lot of big games.

"I like 'em, but I don't have any real feelings about bowls," Bryant said. "From a personal standpoint, they mean little to me. I would rather stay at home during the holiday season and eat turkey.

"But I've always said a bowl invitation should be a reward for the players for a job well done and when they earn a bid, I'm sure not gonna stay home and keep them from playing. And we've had our share of teams which have earned the chance to represent our school in bowl games.

"We've had a couple of teams which were not bowl-caliber, yet received bowl invitations, too. That's where the tradition comes in. Tradition probably got us bids those years.

"I'm not sure Alabama has the greatest bowl tradition in the country, because I don't know anything about the other schools. But I know we have a tradition we can be extremely proud of."

Alabama football got in the bowl business in 1926 when twenty-two Crimson Tide players traveled west waving a Southern banner to defeat Washington in the Rose Bowl. Since then—through victory, defeat, and deadlock—the bowl list has grown and the stories, which seem to better with age, have become plentiful.

Movie stars have been born, faces have been bloodied, national championships have been won and lost, and through it all, Alabama football has gained national attention and respect.

Whether in the snow at Philadelphia, under balmy skies at Miami, amidst much festive fanfare at New Orleans, in frigid temperatures at Memphis, in comfortable room temperatures at Houston, or in bitter winds at Dallas, the Crimson Tide and its long list of colorful players have built a proud tradition.

As the fight song, "Yea, Alabama," says, "Remember the Rose Bowl, we'll win then . . . You're Dixie's football pride, Crimson Tide."

The Changing of the Guard

A Tribute to Paul "Bear" Bryant

Paul "Bear" Bryant appeared troubled. His twenty-fifth University of Alabama football team had been defeated by Louisiana State, 20–10, and he was not smiling when he greeted the news media in a trailer parked behind Legion Field in Birmingham.

Nor was he scowling as badly as he usually did after a defeat.

On this November afternoon in 1982, Bryant was talking seriously. Many of his longtime observers doubted his sincerity when for what seemed like the hundredth time he mentioned retiring as coach of the Crimson Tide. "The time has come for a complete review of our program, starting at the top, with me," Bryant said less than a year after becoming the winningest collegiate coach in history.

But he sounded somewhat convincing two days after his team had lost for the third time in five games to drop its record to 6–3.

"Fifteen years ago I could get them to play," said the 69-year-old Bryant after the loss to LSU. "I could've won at Vassar. I was surrounded by good people. I still am. But I can't get them to play like I used to.

"The good Lord willing, I'm going to do better. If that's not good enough, I'll ask the good Lord to let me know. I'm not a spring chicken any more. If it was fifteen years ago, I know I could do what it takes. But I'm older now, more frail, broken down, and times have changed.

"The University of Alabama has done more for me than anybody I know. There's no way I could pay back my school for what it's done for me. I've got a strong obligation to my players and staff. That's why I'm wondering if I can still give my school what it deserves.

1

"There are a lot of unhappy fans out there. I know that. I'm one of them. I'm not satisfied unless we win the national championship, like they are, and that's good. We're not in contention now. That's bad. Oh, those fans come up and say, 'Let's do it one more time, Coach Bryant, for the sake of old times.' That's nice. I know people love me. But that doesn't do any good when we're not winning games."

Bryant was talking at a predawn hour in his office at Memorial Coliseum in Tuscaloosa. He had welcomed a visitor who had sensed he was serious about retirement just after his postgame remarks in Birmingham, a person who had asked him about the notion and had looked in his eyes in disbelief after he said, "Yeah, I think the time might have come for me to hang it up, to give somebody else a chance." He had only smiled when the visitor on this morning had chastised him for talking about quitting in the middle of the fight, as he had cautioned so many of his players against, for yielding to defeat in the fourth quarter of his career.

Then Bryant dropped the bombshell. He unbuttoned a sleeve on his shirt, rolled it back and displayed an arm that was blue from poor circulation through its veins. He said, "Alfred, I haven't felt good for a while now. My heart doctor said I'll have a stroke if I don't quit coaching. That's between you and me. But that's the way it is. I'm afraid the time has come."

It was obvious at that moment that his time had come, and

With Ara Parseghian at 1973 Sugar Bowl dinner.

gone, although few people wanted to believe it. Bryant began to make preparations to leave a sport he had made much better, to quit coaching young men after turning many of them into model citizens during a spectacular career.

The champion had not lost his will to win. But the physical strength was fading.

Alabama football was about to make a change.

Bryant was about to put the wraps on a career that would end with a 323–85–17 record in thirty-eight seasons, a 232–46–9 record and twenty-four bowl game appearances in twenty-five seasons at Alabama.

Ray Perkins was the man in waiting, the chosen one, a former Crimson Tide all-star end who was coaching the New York Giants.

On November 16, the Liberty Bowl began courting Bryant and Alabama for its December 29 game in Memphis, with happy results. "We've got every indication that Alabama will come play in our game," said Tim Treadwell, the executive director of the Liberty Bowl.

On December 14, a cold and rainy day in Tuscaloosa, Bryant announced at a press conference that his 7–4 team would be his last. He made it official; he was retiring, and Perkins would pick up the torch at Alabama.

"The gloomy weather outside Memorial Coliseum that day matched the mood inside," said Steve Martin, a sportswriter who covered the press conference for *The Tuscaloosa News*.

The universally unwelcomed announcement came in a film room adjacent to the office Bryant had occupied since 1968. The press conference was attended by media members from across the nation. At a simultaneous press conference in East Rutherford, New Jersey, Perkins was announcing that he was returning to his alma mater as coach.

The changing of the guard was taking place.

It was obvious that Alabama football would be strikingly different than it had been. The man with the houndstooth hat was stepping aside.

A little more than four years later, on December 31, 1986, Crimson Tide fans would learn that the stability the program had maintained for so long under Bryant had ended when he announced his retirement. Perkins proved that nothing is forever in sports by announcing he was leaving Alabama to become coach of The Tampa Bay Bucs of the National Football League following a month of rumors to that effect. Once again the program was at a crossroad.

3

Sensing the importance of quick action, on January 3, 1987, Alabama President Dr. Joab Thomas announced that Steve Sloan, coach at Duke, was returning to Alabama as athletic director and that Bill Curry, coach at Georgia Tech, would become the new head coach.

The torch had once again been passed, stirring memories of the day Bryant had announced his retirement.

Bryant followed Alabama President Dr. Joab Thomas into the room. He was attired in a bright red sportcoat. He made small talk and announced that his statement had been prepared by his wife, Mary Harmon, the previous evening as they sat at home.

Bryant said:

There comes a time in every profession when you need to hang it up. That time has come for me as football coach at the University of Alabama.

My main purpose as athletic director and football coach at the University of Alabama has been to field the best possible teams, to improve each player as a person, and to produce citizens who will be credits to our present day society. We have been successful in most areas, but now I feel the time is right for a change in our football leadership.

We lost two big football games this season that I feel we should have won (at Tennessee and against Auburn in Birmingham). We played only four or five games like Bryant-coached teams should.

I've done a poor job of coaching. This is my school, my alma mater, and I love it. And I love the players. But in my opinion they deserve better coaching than they've been getting this year. My stepping down is an effort to ensure they get better coaching from someone else.

It has been a great joy for me personally to have had the opportunity to coach at my alma mater. I know I'll miss the coaching. But the thing I'll miss the most is the association with the players, the coaches, the administration and the competition, all of those things that have made such a strong tradition at Alabama.

I plan to continue as athletic director. I pledge my support to my successor in every respect, particularly in recruiting.

I'm thankful to have had the support of every president I've worked for at Alabama, including our present president, Dr. Joab Thomas, whom I would like to present to you now."

4

Bryant sat down.

Thomas approached the podium.

The president said, "I've discussed this possibility with Coach Bryant for the past year or year and a half. On most occasions, I've been able to talk him out of retiring. My preference would be for him to coach here for the next ten years. But this time Coach Bryant was firm in his decision to step down.

"Coach Bryant is a legend in his own time. He's an institution in himself. He's the best football coach Alabama has ever had and the best this nation has ever had. He has been replicated many times, but we know there never has been an exact replica.

"Never has one coach done so much for so many."

Later in his office, during a private seating, Bryant said, "I'm a tired old man. But I'll never get tired of football or the opportunity to be associated with the people I have been associated with and I am associated with at present. It's just time, that's all."

Bryant admitted he made a suggestion, but not a strong recommendation, when his successor was selected. He pointed out, "No Alabama football fan could ever forget Ray Perkins, how he played on two national championship teams (in 1964 and 1965) and another one (in 1966) that should have made it three national championships in a row."

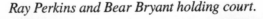

Ray Perkins and Bear Bryant holding court.

Bryant contacted Perkins on a Wednesday night. Thomas talked to him the next morning. A Sunday morning interview was arranged, and the new coach accepted the offer the next morning.

"There wasn't a decision to make," Perkins said the morning his appointment as Alabama coach was announced. "It's something I've dreamed about. It's the happiest moment in my life."

Perkins signed a five-year contract for $100,000 annually, plus numerous fringe benefits. His pay was for the filling of big shoes.

"I'm following, repeat following, the greatest football coach in history," Perkins said. "It's a great honor to go there. If I was scared or intimidated, I wouldn't take the job. You'd have to be a little crazy to do that. I admire the man I'm following.

"Yes, I love Coach Bryant.

"Yes, I admire him.

"No, I'm not intimidated by him.

"Let me put it this way. I'm not following in his footsteps because his are shoes that'll never be filled. I'm merely following the man. I'm just the next man, that's all, and I hope I can carry on the tradition he has established at Alabama.

"There's nothing more to be accomplished at Alabama than that which has already been established. I just hope to sustain it.

"Nobody will ever come close to matching what Coach Bryant has established at Alabama.

"I look at this as a chance of a lifetime. It was an easy decision to reach. I'm more excited than I've been in my life."

Thomas called Perkins "another coach who heard mother call and graciously accepted."

People in Tuscaloosa, as well as in other cities across the nation, reacted to the resignation with universal surprise. It was as if most observers thought the time would never come for Bryant to leave football.

"I'm shocked," said Clem Gryska, who had coached with Bryant twenty-three years. "I knew the time would come someday, but I knew I'd never be completely prepared for it."

"It's sad," said Sam Bailey, who had coached with and worked as a top administrative aide alongside Bryant for almost three decades. "He just couldn't take the pressure and the stress any more."

"It's an unselfish decision on his part," said Charley Thornton, who had worked with Bryant through most of his tenure at Alabama. "Few people who had achieved the pinnacle of success personally would make such a decision based on what's good for the school and its football program. But that's what Coach Bryant has done. That's typical of the man."

Bryant told his players about his decision to retire at an early morning team meeting the day he told the world about it.

"It won't seem the same at Alabama without Coach Bryant, not today, not forever," said Gary Bramblett, a Crimson Tide offensive lineman.

"He's the John Wayne of the football world," said New Orleans Saints coach Bum Phillips.

"It ain't gonna be the same without Coach Bryant, not at Alabama, not in football anywhere," said Grambling coach Eddie Robinson, who would in 1985 become the winningest coach in history, controversially supplanting Bryant because many of his wins came over teams from smaller programs.

The reverence was apparent.

People knew Bryant, a former farmboy from Fordyce, Arkansas, had bled for Alabama. When he died less than a month after his final game, a 21–16 victory over Illinois in the Liberty Bowl, people knew he had given his life for his alma mater, played his game to the hilt, as he so often commanded his players to do on the football field. When he announced he would stay on as athletic director to ensure a smooth transition into the Perkins era, people knew he was helping to construct a bridge for a young man, with the light of his life making the path much easier to navigate.

On December 19, at his pre-Liberty Bowl press conference in Tuscaloosa, Bryant shared the spotlight with Perkins. He said, "I don't know what it'll be like next year, after I'm gone, but I'll probably be off fishing some place and hearing about Alabama winning a lot of football games. I'm sure Ray will do a great job. I'm sure Alabama football is in good hands. That'll make retirement easier.

"I'll be resting while other people are working and sweating."

Bryant never got to enjoy his retirement.

But he did have time to thank the good Lord for his success and his former players and associates for their contributions to his greatness. Two days after he announced his retirement, Bryant began writing personal letters to many of the people who had helped him produce such an astonishing record, including a greeting of gratitude mailed to former Alabama end Dennis Homan.

"It was gripping to receive the letter," said Homan. "It showed how little he thought about himself and how much he thought about the people who played for him and coached under him. It showed a side of the man I wish everybody had been able to know. Fortunately, I was able to enjoy an association with the greatest coach, the greatest man, who ever lived."

The letter Bryant sent to Homan, as well as those sent to hun-

7

dreds of his other players and associates, did indicate a lot about the unselfish way the coach went about putting together teams and stringing together victories.

It read:

> As I contemplate my many years as a football coach during the postretirement period, it is not surprising that my former players and my former associates are the first people who come to mind. Since you are one of those people, I want to personally thank you for the contributions you have made to my happy and rewarding career.

> Also, I want to tell you how proud I am of you, and I want to challenge you to become an even bigger winner in life.

> Frankly, I am sometimes embarrassed by the accolades that have been given me. Never is enough said about the people who have worked so hard for me, individuals like you. I will always count you as a member of my football family and I eagerly await the construction of a museum being constructed in your honor on the campus of the University of Alabama.

> Again, thanks, and may all of your future days prove successful.

> Mary Harmon sends her love.

So comes to mind the story about "The Old Man and the Bridge." It tells about an elderly man who for many years had crossed a river as he went about his daily business. One day he crossed the river, returned to the other side, and began building a bridge. Seeing this, several younger men ran to his side and asked, "Sir, why are you building this bridge when you know you will not pass this way again?"

The elderly man looked at the younger men and said, "Because I want to make the path easier for people who will have to negotiate it after I am gone."

Paul William Bryant understood the meaning of that prose.

Walter Ray Perkins, who continued a marvelous tradition of taking Alabama football teams to bowl games, after starring in three for the Crimson Tide, also understood the meaning.

But Perkins never captured the hearts of Alabama fans.

Nor did the next coach, Bill Curry, who suffered with more serious bouts of unpopularity.

Now, however, the Crimson Tide has found renewed stability under the leadership of Gene Stallings, who is, in reality, the man Paul "Bear" Bryant favored as his successor.

Mary Harmon and Paul Bryant.

1926 Rose Bowl Game

Alabama 20   Washington 19

Oh the crimson of each sunset
And the glowing pink of dawn,
Royal colors of the roses
Holding court upon the lawn.
Oh the joy, the smiles, the fragrance
Of a land that knows no gloom,
Just a peaceful sun-kissed heaven
When the roses are in bloom.

—Francesca Falk Miller

How sweet the smell, how wonderful the memories....

Luny Smith and Hoyt (Wu) Winslett looked at each other with curious expressions on their faces as bystanders at the *Tuscaloosa News* smiled on the gentlemen who had accidentally been reunited.

"Hoyt, how in the world are you?" Smith asked as Winslett stopped in front of him. "You know who I am?"

"Your face looks familiar," Winslett answered with a voice which indicated puzzlement.

Smith pulled his checkbook from his overcoat pocket, opened it, and handed it to Winslett.

"Luny, I be doggone!" Winslett said as he quickly reached to shake hands with Smith. "It has been ages since I saw you last."

It had been almost 50 years since Smith and Winslett had

11

last seen each other as students at the University of Alabama, but the memories they shared on that October morning in 1975 seemed to bridge the time. They had a common bond to gaze upon, a piece of Alabama football history to reflect upon, and the first day of 1926 to rehash in a sudden blaze of glory.

Smith and Winslett, though their roles were different, were parts of the 1926 Rose Bowl team Alabama sent west to defeat powerful Washington, 20-19. It was the first bowl trip for the Crimson Tide, one which allowed Alabama to remove the cloak of inferiority which had blanketed Southern football.

Making the historic trip—although an invitation almost never came—was honor enough for Alabama. Winning the game—also hard to come by—was the first spark in a blazing tradition the Crimson Tide continues to enjoy.

Smith, now a retired educator in Citronelle, Alabama, who gained fame in college as the "One-Man Track Team from Alabama," accompanied the Crimson Tide on the Rose Bowl trip as a team manager and newspaper reporter. He served as an Alabama messenger in Pasadena, California, and sent back reports to newspapers in the South.

Winslett, now known as "Mr. Wu" in his hometown of Tuscaloosa, Alabama, was an end on the first-ever Alabama bowl team. He gained glory as a passing end for the Crimson Tide and played one of his finest games in the victory over Washington.

Regardless of the duties Smith and Winslett had on the trip to Pasadena, they both remember the game in the same manner as almost everyone—as the explosive debut of Southern football for fans around the nation, as one of the most stunning upsets in bowl history, and as the start of a tremendous Crimson Tide tradition.

"It was wild out there," Smith said, "because nobody knew what to expect from a team from the Deep South. The bettors were running from hotel to hotel trying to find out something about Alabama, but they rarely found us because we were stuck in some out-of-the-way hotel outside of town.

"Washington stayed with the bettors, however—right down there in the action—and when they saw how big those Huskies were, the bettors figured they would murder us. At one time, they were picking Washington to win by as much as 51 points."

Smith may have been overzealous in his analysis of the pregame point spread, but most accounts state that Alabama was a two-touchdown underdog one week before the game. The spread was reduced to almost nothing by kickoff time, however.

Winslett, who enrolled at Alabama after a glittering high school career in Dadeville ("the heart of Auburn country," he calls it), remembers the underdog billing, too, but insists Southern Conference champion Alabama paid little attention to the oddsmakers.

"We were too excited about getting to play in the Rose Bowl to pay attention to the bettors," Winslett said. "We kind of took it in stride and tried to look at it as just another game.

"After all, we were the Southern Conference champions and we had been in tough games. But we were underdogs, because there was only one writer on the coast who gave us much of a chance to win.

"We respected Washington, but we were not scared of them. We went to Pasadena to win. We felt an enormous responsibility to our state and to the Southern Conference."

Perhaps Alabama head coach Wallace Wade, who guided the Crimson Tide to a 61-13-3 record from 1923-30, accurately described the heartbeat of his squad of 22 players when he spoke one line at a 1926 Rose Bowl reunion at Tuscaloosa in 1975.

"We were the South's baby," Wade said.

Alabama was the South's baby strictly from the standpoint of representation, for Wade had molded the Crimson Tide into a legitimate football power. National wire reports hailed Alabama as one of four super teams in the country, with Eastern champion Colgate, Southern Conference peer Tulane, and mighty Washington the others.

Alabama and Tulane made it through the 1925 regular season unbeaten and the Crimson Tide was declared champion of the 22-team Southern Conference by writers covering the league. The forward pass, which Alabama refined after it was master-minded by Notre Dame, and a crunching defense were the major forces behind the Crimson Tide's success.

Only one team, Birmingham-Southern, scored on Alabama during the 1925 regular season, with the Crimson Tide defeating its state rival, 50-7, in the second game of the season. In the opener, Alabama whipped Union, 53-0. The other seven Crimson Tide victories came at the expense of Louisiana State (42-0), Sewanee (27-0), Georgia Tech (7-0), Mississippi A&M (6-0), Kentucky (31-0), Florida (34-0), and Georgia (27-0).

The victory over Georgia Tech was the most difficult to

13

The first great coach, Wallace Wade.

secure, the Crimson Tide scoring its touchdown on a 55-yard punt return by Johnny Mack Brown. Pooley Hubert amazed 20,000 fans in Atlanta by knocking down two Georgia Tech players on the game-winning run. The Crimson Tide knocked down all 11 Georgia Tech defenders—and the referee—on the play.

Brown, the brilliant running back who used the Rose Bowl trip to launch an acting career as a Saturday afternoon cowboy movie hero, and Hubert, the quarterback who dismantled the Washington defense with a sparkling second-half performance, were the leaders of an awesome Alabama offense.

But talent was deep throughout the Crimson Tide roster in 1925. Zipp Newman, an outstanding sportswriter covering football in those days, predicted a successful Alabama season before preseason practice got under way.

"Alabama will have the greatest collection of smart running backs in the South," Newman wrote in his *Birmingham News* column. "Alabama will have the class of Southern backfields with Mack Brown, brilliant broken field runner; Pooley Hubert, one of the greatest all-around backs in America; Grant Gillis, a cool and steady punter; Red Barnes, punter and broken field runner; Jimmy Johnston, a linebacker; and Red Pepper, a 200-pound fullback; and Little David Rosenfield, Herschel Caldwell. and Red Brown, the flashy brother of Mack; and Harry Holder, Bill Morrison, and Dick Hammer. Here is a collection of backs that do everything backs are supposed to do and do it well. Wade could shut his eyes and pick a good combination of backs from this collection."

Guard Bill Buckler, an All-Southern Conference selection in 1924; guard Bruce Jones, who was named team captain; tackle Pete Camp; and ends Ben Hudson and Winslett were the top names in an impressive line.

For various reasons, some of the players lauded by Newman in his preseason analysis were not in the Alabama traveling party when the team left for Pasadena by train on December 19. The 22 players making the trip were Brown, Hubert, Gillis, Barnes, Johnston, Rosenfield, Caldwell, Red Brown, Morrison, Buckler, Jones, Camp, Hudson, Winslett, Claude Perry, Fred Pickhard, Sherlock Holmes, Ben Enis, Leslie Payne, James Bowdoin, James McDonald, and H. S. Dismukes.

Much fanfare accompanied the departure of the team, including eloquent remarks from Dr. George Denny, the universi-

Multi-talented Johnny Mack Brown.

ty president. Denny also took time during his speech to suggest the players take their books and devote some time to study since midterm exams were forthcoming.

"Win or lose, this trip means more widespread and sustained publicity for Alabama than any recent event in the history of the state," Denny said.

So Alabama was off in search of fame and fortune in the Rose Bowl and to this day, few people realize how close the Crimson Tide came to staying home that year. The Rose Bowl—the only bowl game at that time—almost became known as the 1926 No-Go Bowl.

Washington, the natural host for the game, balked at an invitation first. A vote among Huskies indicated they were not going to a bowl, despite being called "the finest team ever" by Coach Andy Smith of California.

Then there was the question of whom the Rose Bowl would invite from the East or the South. Alabama? Tulane? Colgate?

An Associated Press wire report said, "For a while it looked as though Colgate would go, but objections to making the trip appear to have developed among parties of influence among the alumni." The story said Dartmouth and Princeton were approached, too, and declined to consider the transcontinental trip. "As the situation now stands, it would look as though the choice lies between Tulane and Alabama."

In selecting Alabama, Jack Benefield of the Rose Bowl said, "This is the first invitation that has been offered by anyone. I did take the matter up with Colgate authorities, but their request for time to consider was out of the question. Tulane, nor any other college, has not been offered an invitation as only feelers have been sent out."

Earlier that week, Alabama coach Wade had said the Rose Bowl was peddling the proposition among various institutions and Alabama would not be interested in the game.

Obviously the Rose Bowl did not take the Alabama vow for declination seriously, because an official invitation was made. Alabama, apparently soothed, accepted.

But what about Washington? Well, the Huskies had changes of heart, and through a newspaper report the Rose Bowl first learned of its scalding matchup—after a lukewarm beginning.

The Washington acceptance said, "In light of an urgent request from the Pacific Coast Conference, the Northwest Huskies agree to reverse their decision and battle in the classic game of the year on January 1."

It was a classic game and the impact it has had on Alabama football cannot be measured. But to Crimson Tide players, it was more than a football game. It was a treat.

"I came from Horseshoe Bend over on the Tallapoosa River near Dadeville," Winslett said while looking back almost half a century, "so you can imagine what an old country boy thought about it out there."

It cost $250 for a round-trip ticket to the Rose Bowl in

1926, but several carloads of Alabama fans joined the squad for the 2,800-mile trip to Pasadena. Among the crowd was Bob McDavid, president of the Birmingham Alumni Association. He startled fellow passengers when he awoke from a nap screaming, "Hooray for Johnny Mack!"

The trip lasted almost six days, the team arriving in Pasadena on Christmas Eve. Several stops were made along the way, including one at the Grand Canyon—for educational purposes—and another in Williams, Arizona, for a practice session.

"It took a long time to get there," said Camp, a standout tackle at Alabama and now a successful physician in Jasper, Alabama. "We were unable to eat in the dining car, so we stopped along the way at the Harvey Houses.

"And we would stop ever so often, get off the train, throw the ball around, and take exercises. There was no time to think about getting tired."

Alabama players were showered with invitations in Pasadena. "It would require two months to fill all the invitations," Newman wrote in the *Birmingham News.*

As it worked out, pleasure lasted a much shorter time, because Coach Wade halted all non-football activity on December 28. "In order to get in the right mental attitude, no more entertainment will be indulged in after Monday," Wade told the team.

Kickoff was drawing near and Wade, a man Winslett described as "very thorough and very tough," was taking the first step in final preparations with an Alabama team which would face George (Wildcat) Wilson, who had been labeled the best player in America, and his Washington teammates.

Wilson, a hard-driving runner, turned down a then-incredible sum of $3,000 to become a professional shortly after Alabama accepted the Rose Bowl invitation.

"He passed up the handsome offer in order to test his line-crashing power against the pride of the South," a newspaper report explained.

Talk concerning Wilson and Washington superiority put fire in the eyes of Alabama players after they arrived in Pasadena. As Crimson Tide running back Brown said, "Superman, my eye; Wilson is only one guy, isn't he?"

But the talk continued in the Alabama dressing room before the game, where Wade instructed quarterback Hubert— whom the Crimson Tide coach called "my coach on the field."

"Run the game any way you want, Pooley," Wade told the Alabama leader, "but don't run the ball yourself or they'll kill you. Remember, those Washington players once knocked out Ernie Nevers (an All-American running back at Stanford)."

"A very thorough and very tough" Coach Wallace Wade.

Hubert followed instructions and by halftime Washington had a 12-0 lead. The crowd of 45,000 gave Alabama a polite ovation as the Crimson Tide ran to the dressing room at halftime, fairly convinced the West Coast Huskies were on their way to a cakewalk victory.

Wilson had lived up to his billing in the first half and finished the game with commendable statistics—134 yards rushing and five pass completions for 77 yards and two touchdowns. But the Washington star missed the third quarter due to injury and Alabama capitalized by scoring all of its 20 points during a seven-minute span.

Winslett is credited with sidelining Wilson. How the injury came about is a source of debate.

"I tell you one thing," said manager and sportswriter Smith, "Hoyt won that game for Alabama. He put Wilson out of the game by kneeing him in the throat."

"I ran a reverse at Wilson," Winslett said, "and they say he didn't get up. But I don't want to talk about that...too much egotistical slant."

Although it trailed by 12 points at halftime, Alabama had showed some spark late in the first half, driving to the Washington 22-yard line as the clock ran out. The Crimson Tide continued its assault early in the second half when Hubert got in the offensive action.

Hubert ran 27 yards after a Washington punt, then ran four straight times for a touchdown. Buckler kicked the extra point and Alabama trailed, 12-7.

Alabama struck again quickly, Gillis passing 63 yards to Brown for a touchdown and a Crimson Tide lead. Brown caught the ball on the Washington 25 yard line.

"All I had to do was sidestep one man and I was across," Brown said.

Buckler again kicked the extra point.

A fumble gave Alabama another chance to score, Enis recovering the ball at the Washington 33 yard line. On first down, Hubert told Brown to run as fast as he could for the goal.

"When I reached the three, I looked," Brown said about the pass play. "Sure enough, the ball was coming down over my shoulder. I took it in stride, used my stiff arm on one man, and went over carrying somebody. The place was really in an uproar."

Buckler missed the extra-point attempt and Washington

Johnny Mack Brown, super runner to super actor.

scored another touchdown in the fourth quarter. But an amazing comeback was in the record books.

The Alabama mission had been completed. The eyes of the
nation were glued on Southern football.

"The Rose Bowl's greatest game," is the way Maxwell
Stiles described the Alabama victory in his historical book on
the New Year's Day extravaganza. "One of football's most sav-
age counter-attacks to storm the heights of victory in the face
of what seemed certain and overwhelming defeat. One of the
most magnificent one-man stands since Horatius held the

bridge. This game was all of these."

Yes, Alabama was suddenly in the football spotlight with the names Hubert and Brown becoming wholesale around the country and almost all of the other 20 names easily recognized in Crimson Tide country.

"Seldom have the spectators at these annual New Year's Day struggles been privileged to see the performances of such marvelous individuals as George Wilson and Pooley Hubert," wrote Paul Lowry in his *Los Angeles Times* game story. "Nobody made a mistake in naming Wilson an All-American, but how in the world they overlooked Hubert on the first team is a mystery."

To which Hubert says, "It was quite a surprise that we even had the opportunity to go to the Rose Bowl. We had some indication that we might get to, but we were afraid to even hope.

"It was a right pleasant trip going out there, but coming home was the best part about it, because we had been out there representing the South.

"We never thought about losing."

Times have changed little at Alabama....

1927 Rose Bowl Game

Alabama 7   Stanford 7

One New Year's Day, nineteen twenty-seven
Alabama's Crimson Tide met Stanford's eleven,
Having journeyed far away from their goal
To the Pacific Coast, California's Rose Bowl.

In the city of Pasadena this feat was held
In the presence of some sixty-thousand fans,
Who witnessed the battle between these teams
For athletic honors, the laurel wreath.

In the first quarter of play
Stanford's men carried the day,
And a mighty bout was rendered to heaven
As the score stood Alabama zero, Stanford seven.

In the next quarter of the affray
Neither team could gain, but battled away,
Until this period ended the first half of play
With Alabama defeated, Stanford carrying the day.

The Californians were happy in the knowledge
That all was well with their Stanford College,
But Alabama was still in the fray
For there was another half to play.

With determination the South once more
Met the West out on the Pacific shore,

23

And held Stanford's husky line
To another scoreless period of time.

But in the last quarter of play
It looked as if Stanford had won the day,
But Southern pride began to soar
And the Crimson Tide made her score.

Right in the last minute of play
Winslett and Johnson saved the day,
And the fans were held spell bound
At the valour of the boys from a Southern town.

So the score stands seven-to-seven
With Alabama's Crimson Tide and Stanford's eleven,
To the world proclaiming from North to South; from sea to sea
The prestige of Alabama's great University.

—J. H. Cooper

An outstanding poet, 'tis said, has the ability to see things not easily seen by non-poetic individuals. J. H. Cooper, the originator of the preceding verse, cannot be considered outstanding.

Cooper, a University of Alabama football fan in 1926, composed his poem for the *Tuscaloosa News* in early January 1927. The verse appeared in print six days after Alabama and Stanford battled to a 7-7 tie in the 1927 Rose Bowl game.

Flair withstanding, Cooper must be given credit. His poem hit the nail on the head. It got the point across, for Alabama's second bowl appearance was a delight to Crimson Tide fans—a game Southern loyals viewed with pride and honor.

Present Alabama head coach Paul (Bear) Bryant once said, "A tie is like kissing your sister." But tying mighty Stanford was much more rewarding to Crimson Tide fans.

The come-from-behind tie pushed the Crimson Tide another step in boastful spotlights, wrote another chapter in the book, *Southern Football Shall Rise Again*, and gave fans another reason to celebrate the success of Alabama.

Having made its glowing bowl debut by defeating Washington in the Rose Bowl a year earlier, the 1926 Crimson Tide team was saddled with the responsibility of proving the stunning 20-19 victory was no fluke. On New Year's Day 1927, be-

*"A tie is like kissing your sister," says Coach
Paul (Bear) Bryant.*

fore a record Rose Bowl crowd of 57,417, unbeaten Alabama
ended all doubt by earning its deadlock with unbeaten—and
thought to be unbeatable—Stanford.

"We regarded the contest with Stanford as just another
game," said Leslie Payne, a center on the 1927 Rose Bowl team,
"but every Alabama player had in his own mind that we were
representing a lot of people in the South. There was more than
a handful of people counting on us to do well.

"We had a job to do when we went to play Stanford and I
think we did it well."

Payne, a retired businessman in the New Orleans area who
was nicknamed "Misery" by teammates at Alabama, probably
enjoyed the Rose Bowl trip more than most Crimson Tide players, for it paid dividends on a gamble he made before his freshman season. An outstanding high school player in Bay Minette,
Alabama, he became a Crimson Tide player in a most unusual
way.

"When I got out of high school," Payne remembered, "Alabama did not offer me a scholarship. I only weighed 185 pounds and Coach Wallace Wade was looking for guards and tackles who weighed at least 200. So I signed with Georgia Tech and reported to Atlanta on July 1.

"At that time, the *Birmingham News* gave a scholarship to state schools and I had applied for the one to Alabama, but I didn't figure on getting it.

"Well, I was in Atlanta working this job Georgia Tech had gotten for me when I got a telegram from a lawyer in Bay Minette. He said the *Birmingham News* was going to offer me the scholarship to Alabama, but they wanted to know if I'd accept it. I told them to give it to somebody else, because I was happy at Tech.

"The next day I received another telegram saying I had been awarded the scholarship and for me to be in Tuscaloosa the next day to sign up. They also said $50 would be waiting for me there.

"I thought about it, then slipped off in the middle of the night. I never went back to Georgia Tech and as things worked out, I'm proud I made that decision."

Payne was not considered a star on Alabama teams in 1925, 1926, and 1927, but on a squad which numbered 32 in 1926 he was valuable as a utility player. In terms of today, he would have been considered a "super-sub" capable of playing a

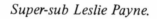

Super-sub Leslie Payne.

number of positions.

"I had a good memory, so Coach Wade used me to carry in plays and messages," Payne said. "In those days a coach might change the game plan eight or nine times during a contest and I was the man who would carry the changes from the bench."

Payne was a guard and tackle most of his Alabama career, but midseason despair led to his becoming the starting center during the 1926 campaign. Sherlock Holmes and Jim Smith were the Crimson Tide centers, but both were sidelined— Holmes by injury and Smith by his own choice.

"Holmes broke a bone in his foot during a game at Birmingham," Payne said, "but we didn't worry because we had Smith to take his place. Well, Smith did a good job in that game and when we got back to Tuscaloosa we thought everything was okay.

"But the next day I got a telephone call from Coach Wade and he sounded frantic. I thought I was getting kicked off the team, but he said, 'Congratulations, Payne, you are the first-team center at Alabama.'

"It seems Smith was a little worried about being a regular so he packed up and left town. We never heard another word from him and to this day I don't know what happened to that boy."

Holmes returned to the Alabama lineup a couple of games later, thus demoting Payne back to reserve status, but "Misery" had earned his spot on the Rose Bowl traveling squad.

Alabama had already earned its invitation back to the Rose Bowl, because the selection committee told Coach Wade the Crimson Tide could return to defend its championship if it had an outstanding 1926 regular season.

Alabama delivered, winning all nine games, its third consecutive Southern Conference championship, and its second consecutive Helms Award, given to the national champion.

The success enjoyed by Alabama during the 1926 regular season was surprising since the Rose Bowl championship team from the year before had been loaded with graduating seniors. Nobody was more surprised by the outstanding season than Wade, who was not optimistic in his preseason analysis of the team he would coach.

"The University of Alabama football team has been defeated by a Southern Conference team only once during the past three years," Wade said before practice started. "This record has been made through the good fortune of having a large part of the team remaining intact for three straight years. As a result of these men staying together for a long while and a rather intensive spring practice campaign, the Alabama team developed unusual versatility and ability. The outstanding strength of the team lay in good blocking, excellent defensive line strength, accurate forward passing, good open field running, and defensive generalship.

"The interesting question is how the 1926 team is going to compare with that of 1925. Through the loss by graduation of three all-Southern backs—Hubert, Brown, and Gillis—the men who contributed the generalship, forward passing, and open field running, it will become necessary to develop an almost entirely new offense....

"Alabama has undoubtedly lost a large part of its football team and has no players as experienced and as skillful with which to replace the losses. The most encouraging aspect of the situation is the fact that a great deal of progress toward rebuilding was made during the Spring practice period....

"The prospects are that Alabama will have a good team, probably almost as good as any team in the South. But the prospects of Alabama winning another Southern Conference championship are very slim."

Alabama promptly went out and won another conference championship, opening the season with a 54-0 win over Millsaps and ending it with a 33-6 win over Georgia. In between, the Crimson Tide defeated Vanderbilt (19-7), Mississippi A&M (26-7), Georgia Tech (21-0), Sewanee (2-0), Louisiana State (24-0), Kentucky (14-0), and Florida (49-0).

The Sewanee victory, the toughest one of the season, was insured when Alabama blocked a punt and it rolled out of the end zone for a safety in the last minute of the contest.

"I suspect our 1925 team was a little better than the 1926 team," said Hoyt (Wu) Winslett, an All-American end in 1926 and one of the heroes in the standoff with Stanford. "But we had some grit about us in 1926."

What the 1926 Alabama team lacked in talent, it made up for in poise. Players from the first Rose Bowl team admitted awe as they boarded the train which took them to Pasadena. The 1926 team, on the other hand, took the trip in style.

"We knew what the bowl business was all about when we made the return trip to Pasadena," said Payne. "We were full of confidence, not overconfident, just knowing what we had to do.

"More than anything else, the trip meant fellowship for me, the chance to talk to people I wouldn't have gotten to chat with otherwise. I particularly enjoyed talking with Dr. George Denny. He was our school president, but I doubt I would have ever gotten the chance to talk with him had it not been for our trip. And of course we got to see the so-called royalty in California, you know, the big stars and everybody.

"We just took it easy on the way out there. We talked, laughed, and played cards."

The best poker player on the team? "Well, I did pretty well," Payne said, "but nobody ever won more than 50 or 75 cents in a day."

Several carloads of Alabama fans accompanied the team on the trip. One fan from Tuscaloosa sent letters back to the newspaper.

"There are two parties here in California," the first letter said, "the principal party consisting of the team, Coach Wade, and his close associates and us fans who call ourselves The Wrecking Crew. The team is staying in Pasadena, while we are holding complete sway at the Hotel Rosslyn in Los Angeles."

The Wrecking Crew reported twice in the *Tuscaloosa News*—once on December 27, then again on January 4. The last letter was written on January 1 as fans headed to the famed Tournament Of Roses Parade.

"Tickets to the parade are $5," the writer said, "so I guess we'll have to climb a telephone pole or a palm tree. The trees here are almost as big as the oaks we have back home."

The parade itself was history-making, for Czechoslovakia was the first nation to enter a float. Each float portrayed some famous song with the Beverly Hills entry, "Sitting on Top of the World," winning competition.

Newspaper reports said that the sight of girls' legs proved shocking to some spectators. The biggest of pregame shocks did not come at the sight of skin, however. It came when Stanford players showed up at practice wearing red silk pants.

Stanford was the betting favorite in the game, but Indians head coach Pop Warner decided to dress his team in silk pants because he figured his players would be faster, thus overcoming Alabama's apparent overall speed.

Speed was not the only plus Alabama had entering the game. The Crimson Tide was also benefiting from psychological uplifts as writers, fans, and some Stanford players continuously talked about West Coast superiority.

Former Stanford standout Ernie Nevers said two touchdowns would be the least possible winning margin for the Indians. One writer said Stanford "has no parallel in coast history." Another said the home team "has made a lot of us believe that no team that ever played could beat it."

Alabama players became outraged by the remarks.

"I'm going to get me a pair of those red silk pants for a souvenir," said Alabama's Fred Pickhard.

"Swan will have plenty of time to get acquainted with us on New Year's Day," said the Crimson Tide's Lovely Barnes, after Stanford's captain paid pregame respects to Coach Wade but refused to meet Alabama players.

Thus the stage was set for another Rose Bowl game, one which was so attractive that tickets were being sold for $50 per pair, unheard-of prices in that time.

Whether the game was worth the money merits argument. One writer labeled it "frowsy football" while others walked away shaking their heads in dismay, wondering how the Rose Bowl managed to match teams so talented.

Stanford scored its touchdown late in the first quarter when George Bogue passed 5 yards to end Ed Walker, who ran the remaining 15 yards for the score. Bogue kicked the extra point and that ended scoring until Alabama pulled off a late-game rally to escape with the tie.

Only four minutes remained in the game when Alabama's Babe Pearce clawed his way through the line and blocked a Stanford punt. The ball was recovered by the Indians on their 14 yard line, but the Crimson Tide took over on downs.

Jimmy Johnson, who had missed much of the season with a dislocated shoulder, entered the game for Alabama at halfback and he and Winslett provided the spark which led to a Crimson Tide touchdown.

Winslett gained three yards on the first play, Johnson seven on the second. Winslett gained three more to the one yard line; then Johnson bulled into the end zone for the touchdown.

In postgame remarks, Lovely Barnes said, "Jimmy Johnson gave the team strength to rally. He could still be running and only the Pacific Ocean could stop him."

To which Johnson said, "It was the line which opened up a hole as large as a wagon track and it only remained for me to run through that hole."

Regardless of who was most responsible for the touchdown, it cut the Stanford lead to only 7-6. A bit of trickery—Alabama's now-famous "Signals-Off Play"—allowed the Crimson Tide to tie the game.

When the teams lined up for Herschel (Rosy) Caldwell to attempt the extra point, Stanford was set for an all-out rush in an attempt to block the kick. Suddenly Barnes, who was calling signals, screamed "signals off" and Stanford players stood at ease in anticipation of new signals. As the Indians relaxed, Holmes snapped the ball to Winslett, who was holding for the kick, and Caldwell, under no pressure, kicked the ball through the uprights.

"Herschel was cool as a cucumber," Winslett said about the play. "As we lined up, I said, 'Well, old boy, right through the middle.'

"I think Coach Wade had thought up the play. That was the only time we used it."

All told, Alabama was fortunate to get out of Pasadena with a tie. Stanford gained 350 yards, Alabama 117. Stanford had 12 first downs, Alabama 6.

But all that remains from that hot afternoon under a brilliant California sun is an Alabama—Stanford deadlock and memories nourished by a complimentary press and proud Southerners who greeted the home-traveling Crimson Tide like it had just won a world war.

"Alabama's Crimson Tide, the pride of Southern gridiron, battled long and without effect at the Stanford dyke until with four minutes of the end of play here today, then rolled into brilliancy at a lucky break and tied Palo Alto's chances of victory into a hopeless knot with a 7-to-7 tally," the Associated Press game account said in newspapers across the country January 2.

"Twice in two successive New Year's Day appearances in the Rose Bowl, the lads from the South have risen to real heights, last year to win from Washington and this year to hold the mighty Cardinals, bosses of the Pacific Coast Conference, to an even break."

The *Tuscaloosa News* apparently had trouble accepting the fact that Alabama had been tied. An editorial in its January 3 edition said, "...While on the subject of the Crimson Tide, it can still be figured that Alabama is still one point ahead of the Pacific Coast—The total number of points registered against that conference is 27; 20 in the Washington game and 7 in the Stanford game, while Washington registered 19 points and Stanford 7 making a total of 26.

"And Washington whipped Nebraska, which whipped New York University, which whipped a flock of strong Eastern teams, and Stanford decisively whipped Washington and Alabama tied Stanford. Get out your tablet and figure out how Alabama stands in the football world."

The day after the game, it was announced in the *Tuscaloosa News* that local businessman Fred Neilson would be in charge of the celebration and parade when the team returned from Pasadena. Merchants were asked to close their businesses, money was solicited to cover arrangements, and a general committee was formed to decorate Tuscaloosa.

That same edition, the paper carried the sad news that Judge James J. Masfield, former Supreme Court justice in Alabama, had died in Montgomery while listening to radio accounts of the game.

A movie advertisement in the paper announced that the first film of the Rose Bowl game would be shown January 8 at the Belvedere Theatre in Tuscaloosa, sharing top billing with a double-feature—Madge Bellamy in *Sandy* and *Going Crooked* with Bessie Love. Ironically, Bellamy, a star actress, rode a float in the Tournament of Roses parade that year.

When the team arrived in Tuscaloosa, the town went crazy. The parade was led by the Alabama Million Dollar Band, with the team following in student-drawn wagons. Cars carrying Governor-elect Bibb Graves and university president Denny fell in line behind the team.

The mood of the day was probably best exhibited by speeches presented by Denny and Graves.

"I come back with my head a little higher and my soul a little more inspired to win the battle for this splendid Anglo-Saxon race of the South," Dr. Denny said, only to be topped by Graves.

"The hearts of all of Dixie are beating with exultant pride," Graves opened his speech. "We are here to tell the world that the Crimson Tide is our Tide and an Alabama troop of heroes. It upheld the honor of the Southland and came back to us undefeated. It fought the greatest fight ever fought on an athletic field."

1931 Rose Bowl Game

Alabama 24   Washington State 0

Hold 'em, Bama stalwart sons,
Stop each rush and nail all runs;
Play your game, we know you're right,
We ask no more, we've seen you fight.

At the final gun and you leave the field,
To this opinion we can't help but yield;
The Cougar will be driven from the lair,
His bite removed and stripped of hair.

So on with the game, we believe in you,
Charge 'em hard, "Wade" straight through;
For glory to old Bama and all Dixie land,
That waits to extend the old glad hand.

—T. K. K., 1931
Los Angeles Evening Express

Memories of the 1931 Rose Bowl football game come easily to University of Alabama All-American running back John Henry (Flash) Suther. All he has to do is look in the mirror every time he brushes his teeth.

Four of his teeth are missing and have been since New Year's Day 1931, when Alabama soundly defeated powerful Washington State, 24-0.

"I left those teeth somewhere in the Rose Bowl," Suther said while looking back at one of the greatest Crimson Tide bowl appearances in history. "I'm not sure where they are, but I left them laying in that stadium."

Suther, a 70-year-old retired businessman who was known as the "Flying Dutchman" during his playing days at Alabama, lost his teeth while making a tackle on Washington State fullback Elmer (The Great) Schwartz. The mishap came long after the Crimson Tide had sewed up its second Rose Bowl victory in three trips to Pasadena.

"It happened about a minute before the end of the game," Suther said. "Schwartz came at me and I stuck my head right on top of his helmet.

"We didn't have all the fancy protective equipment in those days, so we had to throw all we had at an opponent. I knocked him down, but Schwartz got the best of me on the play.

"I was back at the hotel before I came to my senses. I knew I had been playing in a football game, but I wasn't the least bit sure where.

"I did know I wasn't having a good time like the other guys were."

The easy victory was fun all the way for Alabama. It ended a three-year bowl appearance drought for the Crimson Tide—after a victory and a tie in the 1926 and 1927 Rose Bowls, respectively. It allowed Head Coach Wallace Wade to end his remarkable career at the Capstone with an undefeated season. It reinforced the idea that Southern football was at a summit.

And it was a victory which allowed Alabama the liberty to claim national superiority, although Notre Dame was named national champion that season.

"The Rose Bowl was the only bowl, so it was our goal to get there," Suther said. "We wanted an invitation badly, because once you got there and won, you considered yourself the national champion. It was like the World Series. Who could argue about the worth of the winner?"

For Suther, the Rose Bowl victory provided a glory-filled swan song at the end of an illustrious football career—including high school and college.

At Tuscaloosa High School, Suther played on Black Bear teams which did not lose a game in his four years there. In fact, the school went seven seasons without tasting defeat, while playing postseason games with teams from St. Louis; Lakeland,

Florida; and Chicago.

"We probably had the greatest high school coach ever in Paul Burnum (later an Alabama assistant coach)," Suther said. "Of course we had some pretty fair players, too."

In 1926, Suther's senior season at Tuscaloosa, the Black Bears scored 504 points in winning all 10 games, including the final 42-0 victory over Senn High of Chicago for an unofficial national championship. Suther scored 361 points that year and was named All-Southern as a running back. Since he was a home-grown product, Alabama took it for granted he would become a Crimson Tide player.

"Nobody went out and made propositions in those days," Suther said, "but it did strike me as funny that Alabama did not say anything to me about my collegiate future. I kind of expected something like that from Coach Wade, however. He was a funny fellow. Shoot, he never talked to me about Alabama. Of course, he rarely talked to anybody about anything."

Suther was heavily recruited by Florida, but decided to stay home, where he received the standard scholarship—$17.50 per semester for tuition and $16.50 per year for room and board. Although his first three seasons at Alabama were lean from a Crimson Tide victory standpoint, the 1930 season made what little money a player received seem incidental.

In 1927, following an unbeaten and Rose Bowl championship season, Alabama posted a 5-4-1 record. The next two years the Crimson Tide had 6-3 records and critics began calling for Coach Wade's resignation.

Wade gave them one on April 1, 1930, stating his intentions of becoming the head coach and athletic director at Duke.

"Coach Wade gave no reason for leaving the university, after being offered a five-year contract at Alabama," wrote *Birmingham News* reporter Zipp Newman. "The Alabama coach informed this writer last fall that he would coach only one more year at the Capstone."

After tendering his resignation, Wade continued to treat the situation with silence. According to Suther, team members did not officially get word from their coach until a few days before the opening game of the season against Howard.

"He called a team meeting just before the first game," Suther said, "and it was an emotional one. His remarks built a fire under us.

"Coach Wade said it would be his last year at Alabama,

National Football

Hall of Fame

Coach Wallace Wade
Vanderbilt University-University of Alabama
Duke University

has been granted the highest honors of the National Football Hall of Fame, in recognition of his outstanding coaching ability as demonstrated in intercollegiate competition, his sportsmanship, integrity, character, and contribution to the sport of football, this certificate bears witness that his name shall be forever honored in the

National Football Hall of Fame

Elected:

June 21, 1955
New Brunswick, N.J.

Bill Cunningham
Chairman, Honors Court

because some of the radicals in the state didn't care for the way he was running things. Then he gave us all a challenge.

"'Gentlemen,' Coach Wade said, 'I'm gonna win this damn championship this season and if you want to be a part of it, you can. If not, get out of here now.'

"Well, we got with it. I mean we really buckled down and worked for him. You know the rest. By the end of the year, those radicals were begging Coach Wade to stay and it's obvious what he told them.

"Coach Wade was like a blood-thirsty army officer. We all wanted to hate him, but when it got down to it, we loved him. He was a helluva coach who developed us into an outstanding team in 1930."

The 1930 team was not picked in the top five in Southern Conference preseason polls, but sportswriter Newman had a vision for the Crimson Tide. "For a team not picked to go anywhere in particular, the Crimson Tide will be a most feared opponent," Newman wrote. "A team dreaded worse than the plague. And why? Because Wade will have another bone-crushing line and a squad that will outfight its weight in wildcats."

Alabama boasted a talented roster of 35 players in 1930, led in the backfield by Suther and sophomore quarterback and punter Johnny Cain and in the line by All-American tackles Fred Sington and C. B. (Foots) Clements, who was elected team captain after the Rose Bowl victory.

Wade was optimistic in his preseason analysis of the last Alabama team he was to coach. "Alabama will be exceedingly hard to score upon," Wade said, "but Alabama opponents are going to be just as hard for Alabama to score upon, if not harder. We have despaired of uncovering a triple threat, even a great passer. Given a Pooley Hubert or Bobby Dodd, I would rate Alabama's chances with Tennessee, Georgia, and Vanderbilt."

Alabama defeated all three of the other contenders en route to the Southern Conference championship and its Rose Bowl berth. The Crimson Tide scored 247 points and allowed only 13 during the season.

"People are always talking about defense, defense, defense," Suther said while looking back on his senior season. "Well, we had some kind of defense that year."

Alabama opened the regular season by defeating Howard, 45-0. Then came victories over Mississippi (62-0), Sewanee (25-0), Tennessee (18-6), Kentucky (19-0), Florida (20-0), Lou-

Fred Sington: best lineman in America.

isiana State (33-0), Vanderbilt (12-7), and Georgia (13-0).

The wins over Vanderbilt and Georgia iced the Rose Bowl invitation.

"Rumors started flying about the Rose Bowl just before the Vanderbilt game," Suther recalled. "Well, Coach Wade refused to talk about it.

"But there was no way to hide it before the Georgia game. They had only lost once and the Rose Bowl had indicated the winner in our game would receive an invitation."

Cain led Alabama to the victory over Georgia. His high punts, accompanied by coverage by Sington, Albert Elmore, Jess Eberdt, and John Miller, kept the Bulldogs at bay. He also ran 24 yards to set up a Monk Campbell touchdown in the third period. Campbell returned a punt 58 yards to set up a Cain touchdown in the fourth quarter.

Ed Danforth, sports editor of the *Atlanta Georgian*, praised the Crimson Tide—"Were there any way to reassemble those two older teams (1925 and 1926 Rose Bowl) and play them against this 1930 team on succeeding Saturdays, I'd take the new generation to win."

Perhaps a headline in a Philadelphia newspaper summed up the season best—"South's Big Need Is Relief From Crimson Tide."

Fans and sportswriters in the South and East were convinced Alabama was a powerful football team in 1930, but the Crimson Tide still had doubters on the West Coast, including a Washington State team which had won all nine of its games that season.

It was on December 19 that 170 Alabamians boarded a train and started west on the third Crimson Tide power-proving trip. Initial plans said only one non-scheduled stop would be made—at the Grand Canyon—but Wade changed them as he did on the two previous trips to Pasadena.

One stop was made in San Antonio, Texas, where the team held a practice scrimmage, while another special stop was made in Picayune, Mississippi, so the mother of player Frank Howard could ride with her son to New Orleans.

"We were a serious bunch on the trip to Pasadena," Suther said. "We knew we would be facing a tough team."

Washington State was known as the "wonder team" because the Cougars were the surprise squad in the West Coast Athletic Conference. Schwartz was the top name on the Washington State squad and was compared to George (Wildcat) Wilson, the Washington star in the 1926 Rose Bowl game.

Alabama found itself rated a slight favorite in the game when it arrived in Pasadena on December 23, a contrast to the two earlier trips. But the squads were rated almost evenly, so evenly matched that betting was limited.

Los Angeles Evening Express sportswriter Sid Ziff wrote, "Washington State College and the University of Alabama are all set to usher in the New Year with a great exhibition of football tomorrow at the Pasadena Rose Bowl.

"From a standpoint of football, there is every reason to believe it will be the best game of the season in Southern California. The result should be a smart, clever game of football on both sides...something we haven't seen as yet in Los Angeles this season.

"Critics who have followed the workouts here have been greatly impressed with the huge, hairy-chested Southerners. In practice they have growled menacingly at intruders—played seriously. They impress you as a team with a genuine record."

Ziff was not impressed with Alabama the next day. He picked Washington State to win.

As it was, Washington State showed up on the field dressed head to toe in Alabama red. After the game, the Cougars burned the uniforms.

"We didn't care what color their uniforms were," Suther said. "We knew they were the opponent and that's all that mattered."

The highlight of pregame talk centered around one question—would Alabama coach Wade start his second team as he had during the regular season, then unleash the first unit in the second quarter?

"We knew the second team would start, because Coach Wade said they would," Suther said. "Our question was whether we (the first unit) would get in the game. He was mad at us at kickoff because he thought we had been loafing in practice, and before the game he told us we might not play.

"Well, the Shock Troopers—that's what we called the second team—held Washington State to a scoreless tie in the first quarter and, when it ended, us first-stringers were sitting there with our helmets on ready to go in the game. Coach Wade didn't even look our way, so we started thinking, 'Bull, we came all the way to Pasadena and he's not gonna let us play.'"

Wade mellowed early in the second quarter and sent in the first team, which scored 21 points in six minutes.

The first touchdown came when left end Jimmy Moore took a lateral from fullback Cain and rifled a pass to Suther on the Washington State 22 yard line. Flash trotted into the end zone.

"I sneaked behind the Washington State defense," Suther said, "and I was all alone when Jimmy threw the pass. We scored five or six touchdowns on that play during the year.

"Scoring that touchdown was the greatest thrill I've ever had. It makes a man feel proud to see his teammates running toward him to shake hands."

Campbell scored the next Alabama touchdown on a 1-yard run, after Eberdt intercepted a Washington State pass and Moore passed 46 yards to end Ben Smith.

Campbell scored the final touchdown on a 43-yard run. J. B. (Ears) Whitworth, who coached Alabama from 1955-57, kicked all three extra points and added a 42-yard field goal in the fourth quarter.

"There was one writer on the coast who kept insisting Washington State would beat us on a field goal," Suther said. "That kind of got away with Coach Wade, so I think he had 'Ears' kick that field goal to rub it in a little. It was icing on the cake."

Whitworth was labeled the "Educated Toe" by sportswriters after his long field goal. Alabama players made the best of the nickname, forcing Whitworth to cut a hole in his sock on the trip home and show his toe to every lady on the train.

Cain, the inexperienced sophomore who later became an All-American, captured the imagination of the crowd of 60,000, however. He averaged 46 yards per punt and directed an almost-unstoppable offense.

"The vaunted defense of the Western champions crumbled like the walls of Jericho," wrote Royal Brougham in the *Seattle Post Intelligencer*. "The freckle-necked Southern gentleman (Wade) won this game with his noodle. He used Shock Troops to give him time to dissect his opponents' strengths and weaknesses, then he sent his regulars in to win the game."

Maxwell Stiles of the *Los Angeles Examiner* described the game, "Washington State was like a trout in the rapids. The trout knew that he was in a lot of running water, but he didn't know where it was coming from."

41

It was simply an Alabama day, one probably best remembered by Crimson Tide player Bruce Bell.

"Bruce was not a regular on the team," Suther said. "In fact, he didn't play in a game all season. But he wanted to go to the Rose Bowl with us, so we covered him up with equipment and sneaked him on the train.

"When we got to Pasadena, Bruce walked up to Coach Wade and asked if he had a ticket to the game. Wade said he didn't, but since Bruce was there he could put on a uniform and sit on the bench with us.

"Late in the game, when everybody else had played, Coach Wade put Bruce in for a couple of minutes. That tickled us all to death.

"Yep, that's what it was all about in those days."

1935 Rose Bowl Game

Alabama 29   Stanford 13

Afar from the deep, with a mighty leap,
The Crimson Tide rolls high.
And the speed and grace of its thundering pace,
Is electric to the mortal eye.

Up and down the strand it crashes the sand,
The dunes are lost in its hold;
Beneath foam and fleck, it flings the wreck,
Into depths that cannot be told.

And the Crimson Tide through the years will abide,
A force to be reckoned with awe;
A force with control in its conquering soul,
That batters you naked and raw.

—Nell Robert Murphy
Gainesville, Georgia

Paul William Bryant, known simply as "The Bear" in this day and age, has had many eventful afternoons in a life pretty much filled by college football. The University of Alabama head coach has a full memory bank.

But few afternoons, if any, hold a spot as near the Bryant heart as the first one in 1935. On that day, the legendary coach played for Alabama in the Rose Bowl game, a 29-13 victory over Stanford which pushed the sparkling Crimson Tide bowl record to 3-0-1.

"People ask me if I remember much about the 1935 Rose Bowl game," Bryant said. "I remember everything about it.

"I remember how the cold chills ran up my back, and still do thinking about a telegram our team received from Stanford before our final regular-season game with Vanderbilt. The telegram said, 'If you win decisively today, where can we reach you after the game?'

"I remember the train trip cross-country. How long it was. And all that free food.

"I remember falling in love with California.

"I remember there were movie stars all over the place.

"I remember every minute of the game—their great tailback Bobby Grayson running for a touchdown in the first quarter to put Stanford ahead, 7-0.

"I remember Dixie Howell hitting off me and spinning out and running for the touchdown that should have tied the game, but Riley Smith missed the point-after.

"But I remember we had the game won by the fourth quarter. By then it was 29-13...."

In his book *Bear*, Bryant says there are two other things which stick out prominently in his mind about the fourth consecutive successful trip for Alabama to the Rose Bowl. He jokingly says he would just as soon forget.

Bryant is married to the lovely and gracious Mary Harmon Bryant, a former college beauty queen at Alabama. They have been married more than 40 years. Bryant will not admit it, but he probably spoke part of his vows on the Rose Bowl trip.

"I had begun dating Mary Harmon that year, but she was so popular I had to spread myself around a little just to keep the scales balanced," Bryant remembers. "And I invited a good-looking girl from Pine Bluff, Arkansas, named Barbara Del Simmons to be my Rose Bowl sponsor.

"When we got the Rose Bowl bid I wrote her and asked her to come out. She wrote back that I'd have to write her daddy. I did, but I didn't get a reply.

"In the meantime, I was putting the pressure on Mary Harmon and she told me she could go. She would be my sponsor. Mary Harmon and another girl named Grace McGhee were elected game sponsors, with Mary Harmon getting all the votes but two. And darned if that day Barbara Del Simmons doesn't show up. Talk about shocks.

"Barbara Del wound up having a good time, squired

Mary Harmon Bryant and coaching husband.

around by Happy Campbell and some of our Arkansas boys. But we didn't say two words to each other the whole time."

After possibly winning Mary Harmon for a lifetime two days before the game, the game itself found Bryant letting what must have seemed like a small fortune slip from his hands.

"Just before the game ended, Stanford was back in a huddle and I looked down and on the field right next to my knee was a big pile of silver," Bryant recalled. "Dimes, quarters, half-dollars. I don't know where it came from, but I knew for sure that somebody up there not only liked me, but was leaning my way. A lot of money. About $3 in change.

"I scooped it up real fast and was holding it to take to the bench between plays when, lo and behold, here comes Grayson on a sweep around my end. It was the only decent tackle I made all day. And I lost my money."

Bryant's loss of money was about the only thing Alabama lost that season. The Rose Bowl victory capped an amazing year for the Crimson Tide and gave its coaching genius, Frank Thomas, his first taste of postseason magic.

Actually, it was Thomas' second trip to Pasadena, California, with Alabama. The former Notre Dame player under the fabled Knute Rockne traveled with the 1931 Rose Bowl team because he was taking over as head coach from Wallace Wade.

Wade was the man most responsible for Thomas getting the Alabama job because he told Dr. George Denny, university president, to hire the man who would lead the Crimson Tide to great heights. Thomas and Denny met in Birmingham and sealed the deal while the new Alabama coach was still employed as backfield coach at Georgia.

The official contract was signed on July 15, 1930, at which time Denny said, "Mr. Thomas, now that you have accepted our proposition, I will give you the benefit of my views, based on many years of observation. It is my conviction that material is 90 percent, coaching ability 10 percent. I desire further to say that you will be provided with the 90 percent and that you will be held to strict accounting for delivering the remaining 10 percent."

Thomas called the remarks "the hardest and coldest words I ever heard," but apparently was not shell-shocked. After four seasons at Alabama—entering the 1935 Rose Bowl game—Thomas' record was 33-4-1.

Under Thomas, Alabama won the first-ever Southeastern

Coach Frank Thomas: gallant and successful.

Conference (the Southern Conference split that year) championship in 1933 with a 7-1-1 record, but the Crimson Tide coach was licking his chops looking down the roster he would work with the next season.

Dixie Howell was the 1934 quarterback and Don Hutson was an end. The H-and-H duo became one of the greatest pass-catch combinations in collegiate history.

Other than a hard-fought 13-6 win over Tennessee, Howell and Hudson led Alabama through an easy undefeated, untied regular season. Howard fell in the opener, 24-0, followed by Sewanee (35-6), Mississippi State (41-0), Tennessee, Georgia (26-6), Kentucky (24-14), Clemson (40-0), Georgia Tech (40-0), and Vanderbilt (34-0).

At midseason speculation began concerning possible match-ups in the Rose Bowl. Stanford appeared to have the best team on the West Coast, so the Indians were en route to hosting the game. Minnesota was unbeaten and shared the top spot with Alabama as another candidate.

It was before the Vanderbilt game that Thomas first mentioned a possible Rose Bowl invitation to his team. He sent everybody except the first team out of the dressing room and read the telegram from the Stanford graduate manager.

"Vanderbilt didn't have a prayer," Bryant remembered. "Howell and Hutson played great and I got in the way of Vanderbilt's All-American tackle Dick Plasman enough times not to be embarrassed. And it just so happened that when Coach Thomas took me out in the fourth quarter the band was playing "California Here I Come."

Minnesota beat Wisconsin, 34-0, the same day Alabama whipped Vanderbilt, so there were anxious moments concerning the pending invitation. The official invitation came when the team got to its Birmingham hotel, prompting a wild celebration which continued when the team returned to Tuscaloosa.

Alabama embarked on its trip west on December 21, but the team was late getting to the train because it was practicing. Thomas did not like the way a scrimmage had gone the day before and ordered the team back on the practice field at eight o'clock that morning.

"They had to hold the train for us until Coach Thomas was satisfied he had made his point," Bryant said.

Alabama stopped in Tucson, Arizona, to practice. Thomas had his players run numerous wind sprints. "We almost col-

Bill Lee - Captain
All American Tackle

Riley Smith
Quarterback

Dixie Howell
All American Halfback

Joe Demyanovich
Fullback

Jimmy Angelich
Halfback

Don Hutson
All American End

Riley
Back

K. Francis
Center

Joe Dildy
Center

Charles Marr
Guard

Ralph Gandy
End

Paul Bryant
End

Tilden Campbell
All Captain - Quarterback

Morrow
Guard

Young Boozer
Halfback

Alabama	24		Howard	0
Alabama	55		Sewanee	0
Alabama	41		Miss. State	0
Alabama	13		Tennessee	6
Alabama	26		Georgia	6
Alabama	34		Kentucky	14
Alabama	40		Clemson	0
Alabama	40		Ga. Tech.	0
Alabama	34		Vanderbilt	0

Frank Thomas
Head Football Coach

Sonny McGahey
Tackle

Ben Baswell
Tackle

Whatley
Tackle

Roy White
Halfback

National Champions 1935
Rose Bowl Game
Alabama 29, Stanford 13.

James Walker
End

Bill Young
Tackle

McLeod
Halfback

Thomas Keller
End

Charles Stapp
Halfback

Gilman Walker
End

Ernest Ellis
Center

Clarence Rhoeram
Fullback

Hubber Nisbet
Fullback

Burlatti
Guard

Lamar Maye
Center

Walter Fahlkamp
Guard

Bill Peters
Guard

Leroy Goldberg
Quarterback

Temple Williamson
Quarterback

Tarzan White
Guard

lapsed in the thin air," Bryant said.

When Alabama arrived in California, it found that football fans there were not pleased with the fact the Rose Bowl had selected the Crimson Tide instead of Minnesota. But the game was a sellout, with 84,474 fans buying tickets. Scalpers were selling tickets for $25 each. One thousand extra seats were erected.

"Alabama is the most impressive football squad I have ever seen come from east of the Rockies and Alabama is going to play the best Stanford team in history, a team as great as Southern Cal in 1931," wrote Braven Dyer of the *Los Angeles Times*. "If Alabama can beat Stanford, the Pacific Coast will give Alabama full credit for the greatest team ever to play in the Rose Bowl."

After an early scare, Alabama won easily, scoring 22 points in the second quarter, after Stanford got its early touchdown. In those 15 minutes, Alabama amassed 150 yards on passes and another 106 on the ground. Howell passed for 96 yards—four completions to Hutson and three to Bryant—and ran for 96 yards, including a 67-yard sprint for a touchdown.

Howell and Hutson clicked again in the fourth quarter to put the icing on the cake—a 59-yard touchdown.

Howell left the field late in the game, after a 52-yard punt, and received the loudest ovation ever given a visiting player. He had gained 111 yards running, 160 yards passing with nine completions in 13 attempts, and had punted six times for a 43.8-yard average.

"No team in the history of football, anywhere, anytime, has passed the ball as Alabama passed it today," wrote Ralph McGill of the *Atlanta Constitution*. "And no man ever passed as did Dixie Howell, the swift sword of the Crimson attack."

All-time great sportswriter Grantland Rice wrote, "Dixie Howell, the human howitzer from Hartford, Alabama, blasted the Rose Bowl dreams of Stanford today with one of the greatest all-around exhibitions football has ever known."

Mark Kelly, a West Coast sportswriter, wrote, "...Then like arrows from Robin Hood's trusty bow, there shot from Howell's unerring hand a stream of passes the like of which have never been seen in football on the Coast. Zing, zing, zing! They whizzed through the air and found their mark in the massive paws of Hutson and Bryant."

Bryant, known on the team as the "other end" because of

50

Hutson's greatness, probably summed it up best—"It had all seemed like a dream come true to me—the thrill of being invited, of going, of getting to play in front of all those people. All those things are rich in my memory."

1938 Rose Bowl Game

California 13   Alabama 0

Onward Alabama!
West has challenged you;
Raise your flag of Crimson,
'Gainst our skies of blue.

Charge them, Tide of Crimson,
Crush this valiant foe;
Forward into battle,
Watch our team work score.

Onward Alabama!
Crimson tints the West;
The Bowl is full of Roses,
Victory's our quest.

—Miss Lilian Bell

Somebody, somewhere, at some time said a football team often reflects the personality of its coach. Whoever came up with those words of wisdom must have been inspired after watching the 1937 University of Alabama squad.

That Crimson Tide team was fortunate. It inherited from two sources—a persistent, quick-to-anger, slow-to-forgive head coach named Frank Thomas and a gladiator-like assistant coach named Bill Peters.

Thomas, who compiled a 114-24-7 record in 15 seasons at Alabama, coached under the principle there was only one correct way to do things—his way.

Coach Frank Thomas observes practice.

Peters, a student of Thomas who followed the fabled coach south from Indiana (Notre Dame country), refused to take no for an answer, a trait which became a trademark of the 1937 Alabama team.

On December 6, 1937, a week after Alabama had completed an unbeaten, untied regular season and had accepted a Rose Bowl invitation, Peters displayed courage typical of the Crimson Tide he helped coach. He wrestled a 160-pound buck on a hunting trip, broke the deer's neck, and hauled it almost two miles to his car.

The deer was shot by four hunters, but refused to die. The wounded animal charged toward Peters who, aided by eight dogs, charged too. After 10 minutes, a tired Peters lugged his trophy from the woods.

Alabama, like Peters, scrapped, clawed, battled, and, yes, lugged its way to the 1938 Rose Bowl game, where, like the deer, the Crimson Tide lost 13-0 to California.

The 1937 season was one of Thomas' best coaching jobs since he took a 33-man squad made up mostly of unproven players and molded it into another Southeastern Conference champion. There were three All-Americans on the squad—halfback Joe Kilgrow, tackle Jim Ryba, and guard Leroy Monsky, but the Crimson Tide lacked the explosive element.

"We don't have the big guns we had last time we went to the Rose Bowl," Thomas said early in the regular season, "but we have some men who will fight you."

Monsky, known as "Mad Monk" during his senior season at Alabama, was probably the toughest of the big-hearted players Thomas had. He was captain of the team and is now a successful businessman in Birmingham.

"We lacked ability on that Rose Bowl team, but we all had a tremendous will to win," Monsky said after hailing himself as "the only Crimson Tide captain on a losing Rose Bowl team. We had a scrappy team made up of a bunch of poor country boys.

"There were no big names on our team. We prided ourselves on teamwork, molding together for one purpose—winning. We had a close outfit.

"You know, I wake up two or three nights a week wishing we had another chance to play California. But had we won, considering the players we had, I guess they would have had to call us the Miracle Team of Alabama."

Monsky was important to the Alabama offense, because under Thomas' Notre Dame style, guards were constantly in motion. "I pulled and led blocking on 99 percent of our plays," he said. On defense, Monsky was all over the field. He intercepted four passes during the 1937 regular season. "I was a drifter. I'd hold my blocker off and go wherever the ball went."

How tough was Monsky? Well, he tells a Rose Bowl story which pretty well describes himself.

"We stopped in San Antonio, Texas, for a practice session on the way to Pasadena," Monsky said. "During our scrimmage there, we ran the old shift-right-82 play, which meant Lew Bostic—the other guard—and I were supposed to pull and lead blocking. We had a problem, though. I pulled right—the correct way—and Lew pulled left. We collided in back of the center and my eye got busted up.

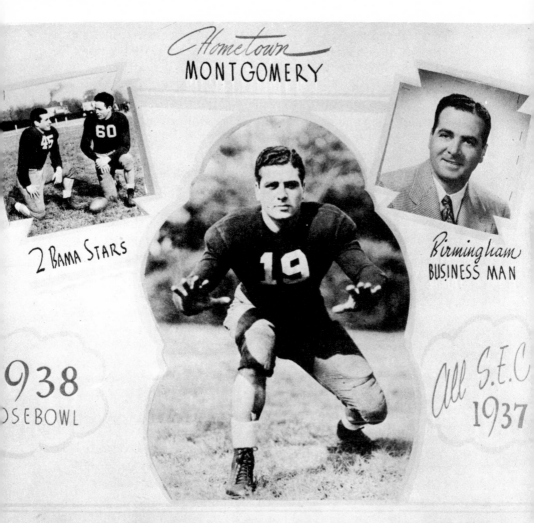

Hometown
MONTGOMERY

2 BAMA STARS

Birmingham
BUSINESS MAN

938
OSEBOWL

All S.E.C
1937

LEROY MONSKY
GUARD
ALL AMERICAN

215

1937

"They had to put 14 stitches and a drain on my eye. I looked pretty bad. In fact, my mother saw a picture of me in the newspaper and thought we had been in a train wreck.

"Well, the next day three doctors came up to me on the train and said they were going to make an emergency stop and give me a lockjaw shot. But then they came back and told me they weren't going to give me the shot, because sometimes it caused a violent reaction and they were afraid I wouldn't be able to play in the game. As soon as they told me, my jaw started hurting.

"When we got to Pasadena, the trainers took me down to a harness shop and got a bar put on the front of my headgear, but to see, I had to look up, so I forgot that.

"Well, we kicked off and here we all went down the field in front of 105,000 people to cover the kick and, lo and behold, California's big 225-pound quarterback Johnny Meek was running the ball at me. I didn't want to put my face on him, but with all those people reaching up to the sky watching, I had to.

"The next thing I remembered was waking up on the sidelines next to Coach Thomas. It was the second quarter and my face was torn open again. I said, 'Coach, how long have I been out of the game?' He said, 'Monk, we just took you out.'

"Well, I had played the first quarter and part of the second without knowing where I was. But you know, I went back in and played the rest of the game and did okay for myself.

"All of us had that kind of fight in us."

Alabama did its share of battling most of the regular season, but the kicking of Sandy Sanford, a transfer end from Arkansas Tech, turned out to be the chief Crimson Tide weapon. He literally kicked the team into the Rose Bowl.

During the season, Alabama defeated Howard (41-0), Sewanee (65-0), South Carolina (20-0), Tennessee (14-7), George Washington (19-0), Kentucky (41-0), Tulane (9-6), Georgia Tech (7-0), and Vanderbilt (9-7).

The Rose Bowl did not show much interest in the Crimson Tide until after the victory over Tulane, but did show some at mid-season. "California's Golden Bears, Pasadena bound at the moment, have their eye officially on either Dartmouth or Yale as a Rose Bowl football opponent here January 1," the Associated Press reported in early November. "Some sentiment has been expressed that Alabama, a frequent and successful guest, has played none too representative opponents. That's a good out for any inviting Western team."

It was two weeks later that Sanford began his kicking heroics. He kicked a 32-yard field goal with three minutes left in the game to beat Tulane at New Orleans. Then after the Crimson Tide barely beat Georgia Tech in front of 22,000 fans at Birmingham, Sanford kicked another field goal to beat Vanderbilt at Nashville on Thanksgiving Day.

The victory over Vanderbilt left Alabama as the only unbeaten, untied team in the country, yet ranked behind Pittsburgh, California, and Fordham in the Associated Press poll. Speculation about bowl matchups reached a high peak, with the Crimson Tide listed as a possible participant in both the Rose and Sugar bowls.

"I haven't heard anything from any bowls," Thomas said on November 27.

The next day, the Associated Press did an interview with California graduate manager Ken Priestley in an effort to clear up the bowl matchup mystery.

Asked if he followed Alabama's victory over Vanderbilt, he said, "Sure, I always read the football scores—all of them. They played some good games, didn't they?"

Asked about Dartmouth, Minnesota, Yale, Nebraska, and some other dark-horse candidates, he said, "Fine schools, all of them. Nice weather we're having down here, isn't it? Hope we have the same January 1."

Asked if California would invite anybody, he said, "Yes."

On November 30, Thomas received a telephone call inviting Alabama to play unbeaten but once-tied (by Washington) California in the Rose Bowl.

Immediately after accepting, Alabama was made a decisive underdog to a California Golden Bear team with a terrific balanced attack.

"Dixie football fans are blowing hot air into high hopes, but, actually they are somewhat skeptical of the Crimson Tide's ability to cope with powerful California on January 1 at Pasadena," a *New York Times* story said on December 8. "Alabama's unbeaten Rose Bowl record is in jeopardy. The Crimson Tide will probably find out you get a thorn with every rose."

Alabama players were upset every time they read about the chances of losing.

"We ain't going out there to get beat," tackle Ryba told a throng of well-wishers as the Crimson Tide boarded the train for Pasadena. "We'll get 'em," said Kilgrow. "We're ready for those Teddy Bears."

Thomas, who labeled his Alabama team a one-touchdown underdog, refused to predict a Crimson Tide victory. But on December 27 he spoke fondly about his team, one he later called one of his favorites.

57

"This is the durndest team I have ever coached," Thomas said in a West Coast interview. "All the boys believe they are red-hot and that nothing grown out here can cool them off. They felt the same way through the season.

"I tell you one thing—the Rose Bowl customers are going to see the fightingest Alabama team that ever came out here. It may not be the most powerful or most versatile, but this bunch can really get down on the ground and fight it out with you.

"The boys are ready to play anytime, anywhere. They could ring the starting bell at four o'clock tomorrow morning and five minutes later every one of those boys would be there fully dressed and ready for the kickoff.

"The Civil War will be just one war they will fight. They won't get around to the Civil War until late in the third period. Before that one is reached, these kids will have fought the Seven Years War, the War of 1812, the Spanish War, all the expeditionary excursions into Mexico, and the Crimean War."

As it worked out, the War of the Roses was too much for Alabama. California demonstrated too much power and speed for the Crimson Tide. The Golden Bears scored touchdowns in the second and third quarters, while Alabama was losing four fumbles and was having four passes intercepted.

A rowdy crowd watched the encounter which O. B. Keeler of the *Atlanta Journal* described: "The other fellows may write all they please about the pitcher who went to the bowl once too often, but my line is that it is a long worm that has no turning and I'll stick to that.

"The Pacific Coast worm in this instance was a Python, a mighty Anaconda from Berkeley; a blue Boa Constrictor disguised as a Golden Bear. And he turned on the Crimson Tide, which in four previous expeditions had never been beaten."

When the Alabama train stopped in Birmingham on its return trip from Pasadena, few people were at the station to greet the Crimson Tide. "Nobody likes a loser," Thomas said when he saw the small welcome.

But when Alabama arrived home in Tuscaloosa, 5,000 fans turned out to give the team a heroes' welcome.

Everybody likes a fighter with a big heart....

1942 Cotton Bowl Game
Alabama 29   Texas A&M 21

Roses we will remember,
The mighty Tide;
Though those days are over,
The long train rides.

A new birth of Crimson,
As glorious as the old;
The banner of Alabama,
In Dallas, the Cotton Bowl.

—Author unknown

A heavy cloud hovered over Dallas, Texas, on January 1, 1942, as 41 University of Alabama football players ran onto the field at the Cotton Bowl.

But a heavier cloud was hanging over the world. A war was being fought—World War II—and the unrest was taking its toll on the mind of Holt Rast.

"The Japanese attack on Pearl Harbor came only a few days after we accepted the invitation to play Texas A&M in the Cotton Bowl," said Rast, an All-American end on the 1941 Alabama team and now a businessman in Birmingham. "It distracted from the football game. The whole mood of the country was downcast.

"We knew we were in a war and I was kind of anxious to get the game and my college degree behind me so I could join up and help the country."

If Rast, who called Alabama offensive signals from his end

59

position, was thinking about anything except football during the Cotton Bowl game, it did not hinder his performance. He was one of the driving forces behind a 29-21 Crimson Tide victory and earned a spot on the All-Time Cotton Bowl All-Star Team selected in 1960.

"Winning the game is my fondest memory of the Cotton Bowl," Rast said. "Of course, playing well enough to make the all-star team was a tremendous honor, too. It was a great way to end a college career, being a positive part of a winning effort."

The Alabama win over Texas A&M remains as one of the most bizarre bowl victories in history. The Crimson Tide made only one first down in the game, while the Aggies made 13. Alabama had only 75 yards total offense, Texas A&M 309. Alabama ran only 32 plays and completed only one pass, while Texas A&M ran 79 plays and completed 13 passes.

But the Crimson Tide intercepted seven passes and recovered five fumbles and had a 29-7 lead before the Aggies charged in the fourth quarter.

"They fumbled around and we fell on the ball," Rast said. "It was simply our kind of day."

Texas A&M scored first for a 7-0 lead in the second quarter, but Alabama recovered a fumble on the enemy 24 yard line and Russ Craft ran for an 8-yard touchdown to tie the game.

In the third quarter, Jimmy Nelson, Alabama's All-American halfback, returned a punt 72 yards for a touchdown. Later in the period, Nelson ran 21 yards for a touchdown after Sam Sharpe recovered a fumbled punt.

In the final quarter, after an interception, George Hecht kicked a 31-yard field goal to push the score to 23-7. Rast scored the last Alabama touchdown late in the game when he ran 10 yards with an intercepted pass.

Nelson, the Alabama statistical leader all season, dazzled the 50,000 fans in attendance on a cold afternoon. He was selected player of the game.

"A ghost in a Crimson shirt skipped through the Texas Aggies Thursday as Jimmy Nelson carried Alabama to a 29-21 victory in the sixth annual Cotton Bowl football game," the Associated Press game story began.

"The rangy black-haired scourge of Southeastern Conference gridirons broke the Aggies backs with a 72-yard touchdown dash in the third period and before the quarter ended stormed 21 yards for another score...."

All-Time 'BAMA END

HOMETOWN, BIRMINGHAM, ALA.

ALABAMA-9-TENNESSEE 1941

...RIZED TROPHY

Honor Student
SCHOOL OF ENGINEERING

L S.E.C. FIRST TEAM '40-'41

President
"DIXIE BOWL"

HOLT RAST
END   180 lbs.
...L AMERICAN   1941

For Alabama, the Cotton Bowl victory capped a roller coaster year which saw the Crimson Tide reach two lows—the losses the team had during an 8-2 regular season. The Crimson Tide drew national attention again in 1941, after three non-bowling seasons with 7-1-1, 5-3-1, and 7-2 records.

Thomas expected an outstanding team in 1941. "I've never

seen as many great backs on one team," he said after watching Nelson, William Harrell, Julius Papias, Sumpter Blackmon, Paul Spencer, Al Sabo, Vaught Tollett, Carl Mims, Howard Hughes, Bart Avery, Russ Mosley, Lou Scales, Dave Brown, George Gammons, Craft, Don Salls, and Mackey McCoy at practice.

Thomas did not own a patent on preseason praise of the Crimson Tide, however. Ed Danforth, sports editor of the *Atlanta Journal*, colorfully labeled Alabama a powerhouse after an early-September trip to Tuscaloosa.

"Alabama led in all the polls this summer—Gallup, trot, and pace—as the team likely to succeed at football," Danforth wrote. "And as your correspondent went racing around the circuit, he heard so much about Alabama that he became slightly ill at the mention of the Crimson Tide. On arriving in Tuscaloosa, he found the air filled with British boys learning to fly planes. As he craned his head upward to watch them, he inhaled deeply of the fumes of the paper mill that in these days suggest the delicate scent of a battlefield that has not been cleaned up.

"So he was in the mood to see nothing good in the Crimson football team. Besides, they couldn't be as classy as everybody said they were.

"Friends and enemies, they are just that good. Maybe better."

Alabama opened the season against Southwest Louisiana—coached by former Crimson Tide star Johnny Cain—and won, 47-6. But the next week, the Crimson Tide was stunned by Mississippi State, losing 14-0 in Tuscaloosa.

The loss to Mississippi State sent waves of panic throughout the state. On Tuesday, following the loss which received nationwide coverage, Zipp Newman wrote a column in the *Birmingham News* which described the situation.

"A heavy pall hung all over all Alabama Sunday and Monday. Sports fans went their way in sorrow. The crowds waiting for the trains stood silently while the papers were unloaded. Newspaper boys with those usually bright faces whispered words of consolation and looked like they had lost their pay envelopes. Close attention was paid to the morning services. No one wanted to face the great tragedy that had struck over the weekend. Sports morale never was lower.

"And in one sweeping blow the hopes of Alabama fans were crushed as they never have been before. Doom's Day, it was all over the state."

Alabama bounced back the next weekend to defeat Howard, 61-0, soothing the wounds of defeat. Then came a tremendous 9-2 victory over Tennessee at Knoxville, a 27-14 win over Georgia, a 30-0 win over Kentucky, and a 19-14 come-from-behind victory over Tulane at New Orleans, which put the Crimson Tide back in the bowl picture. Georgia Tech fell, 20-0, but Vanderbilt handed Alabama its second loss, 7-0, at Nashville before Alabama ended its regular season with a 21-7 win over Miami.

Several teams had better records than Alabama in 1941, but few teams played a schedule as tough as the Crimson Tide. Taking the schedule into consideration, the Cotton Bowl issued its invitation on December 1.

The Associated Press announced the Alabama invitation by saying, "Colorful Alabama—the famed Crimson Tide that swept to three Rose Bowl triumphs—will come to Dallas to play Texas A&M, champions of the Southwest Conference."

Dan Rogers, president of the Cotton Bowl, said, "The decision was reached after a very close study of the schedules played by various teams under consideration and we are of the opinion that Alabama's season record is among the very best. They have a colorful ball team and we are mighty happy to have them here as an opponent of Texas A&M College."

Crimson Tide fans were joyous upon hearing of the invitation. The usual parties were thrown all over the state, but only 77 people accompanied the team to Dallas by train—a far cry below the number of fans who joined Alabama on its trips to the Rose Bowl. Those who went were treated to a surprise, however.

"The Alabama delegation, some 77 strong, got an idea what to expect from Dallas when their train was halted at Ennis, 30 miles from Dallas, by a holdup staged by synthetic cowboys and beauteous cowgirls amid much firing of blank cartridges," an Associated Press story reported.

More fanfare awaited the team upon its arrival in Dallas. It was greeted by booted, pistol-carrying Chamber of Commerce cowboys. Team members were given 10-gallon hats, then boarded onto fire trucks for a ticker-tape parade through town.

Texans marveled at the sight of Alabama quarterback Roy Johnson wearing his big cowboy hat. A sophomore, he was probably the smallest major college player in the country that year, standing 5-feet-2 and weighing 135 pounds.

National Football
Hall of Fame

Coach Frank W. Thomas
University of Alabama~University of Georgia and
University of Chattanooga

has been granted the highest honors of the National Football Hall of Fame, in recognition of his outstanding coaching ability as demonstrated in intercollegiate competition, his sportsmanship, integrity, character, and contribution to the sport of football, this certificate bears witness that his name shall be forever honored in the
National Football Hall of Fame

Elected:
November 3, 1951
New Brunswick, N.J.

Bill Cunningham
Chairman, Honors Court

Rea Schuessler, the director of the Senior Bowl football game in Mobile, who was then news bureau director at Alabama, wrote a feature story about Johnson.

"...This favorite with Crimson Tide fans is little Roy Johnson from Birmingham. Roy wasn't big enough to be accepted in the University's ROTC unit—Johnson looks like a sapling among giant oaks when he takes the field with Alabama's mighty Crimson Tide.

"Coach Frank Thomas calls him, 'The best football player, per inch, I have ever seen.'"

Texans probably remember him as the one-day smallest cowboy in history.

1943 Orange Bowl Game

Alabama 37   Boston College 21

Never doubt the grit,
Of the men dressed in red;
Conquerers they became at Miami,
After being given up dead.

Boston had a powerhouse,
Bama had its Tide;
When a screaming throng left the Orange Bowl,
The Eagles had died.

Roll on, Alabama,
Mightiest in the bowls;
Praises for you, forever,
Roll, Crimson Tide, roll.

—Author unknown

It was early in the second quarter of the 1943 Orange Bowl game when the soldier eased into his seat at Burdine Stadium to watch what remained of a football game between Boston College and the University of Alabama. World War II was in progress but the Southern soldier was taking time out from wartime duties.

Four other servicemen sat with the late-to-arrive soldier. Along with 30,000 Miami, Florida, fans, they were intensely watching the action on the playing field but offered their new companion a drink from the whisky bottle they had half-emptied. He accepted.

Obviously pepped up by his hearty drink and the thrill of watching the game, the Southerner stood up and shouted, "If anybody wants Boston, I have a $5 bill to bet on Alabama."

Fans laughed, the bottle was passed again, and the soldier made another proposition. "My $5 says Alabama will win!" he shouted.

Somewhat annoyed, the soldier sitting next to him said, "Can't you see the scoreboard?"

The Southerner peered at the scoreboard to see Alabama was behind, 14-0.

"Just the same," he proclaimed. "I've still got my $5 and I still say Alabama will win. In fact, I'll spot you the 14 points Boston College has and bet you even."

The last statement was too much for one of the soldiers, who said, "All right, if you don't care how recklessly you spend your money, I'll just take it myself."

The Southerner became a grandstand hero because Alabama promptly scored 22 second-quarter points and went on to take an exciting 37-21 victory over slightly favored Boston College. The win provided the Crimson Tide with a successful debut in the Orange Bowl and pushed the Alabama bowl record to 5-1-1.

While one faithful soldier was contributing to the Alabama cause in the stands, Joe Domnanovich was building a fire under his Crimson Tide teammates on the field.

"Don't give up," Domnanovich told his teammates as they prepared to receive the Boston College kickoff after the second Eagles' touchdown. "We haven't had a chance to go with the ball yet. We're going to receive and we're going to run them into the ground."

When "Captain Joe" talked, which was rarely, people listened. The 190-pound senior All-American center—a leader by example—found exactly the right words to say that day in Miami.

Domnanovich, who enrolled at Alabama after a standout prep career in South Bend, Indiana, the home of Notre Dame, downplays his role in starting the Crimson Tide comeback in the Orange Bowl, but admits he spoke some choice words to his teammates.

"It wasn't as much what I said during the time out as it was what we did to change our defense," said Domnanovich from his Birmingham home. "They had us confused, so we

67

changed some things. I did tell our guys to get in there and not let those guys run over you.

"It worked out well from then on. They got a touchdown just before halftime, but didn't get another one the rest of the day.

"I can't say I was surprised, either. I think we had a pretty fair team. We didn't panic when we got behind and coming back 14 points on that Boston College team is something to be proud of. They had a good club."

Domnanovich called defensive signals for the Crimson Tide and was held in respect by Coach Frank Thomas. "Joe is in my opinion the best center to play at Alabama on any team I have coached," Thomas said at the end of the regular season.

Domnanovich had been a leader since his high school days (he played his first high school game at age 16 with a broken arm) and was elected president of the Alabama lettermen in 1977. He was the first person Thomas told when the Crimson Tide received its invitation to play Boston College in the Orange Bowl.

"We had just been beaten by Georgia Navy Pre-Flight in our last game and some of us guys, about 13 or 14, were in a little place relaxing in downtown Birmingham," Domnanovich remembered. "Well, they told me I had a telephone call and it was Coach Thomas. He said, 'Dom, we just got invited to the Orange Bowl. See what the fellows think about going.'

"I went back to our table and asked the other guys and they all said, 'Sure, let's go.'"

A bowl game was thus born and a gallant Alabama team had the opportunity to stage a comeback.

The Alabama comeback was remarkable, especially in light of the fact Boston College All-American halfback Mike Holovak appeared to be en route to a sparkling afternoon. He exploded on the Crimson Tide in the first quarter, running 65 and 35 yards for touchdowns.

Alabama went to work, however, and the Boston College defense, somewhat suspect entering the game, caved in under the assault. Russ Craft, Dave Brown, Johnny August, and Russ Mosley picked up big chunks of running yardage as the Crimson Tide rallied. Bobby Tom Jenkins ran 40 yards for the first Alabama touchdown. August then took over, running for a touchdown and passing to Ted Cook for the third Crimson Tide touchdown of the second quarter. Boston College came back to take a 21-19 lead, but George Hecht kicked a 25-yard field goal late in the period for a 22-21 Alabama lead at halftime.

Wheeler Leeth scored the only points of the third quarter for Alabama on a 14-yard pass from Mosley. Jenkins ran 1 yard for a fourth-quarter touchdown. Hecht kicked his second extra point after the final touchdown and Domnanovich put the final two Crimson Tide points on the scoreboard by tackling an Eagle in the end zone for a safety.

Howell Stevens, sports editor of the *Boston Globe*, gave the following account of the game in his story the next day. "In one of the highest scoring bowl games on record, a courageous and brilliant Boston College team was vanquished by a powerful, hard-driving, tricky Alabama eleven at Burdine Stadium this afternoon, 37-21, before a capacity crowd of 30,000 thrilled spectators.

"Denny Myers' Eagles completely hoodwinked the Tuscaloosans with electrifying plays launched from the 'T' in the opening minutes...but the pupils of Frank Thomas refused to stay down....

"Never in all gridiron history has there been a more delirious or sensational first half....

"By winning today, Alabama maintained its proud record of being the greatest team in the nation in bowl competition."

The victory concluded an 8-3 season for Alabama and gave Crimson Tide fans something to talk about in 1943, since football was suspended that year due to the war. Alabama losses in 1942 were to Georgia (21-10), Georgia Tech (7-0), and Georgia Navy Pre-Flight (35-19). Victories were registered over Southwestern Louisiana (54-0), Mississippi State (21-6), Pensacola Navy (27-0), Tennessee (8-0), Kentucky (14-0), South Carolina (29-0), Vanderbilt (27-7), and Boston College.

Disaster almost wiped out the Orange Bowl matchup between the two schools. A fire in early December at the Cocoanut Grove Restaurant in Boston killed several people and the Boston College team was scheduled to be there.

An Associated Press story explained, "John P. Curley, graduate manager of Boston College, said the entire Eagle team was to have visited the Cocoanut Grove, scene of the fire tragedy, had it ended the season undefeated. No players attended the planned victory celebration, however, because the traditional rivals, Holy Cross, trounced Boston College, 55-12, Saturday afternoon in the final game for both teams."

BRUCE JONES
GUARD · 1923 - '25
CAPT. '25

FRED SINGTON
GUARD · 1928 - 30
ALL AMERICA '29 · 30
ALL S.E.C. '29 · 30

DIXIE HOWELL
BACK · 1932 - '34
ALL AMERICA '34
ALL S.E.C. '33 · 34

POOLEY HUBERT
BACK · 1923 · 25 · CAPT. '24
ALL AMERICA '25 · ALL SOU. '24 · 25

DON HUTSON
END · 1932 - '34
ALL AMERICA '34
ALL S.E.C. '34

BULLY VANDERGRAAFF
TACKLE · 1912 - 15 · ALL AMERICA '15
ALL SOU. '14 - 15

ALABAMA'S   ALL-TI

BILL LEE
Tackle · 1932·34
Capt. '34
All America '34
All S.E.C. 33·34

JOHN CAIN
Back · 1930·32
Capt. '32
All America '32
All Sou. 30·31·32

AUXFORD BURKS
Back · 1902 · '06
Capt. '05

T RAST
· 1939·41
MERICA '41
E.C. '40·41

JOE DOMNANOVICH
Center·1940·'42
Capt. '42
All America '42
All S.E.C. '42

As it looked in 1943.

E   FOOTBALL   TEAM

So as it was, Boston College carried its famed "T" offensive formation (developed by the Eagles and widely used today) to Miami to challenge Alabama. Crimson Tide loyals fondly and quite appropriately called the victory "The Great Miami 'T' Party."

Romney Wheeler, writing the game for the Associated Press, called the Alabama victory more—"Sarasota is winter quarters of Ringling Brothers' circus, but the greatest show on earth was right here in the Orange Bowl."

1945 Sugar Bowl Game

Duke 29   Alabama 26

From Birmingham came a fellow,
Who passed and ran to fame;
People called him "Harry The Hat"—
Football was his game.

Gilmer jumped high to pass,
The result always the same;
A touchdown for Alabama,
Another opponent left lame.

He led a team called babies,
Who soon became grown men;
The Sugar Bowl was something,
But Harry had just begun.

—Buddy Liles

Harry Gilmer almost blew it. He almost missed the bus, which means fans came close to missing one of the all-time great performances in college football history.

Had Gilmer missed that ride in December, 1944—the bus carrying the University of Alabama football team to the 1945 Sugar Bowl game at New Orleans, Louisiana—a storied career could have gone up in smoke.

But Gilmer, then an 18-year-old Crimson Tide freshman halfback, made the trip, was a hero in a 29-26 Alabama loss to Duke, and became known as the greatest passer in the country.

Alabama, known as the "War Babies" because the team

73

was made up mostly of freshmen and military rejects, was a three-touchdown underdog in the game with an experienced, huge Duke team made up of navy trainees. But Gilmer completed eight of eight passes and the Crimson Tide led 26-20 with less than two minutes left in the game before Duke rallied to win.

After the game, Grantland Rice, the all-time great sportswriter, called Gilmer "the greatest college passer I ever saw, barring neither Sammy Baugh or Sid Luckman. This young Birmingham boy can hit a squirrel in the eye at 50 yards.

"He was the Davy Crockett of the Crimson Tide in a seesaw, whirlwind, wild and wooly contest that changed leads with such dizzy speed that only the scoreboard could give the big crowd the story."

Gilmer, now an assistant coach with the St. Louis Cardinals of the National Football League (he was head coach of Detroit in the NFL and an assistant with Atlanta), looks back on his first year in college and chuckles. He also wonders what would have happened had he not caught the bus which carried him to instant fame.

"I was a foolish young kid in those days," Gilmer said. "I had been up in Birmingham visiting Katherine (now his wife of 30-plus years) and I really didn't care if I made that bus or not. I pulled up just as the bus was leaving.

"But when I got on and got in my seat and saw the look on Coach (Frank) Thomas' face, I sure was glad to be there.

"To tell the truth, we really didn't care that much about playing the Sugar Bowl. We were all young and crazy then and that's one reason we got the 'War Babies' name. All we had were young people and 4-Fs from service examinations. We played, however, and it gave Alabama great exposure."

Not only did the stunning margin of defeat, or near-win as some loyals remember it, give the Crimson Tide exposure, it provided 72,000 Sugar Bowl Stadium fans with a football show not easy to forget.

"For the past 10 years after each Sugar Bowl classic I've written this sentence: 'This is the greatest of all Sugar Bowl games,' said *New Orleans States-Item* sportswriter Fred Digby. 'There'll never be another one like it.'

"This time I'm going to say it again and more. There'll never be another like the 11th classic, won by Duke's Blue Devils over the Crimson Tide of Alabama, 29 to 26. It was not only the greatest bowl game. It was the greatest game I ever saw in more than 30 years.

"Eight touchdowns and a safety—a total of 55 points—were jammed into the 60 minutes of football. A game that kept some 72,000 fans (including 20,000 servicemen and women) in the throes of excitement from start to finish; to the last, last second."

Alabama was shooting for a bowl "Grand Slam" in the game, having already won in the Rose, Cotton, and Orange bowls, but the Crimson Tide was given no chance of defeating Duke. A slaughter appeared in the works shortly after the opening kickoff.

On the first play from scrimmage, Duke halfback George Clark ran 52 yards, then faked a pass and ran for a touchdown on the next play. The point-after kick made it 7-0.

But Gilmer and the "War Babies" did not wilt. Ralph Jones recovered a Duke fumble on the Blue Devils' 35 yard line. Norwood Hodges gained 15 yards, then he and Lowell Tew ran the ball to a first down on the Duke 8. Gilmer passed to Hal Self, who was stopped a foot short of the goal line. Hodges scored, but Hugh Morrow missed the extra point and Duke led, 7-6.

Alabama marched 69 yards for another touchdown late in the first quarter. Gilmer ran 20 yards, but lost 16 when he slipped trying to pass. From the Crimson Tide 40 yard line, he passed to Jones, who ran to the Duke 2. Hodges scored the touchdown on the next play, but Morrow missed the extra point.

Alabama scored in the second quarter when Gilmer passed 51 yards to Jones, then 10 more to Jones for the touchdown. Morrow kicked the extra point for a 19-7 Crimson Tide lead.

Duke promptly rallied and drove 63 yards for a touchdown and it was 19-13 at halftime.

Duke, a massive team, began to wear down the "War Babies" in the third quarter. The Blue Devils drove 63 yards for the tying touchdown and took the lead, 20-19, with the extra point.

But in the fourth quarter, Morrow intercepted a pass and returned it 80 yards for an Alabama touchdown. The point-after kick made it 26-20, Crimson Tide.

Duke drove to the Alabama two-yard line, where the Crimson Tide stopped the charge. But Thomas did not want his team to handle the ball near the end zone and ordered Alabama to take an intentional safety so that Alabama could free-kick the ball into safer territory.

"I was against giving them the two points on that safety," Gilmer said. "But I was a kid and the coach was a pretty successful one."

The plan backfired. Alabama free-kicked 40 yards and Duke returned the ball to the Crimson Tide 40 yard line. Three plays later, Duke scored on a 20-yard run by Clark. The point-after gave the Blue Devils their final margin of victory.

The "War Babies" were not completely finished, however. On the last play of the game, Gilmer passed to Jones, who raced for the end zone. The final Duke defender made a diving attempt to stop Jones, caught one foot, and the Crimson Tide runner tumbled to the ground as the gun sounded ending the game.

"Few people know we came that close to pulling the thing out," Gilmer said.

The loss left Alabama with a 5-2-2 record, but the "War Babies" received ovations nationwide. A moral victory was in the books and Crimson Tide fans pitched a celebration after the game. It started at Antoine's Restaurant and ended at the St. Charles Hotel—just before daylight.

"That game was my greatest thrill in football," Gilmer said.

The 1945 Sugar Bowl game was just the beginning for Gilmer, who would later lead the Crimson Tide to two more bowls en route to becoming a record-breaking passer and runner feared by every Alabama opponent. He was All-American his sophomore and senior seasons and became one of the most colorful figures in Alabama football history.

He remembers how it all began.

"I always lived near Howard College in Birmingham," Gilmer said, looking back at his start in football, "and on my way home from grammar school I used to stop by the athletic field and watch the varsity practice. Often, when practice was finished, a bunch of kids from the neighborhood used to have games there—football, baseball, or basketball—according to the season. I received many a whipping for coming home late, with a torn shirt or muddy trousers.

"I usually played quarterback on the grammar school and neighborhood teams and I was quite a hip blocker. The main

Famed passer Harry Gilmer also could run.

reason I played quarterback was that most of the fellows on the team were bigger than me—I weighed about 110 then—and they picked the choice spots in the backfield and would only let me play if I'd do the blocking at quarterback. So I seldom got to do much passing, running, or kicking in those days.

"I entered Woodlawn High School in 1940 and made the freshman teams in football, baseball and basketball—and finally got to play left halfback. Travis Tidwell, who was called on to play halfback at Auburn, played halfback. He entered the Navy in 1942, so I got to play left halfback. If Tidwell hadn't been drafted, I don't guess I would have ever gotten the chance to pass a football.

"I never tried a pass in a regular game until my senior year at Woodlawn. Of course, I used to pass the ball around in practice and in sandlot games, but until I was shifted to left half-

Crimson Tide leader Hal Self.

back, I never practiced seriously. I don't know why I started to jump or leap nearly every time I passed (he made the jump pass famous during his college years). We had some halfbacks at Woodlawn who did it on a play designed by our coach, Malcolm Laney, so I guess I might have started jumping without realizing it. I kept practicing as a senior and found that I could pass just as accurately when I was running and jumping as I could standing still."

Gilmer was so accurate as a passer in high school that Zipp Newman of the *Birmingham News* wrote, "Harry is as fine a passer as there is in football. This goes for the pros, too."

Colleges were drooling at the thought of having Gilmer play football for them, but he had the same answer for all of them when they came visiting—"I just plan to get me a job and get married."

Thomas was persistent, however. He hired Laney as an assistant coach in hopes that Gilmer would follow his high school mentor to Alabama. The plan worked and Gilmer brought his straggly 155 pounds and strict diet for a stomach ulcer to Alabama.

"I didn't care much about playing football," Gilmer said. "I was in love and spent most of my freshman season in Birmingham. I rarely went to class and there were some days I'd miss practice. I was nothing more than an unsettled kid."

An unsettled kid? Yes, he was, but a talented one. Before his first game as a Crimson Tide player—a 27-27 tie with Louisiana State—Gilmer alarmed Thomas and Laney in a final practice session at Baton Rouge.

Working in informal groups, Alabama players were toning up their muscles. Gilmer was putting on a passing display, trying to see how far he could throw the ball. Laney screamed for Gilmer to stop, but the Crimson Tide halfback did not hear him.

Visibly upset, Laney charged at Gilmer screaming, "What in the name of Pete are you doing, Harry? Stop that before you hurt your arm."

Digesting what Laney had said to him—some of it was not nice—Gilmer shook his head and mumbled, "I'm sorry, Coach. Some of the boys wanted to see how far I could throw. I wasn't trying to be smart...they wanted it and I didn't think it would hurt anything. My arm doesn't hurt a bit."

"How many times did you pass?" Laney asked.

"Just three times," Gilmer answered.

Laney walked down the field to the players Gilmer had passed to and said, "Lay off that stuff, you guys. Don't ever let Harry do that again. Do you understand?"

The players nodded, but Laney continued. "Now that the damage is done, just how far did the passes go?"

One of the players spoke up, "The first one was his worst, Coach, and it went 69 yards. The second was for 72 and third, 71. It was beautiful. He threw straight to us. If one of those LSU boys thinks he can stop that business, he's crazy."

Laney ran over to Thomas and told him what happened. Then he said, "And Frank, do you know how far that boy threw, and dead to his receivers?"

Thomas shook his head.

"Tommy, hold your hair," Laney said, "because he got an average of better than 70 yards in three tries!"

Thomas smiled, shook his head, and said, "Well, make him come in and let's get that arm checked. Apparently that boy has a good one."

1946 Rose Bowl Game

Alabama 34   Southern California 14

Winners never quit,
Quitters never win;
The rallying cry of Thomas,
And his Alabama men.

The noise was subsiding somewhat in the Rose Bowl that lovely January 1, 1946, afternoon. Moments earlier, the stadium had been in an uproar as 93,000 fans cheered wildly in appreciation of a performance by the University of Alabama football team.

Alabama defeated Southern California, 34-14, that sunny Pasadena, California, day, and crestfallen Jeff Cravath—the losing coach—talked with newspaper reporters in a corner of the stadium after the contest.

"There goes a great coach," Cravath softly said as he pointed to Frank Thomas, who was slowly heading for a rousing Alabama dressing room. "I'll never forget what he did today. If he had wanted, he could have named the score."

But Thomas, one of the greatest football coaches and gentlemen in history, did not run up the margin of victory on Southern Cal. He played every available Crimson Tide player in the skirmish, the final score being the result of another awesome performance by an Alabama team that had chalked up a 10-0 record.

"Coach Tommy" was satisfied when he left the field that day. He congratulated his team in the dressing room, then eased off into a corner and cried. It was an afternoon to remember, for it was to be his last bowl game as a coach, although he did not realize it at the time.

Thomas, who compiled a 115-24-7 record at Alabama from 1931 to 1946, did not feel well as his squad stormed past Southern Cal. He was becoming a very sick man, a victim of high blood pressure. His persistent drive was suddenly failing him. His condition would get no better.

After the final regular-season game, a 55-13 victory over Mississippi State, Thomas publicly admitted for the first time that he was weary.

"I do not believe I could have held up all season if my boys hadn't given me such a lift with their great performances," Thomas said. "I'm a worn-out man. I'm glad it's over."

For the latter part of the season Thomas had been under

A Pasadena, California, dog seems unimpressed as Alabama linemen stay in shape for the 1946 game.

the care of his physician, Dr. Joe Hirsch. The doctor made trips with the team and ordered the coach to watch his diet, quit smoking, and curtail outside activities.

Thomas, who was usually busy with speaking engagements and community service in Tuscaloosa, followed orders and looked forward to rest at the end of the season. But when the Rose Bowl called, prolonging the season another month, it was Thomas who persuaded his players to accept the invitation.

On December 1, Thomas dismissed the team, saying, "You deserve a rest. Go out and have fun. Forget football for a few days and report back to me on December 8."

During the week off, Thomas spoke with pride about his team. "I never thought this would happen," he told his wife,

Frances. "This will be our fourth straight bowl game—Cotton, Orange, Sugar, and now the Rose. Haven't my 'War Babies' grown up? These are the greatest kids I've ever coached. I'm sure they will do well against Southern Cal. The Lord has been good to me."

Somewhat rested himself, Thomas worked his team hard in Tuscaloosa, then worked them just as hard on the West Coast. By game day, the team was prepared....But the coach was exhausted.

"I'm dead tired," Thomas told his wife at breakfast, "and the day is only beginning. I'm glad I don't have to play today. I'm happy, too, the players don't feel like I do. I don't know what's wrong with me, but I tire so quickly these days."

Good health never returned to the immortal Thomas. He could not control his blood pressure, but refused to quit. He spent the following summer with specialists in North Carolina, then came back to coach Alabama to a 7-4 record during the 1946 regular season. (He was bed-ridden much of the season and conducted practice while seated on a trailer because he could not stand for long periods of time.) He resigned as coach at the end of the year.

In 1951 Thomas was elected to the Football Hall of Fame. After a gallant fight, he died in Druid City Hospital at Tuscaloosa on May 10, 1954.

"Coach Tommy" lives on, however, at least in the thoughts of Hal Self, the quarterback on his final bowl team.

"We knew Coach Thomas was not well," Self said, "but he was not the kind of man to complain or quit. He was some fellow. Even when he was sick, he worked hard until he could work no more. We all loved him for it, too."

Self, a standout player for the Crimson Tide as a powerful blocker and short-yardage runner, scored the first two Alabama touchdowns in the Rose Bowl victory over Southern Cal, but his fondest memory concerning the game stems from a head-to-head confrontation with Thomas in early December. It assured Alabama participation in the contest.

The Crimson Tide was invited to the Rose Bowl after the sixth game of the regular season, but Alabama players were not sure they wanted to play in the game.

"We accepted the invitation to play as soon as it was issued," Self said, "but we were not sure we wanted to go. We had been training since February and had played in the Sugar

84

Bowl the year before, so we were pretty tired of football. We were just a bunch of kids who wanted to be at home for Christmas. We wanted a rest.

"Well, we were in a skull practice one afternoon just after the regular season ended and Coach Thomas started writing on the chalkboard. He was writing what all we would get if we accepted the invitation. You know, so many tickets, a gold football, a Christmas present...and he was putting a monetary value on the trip.

"I didn't like that much—neither did a lot of the other guys—so I started shaking my head. Coach Thomas didn't care for that, so he turned to me and said, 'Self, I'd like to talk to you alone.'

"He really let me have it and said I had a bad attitude. I guess he talked to some other guys, too, because we all soon agreed the Rose Bowl was the place to go.

Hal Self runs for Alabama.

85

"Well, as usually was the case, Coach Thomas was right. He knew if we declined the chance to play in that game, that we would regret it the rest of our lives. To this day, I'm glad we went."

Alabama stormed through the regular season in 1945, setting a school record for points scored (430). Victories came easily—21-0 over Keesler Air Force, 26-7 over Louisiana State, 55-0 over South Carolina, 25-7 over Tennessee, 28-14 over Georgia, 60-19 over Kentucky, 71-0 over Vanderbilt, 55-6 over Pensacola Navy, and the romp over Mississippi State, 55-13.

The Crimson Tide used the famous "Notre Dame Box" offense in piling up its impressive point total. The attack was spearheaded by halfback Harry Gilmer, the passing and running sophomore whiz who had gained fame a year earlier in the Sugar Bowl loss to Duke.

Regardless of the stunning regular season Alabama had enjoyed, West Coast writers scoffed at the chances of the Crimson Tide defeating mighty Southern Cal, which had won eight consecutive Rose Bowl games. "You've won in the Rose Bowl before," said one sportswriter, "but, Alabama, you haven't played Southern Cal yet."

Lowell Tew steps in for a touchdown.

Self remembers the bad ink the Crimson Tide received. "We were getting awful publicity," he said, "and we didn't care for it. I remember Dick Hyland, one of the writers out there, called us 'Swamp Rats' and that's about the nicest thing he had to say.

"But we didn't let it get to us much. We were a close group—a bunch of kids who grew up together, so to speak. We knew we would be ready for Southern Cal, because when Coach Thomas prepared a team, he prepared one right."

Bad publicity was the least of Alabama's problems entering the Rose Bowl game. Inclement weather plagued practice at Tuscaloosa, an outbreak of flu among team members worsened the situation, and Lowell Tew, a starting halfback, suffered a broken jaw in the final Tuscaloosa workout and made the trip with his teeth wired together.

"No football player has been given any more attention than Lowell Tew was given on the trip to Pasadena," wrote Zipp Newman in the *Birmingham News*. "He was fed on an hourly schedule from early in the morning until tucked in between the blankets at night. In one meal he had the equivalent of 10 pounds of choice beef. Two cases of concentrated foods were put on the train at New Orleans and at every stop new supplies were added for Tew."

By game day, the flu had subsided and six-point-favored Alabama took the field to play one of its greatest games ever.

Alabama scored its first touchdown in the first six minutes of the game, Self bulling over from the one yard line after a fumble recovery at the Southern Cal 14. Hugh Morrow kicked the extra point, the first of a Rose Bowl record four.

The Crimson Tide scored 13 points in the second quarter, Self running 21 yards for a touchdown after receiving a pass from Gilmer and Tew running 1 yard. The score was 20-0 at halftime and Southern Cal's vaunted offense had run 21 plays for a net loss of 24 yards.

"It is difficult to express the feelings I had on those two touchdowns," Self said. "But I can promise you it made me feel good."

In the third quarter, Norwood Hodges bulled his way over center from 1 yard for a touchdown and Gilmer ran 21 yards for the final Crimson Tide touchdown in the fourth quarter.

Southern Cal scored its 14 points late in the game, after Thomas had emptied the Alabama bench. He even sent guard

Nick Terlizzi into action with a broken leg.

"Nick, would you like to be able to say you played in a Rose Bowl game?" Thomas asked on the sidelines late in the game.

"Yes, sir, Coach!" Terlizzi answered.

"Well, go out there, but don't get in any mixups and get hurt," Thomas instructed. "Stay out of the way of all plays."

To the amazement of the crowd, Terlizzi hobbled onto the field.

For the game, Alabama outgained the Trojans 351 yards to 41. Southern Cal gained only 6 yards running. Gilmer, reputed to be the greatest passer in the nation, amazed the fans at the game by running for 116 yards on 16 carries.

The bad press Alabama had received before kickoff became glittering praise. Some samples:

Ned Cronin, *Los Angeles Daily News*: "Ushers were having trouble finding places in the stands for guys wearing white jersies and red helmets who were constantly being thrown up there by the Alabamians. The Trojans can consider themselves fortunate indeed that Alabama didn't go all the way and haul off and throw Rufus Bernhard von Kleinsmid (president of Southern California) clean through the clock at the end of the stadium."

Ben Parson, *Los Angeles Daily News*: "The boys from Tuscaloosa made Troy's men look like guys from Arthritis Academy."

Russ Newland, Associated Press: "USC was outplayed, out-powered, and out-dazzled—never before in the memory of the oldest inhabitants was a Trojan team so humiliated."

Dick Friendlich, *San Francisco Chronicle*: "The beefy but bewildered Trojans were taken in, driven out, whip-sawed, and double-timed by a crisp-blocking outfit that made every movement with sparkling competence."

The kind words of the press meant a lot to Thomas, because he spent most of the train trip home reading in his drawing room while players, fans, sportswriters, and school officials celebrated the victory.

History shows things got worse for the Alabama coach, so bad that it was suggested to him during the next regular season that he should resign with a 4-0 record.

"I can't quit on my kids," Thomas answered the proposal. "This winter maybe, but not now."

Winter came and a legendary era of Alabama football ended.

Lowell Tew heads down sidelines.

1948 Sugar Bowl Game
Texas 27   Alabama 7

Roses are red,
LSU is blue;
Sugar is sweet,
And so is Alabama.

    —Harry J. Mehre,
       sportswriter

    As the sun went falling over the horizon on October 4, 1947, University of Alabama football coach Red Drew wore a face as bright as his first name. To say he was embarrassed would be an understatement.

    To say Alabama football was in the dumps that night at Nashville, Tennessee, would be accurate. The mighty Crimson Tide, picked to win another Southeastern Conference championship, was drowning in a sea of despair.

    Alabama had arrived in Tennessee the day before as a heavy betting favorite to defeat Vanderbilt, but the Crimson Tide lost. It was the second defeat for Alabama in three games that season and the fifth defeat in the last eight games.

    Sportswriters around the nation were writing the Alabama obit. A panic swept the state.

    "Alabama's Crimson Tide, preseason favorite of many experts for the 1947 Southeastern Conference gridiron championship, today stood at the bottom of the conference standings, the result of two successive losses to league foes," wrote Bill Waddell in the *Birmingham Post.*

"Latest defeat for the boys from Tuscaloosa came in Dudley Field here Saturday when an inspired Vanderbilt eleven completely out-played the Crimsons for three quarters and a well-deserved 14-7 victory.

"And unlike their conference opener loss by 20-21 to Tulane, Alabama dropped one here to a surprise contender for Southeastern honors.

"Alabama conceivably could have a disastrous season, despite its veteran senior team."

Drew, who was in his first season as head coach after taking over for the ailing Frank Thomas, was receiving a rude baptism. Critics, making much of the fact that the Crimson Tide roster was loaded with seniors who had played marvelous bowl games as freshmen (1945 Sugar) and sophomores (1946 Rose), were pointing a vicious finger in the direction of the new head man.

But Drew did not waver. He even treated the Alabama misfortune with a bit of humor.

"We could have won the Tulane game," Drew told the Tuscaloosa Rotary Club the week after the loss to Vanderbilt, "but were outplayed last Saturday at Nashville. I think our team has better games in its system.

"We had a hard time making up our schedule for this year, but now we have a pile of telegrams from schools that want to play us."

By the end of the season, few people wanted a shot at Alabama. The Crimson Tide had come back in grand fashion by winning its last seven regular-season games.

Drew, who only two months earlier was considered "backward" in the ways of winning football, was suddenly being heralded as "another shrewd leader" of Alabama football fortunes.

Bowl games were important to Alabama fans in those days--as they are now--and Drew had picked a team up off the ground and sprinkled it with Sugar. The Crimson Tide was invited to play in the Sugar Bowl and all was well and back to normal in the Deep South.

Ray Richeson, an All-American guard on the 1947 Alabama team, remembers well how the Crimson Tide made its miracle turnaround before losing to Texas, 27-7, in the Sugar Bowl.

"As young kids say today," Richeson said, "we just got our heads on straight. I really can't put my finger on what made

us come back the way we did, but I do know it was a great period of self-rededication at Alabama.

"Those first two losses kind of stunned us, especially the one to Tulane. We should have won that one. Talk about turn-arounds, well, they made one on us. We had them 20-0 and before we knew what had happened, boom, they were ahead to stay. We were just a flat football team against Vanderbilt.

"With Coach Drew taking over, there was a new command at Alabama, but that wasn't why we got off to the slow start. The coach didn't lose those games; we players did.

"And it was us players who got things straightened out. After the Vandy loss, we didn't say much, but you could see it on the faces. Everybody had that look like something good was going to happen. I guess what it boiled down to was us saying, 'Hey, we're a good club, so let's get it together and have a helluva season.'"

Richeson, who played at Alabama at a mammoth 6-foot-1 and 225 pounds and later took his ability to Pittsburgh of the National Football League, remembers the pride he felt when the Sugar Bowl invitation came. "We worked hard for it and it meant a lot to us," he said. "It meant the chance to carry on the Alabama tradition. It was really nice getting that invitation, especially the way we had to bounce back and earn it."

After defeating Mississippi Southern (34-7) and losing to Tulane and Vanderbilt, Alabama rode victories over Duquesne (26-0), Tennessee (10-0), Georgia (17-7), Kentucky (13-0), Georgia Tech (14-7), Louisiana State (41-12), and Miami (21-6) into the Sugar Bowl. Actually, the win over Miami was elementary because the impressive LSU performance was proof enough of Crimson Tide worth.

In fact, it took only one play in the LSU game to insure an invitation, according to sportswriter Harry J. Mehre.

"Over in Tuscaloosa, some seconds after the game started Saturday, Harry Gilmer raced down the sidelines some 90 yards for the first Alabama touchdown," Mehre wrote in a Monday followup story. "Even before Gilmer scored, I noticed a big huddle around Red Drew on a fence and thought to myself that Old 'Bama is not letting Michigan get ahead of them. Here Drew is ready to put in a defensive unit.

"Adjusting my bifocals to my binoculars, I saw immediately that I was mistaken. It was just part of the Sugar Bowl committee cornering Drew for his signature to be one-half of the New Orleans show come January 1. The committee had come from the end zone. They were non-partisan and ready and eager to rush to whichever side of the field the winner was on."

Gilmer, the All-American senior halfback who had become the greatest passer in Alabama history, scored two touchdowns in the victory over LSU. Two days prior to the game, his wife, Katherine, gave birth to a daughter in Birmingham.

After the victory over Miami, Drew gave his troops a rest, announcing that practice would begin for the Sugar Bowl on December 15. On December 23, the Crimson Tide traveled to Biloxi, Mississippi, for final workouts, before arriving in New Orleans on New Year's Eve.

When Alabama got to New Orleans, it found itself a touchdown underdog to the powerful Longhorns, champions of the Southwest Conference with a 9-1 record. The Crimson Tide also found a city going mad over football in anticipation of a showdown between passers—Gilmer of Alabama and Bobby Layne of Texas.

"New Orleans woke up this morning from its confetti-laden rootin', tootin', New Year's Eve celebration and went football mad," the *New Orleans States* reported in its January 1 edition.

Harold (Red) Drew with Thomas (Corky) Tharp.

"The climax of the whole Sugar Bowl sports program is today—the game between the mighty University of Alabama and the ditto University of Texas football teams. Colors of the two teams were all over Canal Street, all over the hotels, in every lapel.

"New Orleans is jammed in all crannies with visitors here from all over the globe for the big Sugar Bowl game. And this morning, every mode of transportation was still bringing them in as fast as possible.

"This morning, celebrators shook themselves loose from slumber in the much bedecked Roosevelt Hotel, headquarters for Texas; in the southern-style St. Charles, where Alabama's masses are headquartering; in the Pullman cities in which hundreds of visitors slept comfortably on railroad sidings.

"Celebrities were a dime a dozen, and nobody was so important as the football teams of the two universities.

"The big attraction will be the passing duel between Texas' Bobby Layne, one of the greatest to come out of the Lone Star State, and Alabama's Harry Gilmer, who thrilled football fans before in the 1945 Sugar Bowl game against Duke. These two are expected to add more color to the game than in previous years. Each will be playing his last college game."

For Gilmer, an expected final stroll to stardom became a nightmare. He played one of his poorest games as an Alabama player in his last one. Gilmer had only 5 yards rushing on nine attempts and completed only 3 of 11 passes for 35 yards. He threw a pass to Ed White for the only Alabama touchdown in the game.

On the other hand, Layne was dynamic. He paced the Longhorns in the second half as Texas broke away from a 7-7 halftime deadlock. For the game, Layne ran eight times for 34 yards and completed 11 of 26 passes for 195 yards and one touchdown.

"I'll always remember that Sugar Bowl game," Gilmer said, "because you always remember the bad along with the good.

"But there is something enjoyable about any bowl game. The thrill of being invited to one, the friendships you make, the travel, and a lot more. The extra work you have to go through is worth it."

For Alabama, New Orleans in 1948 must have been all the sweeter. After all, the Crimson Tide played the devil getting there.

1953 Orange Bowl Game

Alabama 61   Syracuse 6

Scoreboard lights flashed,
As Alabama rolled and rolled;
Syracuse was a helpless victim,
Down in Miami's Orange Bowl.

The Orangemen turned Crimson,
As 'Bama poured on the steam;
The Yankees just couldn't stop,
An ever-powerful Tide team.

Sixty-one points in sixty minutes,
That's what 'Bama got that day;
The Big Red just ran over,
Anything that got in its way.

—Papa Stewart

"We just beat the devil out of 'em. We had one helluva football team and we were ready to play. No, I never dreamed we could win by that much, but who did? We just jumped 'em early, got 'em down, and momentum carried us the rest of the way."—Bobby Luna, University of Alabama sophomore halfback who played in the 1953 Orange Bowl football game.

"My boys gave it all they had and I can't ask for more than that. Either Alabama was a lot better than we figured or we were a lot worse."—Floyd Schwartzwalder, University of Syracuse head football coach.

96

The final score was Alabama 61, Syracuse 6.

What else can be said? Who would have ever believed 55 points could separate two football bowl teams?

Well, it happened on January 1, 1953, at Miami, Florida. Under bright, sunny skies, the Crimson Tide of Alabama took Syracuse to the cleaners, so to speak, as 66,280 fans gasped for air in the Orange Bowl and millions more watched on television.

The margin of victory remains the greatest in bowl history and the story will probably always be one of the most frequently told by Alabama fans.

As Zipp Newman wrote in the *Birmingham News* after the mismatch had ended, "Come the years and Alabama supporters will take their grandchildren on their knees and tell them about the time Alabama beat Syracuse in the 1953 Orange Bowl—smashing 12 records in the most record-breaking bowl game in history."

Luna, who went on to make All-American as a senior, set one of the records Alabama established that day. He scored 19 points by making two touchdowns and 7 extra points.

"Beating Syracuse that bad was a lot of fun," Luna said, "but to tell you the truth, the margin of victory was not that special to us. The fact we got to play in the Orange Bowl meant more.

"We had a young team that season. Seven sophomores started and since we were so young, we didn't really give a dern who we played or how much we beat them.

"But it is something to remember and the beautiful thing about the game is everybody we had with us got to play."

Luna exited action after the second play of the second half. He ran 38 yards for a touchdown on the play, then kicked the extra point. The touchdown gave Alabama a 28-6 advantage.

"By then we knew it was all over," Luna said. "Actually, we knew we had them beat after we had the ball the first time. We took the opening kickoff and drove it down their throats. After that, everything fell in place for us."

Syracuse took the ensuing kickoff after the first Alabama touchdown and marched for a touchdown to make the score 7-6. Then the roof fell in on the Orangemen, who were making the first bowl appearance in school history.

Alabama scored 14 points in the second quarter, 20 in the third, and 20 in the fourth. Tommy Lewis joined Luna in pro-

High-scoring Bobby Luna.

ducing two touchdowns, while Corky Tharp, Bobby Marlow, Joe Cummings, Hootie Ingram, and Buster Hill scored one each. Clell Hobson directed the Alabama attack at quarterback, but a freshman named Bart Starr backed him up.

Perhaps Alabama head coach Red Drew summed it up best when he told postgame interviewers, "Boy, were we hot! I just couldn't stop them."

Tackle Van Marcus indicated Alabama did not want to be stopped, however. "We didn't want to leave any still standing."

Alabama established the following records in the game: margin of victory, 55; first downs, 25; passes completed, 22; total offense, 588 yards; players used, 47; conversions after touchdowns, 7; longest punt return (Ingram), 80 yards; leading pass receiver (Joe Curtis), 8; most points (Luna), 19; most conversions (Luna), 7; most points, 61; and best percentage on pass completions, .647 (22 of 34).

Defeating Syracuse, Alabama put the wraps on a 10-2 season and temporarily silenced Drew critics. It was the first bowl appearance for Alabama in five years.

Crimson Tide victories during the 1952 regular season were over Mississippi Southern (20-6), Louisiana State (21-20), Miami (21-7), Virginia Tech (33-0), Mississippi State (42-19), Georgia (34-19), Chattanooga (42-28), Maryland (27-7), and Auburn (21-0). Losses came at the hands of Tennessee (20-0) and Georgia Tech (7-3). Tennessee was en route to the Southeastern Conference championship and Georgia Tech was riding a 22-game streak without loss.

"The Georgia Tech loss hurt us badly, because we had them beaten," Luna said. "Tennessee simply swamped us."

While Alabama was "swamping" Syracuse at Miami, Texas was blanking Tennessee, 16-0, in the Cotton Bowl.

Regardless of scores, Syracuse sportswriter Billy Reddy was calling Alabama unbeatable after the Orange Bowl game. "Alabama was the greatest today," he said. "Alabama would have beaten any team in the nation had they played here this afternoon."

Other samples of post-game remarks:

Don Cuddy, *Washington Daily News*—"The next Lambert Trophy winner the East sends to the Orange Bowl may have to pay its way in. Syracuse came a long way to be shown the pride of the East is not in the same class with the fourth or fifth best club of Dixie."

Clyde Hirt, *New York Daily Mirror*—"Alabama's Crimson Tide, flowing with awesome power on both land and in the air, drowned Syracuse's outclassed Orange in a 61-6 Orange Bowl flood today."

John M. Steen, *St. Petersburg Independent*—"'Get there fastest with the mostest.' Alabama's football juggernaut did just

All-American runner Bobby Marlow.

that, smothering the Syracuse Orangemen under a touchdown avalanche, 61-6."

Charles Israel, *Philadelphia Bulletin*—"Alabama won the

Battle of the Biscuits when those hard Crackers from Tuscaloosa crunched the Saltine Warriors of Syracuse by a one-sided score in the Orange Bowl.

"The game demonstrated the superiority of the Southern teams over any aggregation that the damnyankees could send across the Mason and Dixon line.

"The up-state New Yorkers were ruthlessly butchered to make a Miami holiday. It was cruel and barbarous treatment."

For Alabama's record-breaking, pass-catching end Joe Curtis, it was fun—after he put his hands around catch No. 8. Curtis, Hobson, and Starr conspired on the sidelines to insure Curtis' record-breaking catch.

Early in the final quarter, Hobson got to figuring and found the squad needed four more pass completions to break a record and Curtis figured out he needed only one more reception to establish his record.

"I want to catch one for a touchdown," Curtis pleaded with Hobson as both of them sat on the bench.

"I sure can't do anything about it," Hobson answered. "I ain't playing either."

The duo took their plea to Coach Drew, who agreed to let them try for the record. Hobson threw four straight passes to Curtis, but the end dropped them all. Then Starr threw one to him, which he caught, but a penalty wiped out the play. Finally, Starr flipped a short pass to Curtis and the record was established.

Obviously, Alabama had the liberty to play around some during the game. But what about Syracuse? Well, Art Grace, a sportswriter for the *Miami Daily News*, roamed the Orangemen's sideline during the game and wrote the following:

"Schwartzwalder's ostensible calmness as Alabama poured on the power in the third and fourth periods was a classic example of stoicism. When Luna ran through the Orangemen for 38 yards to make the score 28-6, he merely stroked his chin, turned to his quarterback, and told him what to call on offense.

"A few minutes later Alabama got the ball on the Syracuse one-yard-line and went over to make it 35-6. This time Schwartzwalder turned toward the bench and remarked, 'Come on, gang, let's get the game moving. We can still go.'

"With the score 47-6 and Syracuse obviously going nowhere, Schwartzwalder said, 'Don't let it get you. Just go out there and keep plugging.'

"When the score soared to 54-6, Schwartzwalder became a little discouraged. Turning to Bill Bell, his backfield coach, he said, 'Well, I can't play. There isn't much we can do now. The kids have lost everything. They're lost out there.'"

1954 Cotton Bowl Game

Rice 28   Alabama 6

Tommy felt badly about his fate,
But his honor was strong and true;
Nobody was hurt on his surprise tackle,
So why should he feel so blue?

Moegle was the star in the game,
But Tommy touched millions of hearts;
Rice won, 28-6, and the game is over,
'Bama's Tommy should never feel torn apart.

—Ronald Forrest Mills

Just about everybody has heard the story about Tommy Lewis and how he ran from the Alabama sidelines to tackle Rice halfback Dicky Moegle in the 1954 Cotton Bowl football game. Every year at bowl time, the much-publicized incident comes back to haunt the culprit.

For Lewis, it was a quick dash to fame and misfortune. More people recall that one play than remember the score—Rice 28, Alabama 6.

But even fewer people remember William Oliver, chiefly because the Alabama defensive halfback has kept quiet about the fabled "Lewis Tackle" from the moment it happened.

For those who do not know, Lewis, an all-star fullback, ran bareheaded from the Alabama bench to tackle Moegle as the Rice halfback was running toward the Crimson Tide goal. The Owls were awarded a 95-yard touchdown on the play, which gave them a 14-6 second-quarter lead. Lewis was thus named the "12th Man" on the Alabama team.

Since that day, accounts of the play have said Lewis made the tackle as Moegle was running all alone toward a Rice score. But pictures and films of the incident show two Alabama players—Nos. 33 and 54—were in hot pursuit of the Owl standout as he was nearing the Crimson Tide 40 yard line.

"I had him," said Oliver, No. 33 in the pictures and films. "There is no doubt about it. I would have stopped Moegle on the play. I had him trapped. I had an angle on him. It would have been a simple matter of bumping him out of bounds.

"You can take the pictures of the play and draw a line between me and Moegle and it is obvious I would have stopped him. Tommy knocked him down on the 38 yard line. With the angle I had on him, I would have probably stopped him on about the 35.

"The only thing which could have kept me from making the tackle was if DeLaurentis (Vincent, No. 54) had stopped him. There was one blocker to stop two of us. If he takes DeLaurentis, I take Moegle. If Moegle tries to cut back on me, DeLaurentis gets him. It was that simple.

"But heck, why cry over something that has already happened? Anyway, the play makes better reading the other way."

Oliver, now a successful account executive ("I'm nothing except a country stockbroker") with an Atlanta investment agency, remembers being in a dazed state when he saw Lewis make his famous tackle.

"It took place so fast that I was put in a state of shock," Oliver said. "I remember seeing Moegle with the ball, then I remember seeing him on the ground.

"I thought Moegle was dead. When Tommy hit him, Moegle did a flap-jack flip and landed on his back. He was still as a mouse. I thought he had a broken neck. Thank goodness he was okay, because the place was shaking with boos. It only knocked the breath out of Moegle. Had he been hurt severely, I would have feared for our lives."

As it was, nobody was hurt worse than Lewis. Immediately after the tackle, he dashed back to the Alabama bench, where he cupped his head in his hands and cried. At halftime, he went to the Rice dressing room and apologized to Moegle and other Owl players. He returned to the dressing room and apologized again after the game. Dallas newspapers ran pictures of Lewis and Moegle shaking hands in their January 2 editions.

104

Tommy Lewis: "Too full of Alabama."

"My heart went out to him," said Rice head coach Jess
Neely after Lewis offered his halftime apology. "I told him,
'Don't let it bother you.'"

The day after the game, Lewis sat in the Hotel Stoneleigh in Dallas and told *Dallas Times-Herald* sportswriter Louis Cox

about the incident.

"I can't get it off my mind," Lewis told the reporter. "I

Captains Bud Willis (84) and Tommy Lewis at Cotton Bowl

couldn't even sleep last night for thinking about it. I sat on the side of the bed all night. My wife tried to console me, but it did no good.

"I still don't know why I did it. It was my last game for Alabama and I guess I just couldn't relish the thought of losing.

"I've never done anything like that before and I'm just glad Moegle wasn't hurt. I'm really sorry it happened. I guess I'm just too full of Alabama.

"I saw him coming a long way...the nearer he got the closer I moved to the sidelines. I don't doubt what happened, but I just couldn't realize that I had done it when I returned to the bench. It seemed like a dream."

Lewis received some relief the morning after the game when he read a front-page editorial in the *Dallas Morning News*. "...Tommy Lewis, a genuine competitor even while on the bench, had committed a forgivable error that will live with him forever. He quickly and abjectly apologized to Moegle and the Rice team and he did it three more times, finally, at game's end, walking out of the big stadium with his arm around Moegle.

"Tommy is a very depressed boy, but he has the qualities that will take him far down the road in a country that prospers and survives because of youngsters who compete on or off the bench.

"Texans know competitive spirit. We thrive on it. It might not be a bad idea to drop Tommy a line over at the University of Alabama, Tuscaloosa, Alabama, and let him know he hasn't lost his last friend. He's quite a fighter—and we like them that way in Texas."

Since millions of television viewers saw the game, the incident received instant national exposure, but it was only the start for Lewis. Ed Sullivan called the Crimson Tide player and invited him to appear on his Sunday night show. Lewis, Moegle, and Neely flew together from Dallas to New York for the appearance.

Moegle, who ran for three touchdowns and 295 yards in pacing the Rice victory over Alabama, was quick to forgive Lewis for his overzealous play.

"Tommy apologized quickly and several times after that," said Moegle, now a businessman in Houston. "I told him not to worry about it, that I was not hurt. I could understand how somebody could do something like that."

Moegle remembers the play this way. "As I was running

108

down the sidelines, I caught a glimpse of a player getting off the bench, but I thought he was just picking something up.

"I turned back to watch the two players chasing me and then he got me from the side. He sort of body blocked me. I was dazed for a while since I was not expecting the action.

"I believed I would have scored. At least I think I had a lead on the others. The Alabama players apologized and slapped me on the back practically every time they tackled me after that. They were real gentlemen.

"I don't know if the tackle made any difference in the outcome of the game or not, but I know the Alabama boys were awfully nice to all of us the rest of the way."

Alabama did not make light of the incident, but it was not mentioned in the Crimson Tide dressing room at halftime. After the game, Coach Red Drew kept the dressing room doors locked for 20 minutes as his players quietly sat waiting for newspaper reporters. Lewis was taken into a small room where he is reported to have cried without shame.

In postgame remarks, Drew minimized the incident by saying, "The incident didn't have any demoralizing effect on our team. Of course, they got a touchdown, but I don't believe it made any difference."

Bobby Luna, an Alabama halfback on the Cotton Bowl team, begs to differ with Drew, however. And he lends even more controversy to the play by claiming the Rice touchdown should have been disallowed by penalty.

"The play definitely had an adverse effect on us," Luna said. "Heck, we spent the rest of the game thinking we had to treat Rice nice. I certainly don't have any hard feelings toward Tommy, but I think we would have won the game had it not happened.

"The touchdown shouldn't have counted anyway. I was clipped on the play and off-setting penalties would have called for the play to be run again.

"I was playing safety and a Rice blocker hit me from behind down around our 25 yard line. The official threw his flag calling a clip—you can see the flag flying in the pictures—so I was sprawled on the ground knowing the play would be called back.

"But when the official saw the off-the-bench tackle he picked up his flag and forgot about the clip."

Lewis' tackle is much publicized, but it is not the only

such mistake in football history. Roy Riegels, a University of California halfback, ran 64 yards the wrong way in the 1929 Rose Bowl. He watched the Lewis mistake on television and offered advice to the Crimson Tide player.

"Laugh with them," Riegels told Lewis. "That's all you've got to do."

Riegels recalled his reaction to the Lewis play by saying, "It was pretty funny. We wondered immediately what had happened when we saw it on television. I imagine the fellow felt quite peculiar about it—like a sap. A lot like I did.

"He'll hear about it for a long time. But what the heck difference does it make! It's just a football game.

"But I could feel for him."

1959 Liberty Bowl Game
Penn State 7   Alabama 0

The growling of The Bear,
Has Tuscaloosa much alive;
Though the numbers are skimpy,
There will be a '58 Crimson Tide.

Those not tough are leaving,
Those mean enough will stay;
So you faint-hearted beware,
'Bama will see better days.

The Bear is back and working,
His aim is another championship;
Before this year is over,
Many a team the Tide will whip.

—James Mills

Wallace Wade, Frank Thomas, and Red Drew produced outstanding football teams in their years as head coaches at the University of Alabama. Wade got the Crimson Tide started in the bowl business, Thomas made Alabama a feared name in postseason play, and Drew carried the cause crucial steps forward.

But when "mama called," Alabama was about to embark on a modern era of football which few, if any, schools can match in success, color, and pure and simple old college spirit.

Mama called. The Bear answered and since that December

When "mama called," Paul (Bear) Bryant answered.

3, 1957, when Paul William Bryant became head coach at Alabama, the Crimson Tide has played in 18 bowl games, won four national championships, and has had more than its share of all-star players.

"We have secured, to our way of thinking, the best football coach in the country for the position of head football coach at the University of Alabama," said Ernest Williams, a Tuscaloosa banker who was chairman of the committee named by school president-elect Frank Rose to study the overall Alabama athletic situation.

Bryant signed a 10-year contract as coach and athletic director. Today, any contract he signs with Alabama is a mere formality.

"This is the most difficult thing I ever had to do," Bryant said in announcing his decision to leave Texas A&M for the Alabama job. "The reason, the only reason, I'm going back is because my school called me."

The Bear arrived in Tuscaloosa growling, calling himself "an ordinary coach that works hard" and talking about the importance of recruiting good players to Alabama—"It's the players who make the coaches, my friend, and the mothers and papas have a lot to do with making the players.

"In a situation such as we accepted at Alabama, the main thing is getting the material and teaching your kids to forget a losing complex. Teach them to win."

It did not take Bryant long to produce winners at Alabama. His first team in 1958 had a 5-4-1 record, with a 10-point loss to Louisiana State on opening day the largest margin of defeat.

The teaching process Bryant used on his first players was rugged. Several players quit the team the first week of fall practice.

"If a man's a quitter, I want him to quit in practice, not in a game," Bryant said. "There has been enough of that. I demand all they've got. We've got to know now whether we can get it later."

After losing his first game at Alabama, Bryant was asked if he was satisfied with the overall effort of his team. "I'm never satisfied when I get beat," Bryant answered.

From that point on, people knew what to expect from Alabama teams. The winning trail—the one which leads to bowl appearances—was followed the next year when Bryant coached his second team to a 7-2-2 record and into the Liberty Bowl against Penn State.

The highlight of the season was a 10-0 victory over Auburn, the first for Alabama over its cross-state rival in five years. Two weeks earlier, the Crimson Tide stunned Georgia Tech, 9-7.

"Before the game, we said it'd take a superhuman effort to beat Auburn and I think our boys gave it," Bryant said. "If our team played 100 percent against Georgia Tech, it played 135 percent to beat Auburn."

113

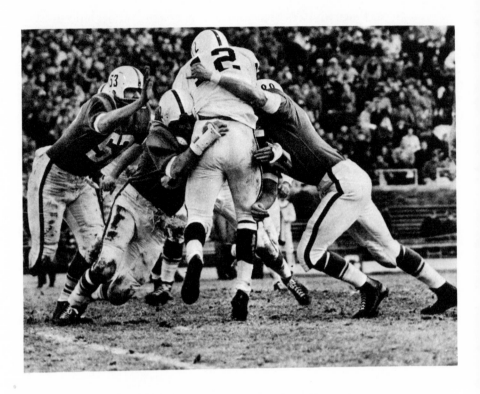

Penn State was tough in 1959 Liberty Bowl.

The victory over Auburn gave Alabama a 7-1-2 record and locked up the berth to the Liberty Bowl. The Crimson Tide was invited to the Blue Grass Bowl at Louisville, Kentucky, but the Liberty Bowl bid was more attractive to Alabama players.

One Alabama starter in the Liberty Bowl game was Billy Richardson, a 5-foot-10, 168-pound sophomore. Now a businessman in Birmingham, he has a sharp memory when the subject is football in the early days of Bryant at Alabama.

"It was rough!" said Richardson, who was a member of the 1958 freshman team that went on to win a national championship during the 1961 season. "Practices were something like none of us had ever gone through. Most of the stories people tell about the early Bryant days are true. It was something.

"I was a high school senior in 1958, so I wasn't at Alabama for the first spring training under Bryant, but I remember it well. The news people were very much aware of what was happening in Tuscaloosa and they showed films of practice almost

Billy Richardson was a star halfback.

every day on television. I remember watching them and getting scared just thinking about showing up for fall practice.

"When the freshmen showed up in 1958, the varsity had already been practicing for a week and I remember looking out on the field and noticing there were only about 30 players left out there. Many of the returnees had already quit and gone home.

"Well, we freshmen got checked in and got our equipment and it was time for our first practice. We went out there scared to death and since there were so few people left, we had to scrimmage full-speed against the varsity the first day. By the time the practice ended, only one quarterback—Mal Moore—was left standing. Pat Trammell and Bill Oliver got hurt.

"I guess everybody out there felt like walking off at one time or another."

The next year was no easier, although Bryant was working with some of his own recruits. "There was little difference," Richardson said. "It was not uncommon for Leon Fuller and me to lose 14 or 15 pounds in one day during preseason practice."

The hard work paid dividends quickly for the 1959 Alabama team. The Crimson Tide lost to eventual Southeastern Conference champion Georgia, 17-3, on opening day, but did not lose again until Penn State took a 7-0 victory in the Liberty Bowl. Victories came over Houston (3-0), Chattanooga (13-0), Mississippi State (10-0), Tulane (19-7), Georgia Tech (9-7), Memphis State (14-7), and Auburn (10-0). Ties were with Vanderbilt and Tennessee, both by scores of 7-7.

"We weren't a very good team," Bryant now says about his 1959 club, "but those fellows got us headed in the right direction. Playing in the Liberty Bowl was a good experience for us."

Since Penn State had some black players on its roster, there was some question whether segregated Alabama would be allowed to participate in the game.

"I got permission from the administration and from Governor John Patterson to make sure we weren't doing anything that would get us in trouble," Bryant remembers. "The governor was highly in favor of the game and went with us."

Alabama and Penn State had the distinction of playing in the first Liberty Bowl game, on December 19, 1959, but according to Richardson, the trip was not very enjoyable.

"It was a fiasco," Richardson said. "We had hoped for a

First bowl for Bryant, 1959 Liberty.

better bowl bid and when the Liberty Bowl invitation came, we were not too excited about it.

"But Coach Bryant called a meeting and started talking about how fine a bowl it was and all the nice gifts we would receive...plus they had arranged a trip to New York for a week after the game. After talking it over with him, we accepted.

"We rode a train to Philadelphia for the game and it was the worst experience any of us had ever had. It must have taken us 20 hours and when we got there nobody was at the station to greet us. We had expected a big crowd, but nobody up there even knew there was a football game scheduled.

"And the game, whew! It was about 25 degrees and the wind was blowing about 40 miles per hour. It just wasn't much fun. I don't think we had our minds on football much, either. I guess we were lucky they didn't beat us worse."

The play which beat Alabama was put in the Penn State game plan by Coach Rip Engle just two days before the game. It was a fake field goal. The Lions scored as the clock ran out to end the first half.

"Our players played the touchdown play perfectly," Bryant said. "Well, not perfectly because they scored. I guess it was more a case of them executing perfectly."

As 32,211 fans sat in Franklin Field and shivered at halftime, Alabama and Penn State players tried to recover from the cold in dressing rooms under the stadium.

According to Richardson, Bryant did not need to get out of the cold. "He raised hell with us at halftime," the former halfback recalled. "He was boiling mad."

Bryant remembers halftime that day, too.

"They had a big pot-bellied stove there in the dressing room and our players gathered around it," Bryant said. "There weren't many players who acted like they wanted to play the second half, so I asked for volunteers. I think we started the second half with volunteers on the field.

"We were a young team and I guess we were fortunate not to get beat by three or four touchdowns."

Alabama was not without its brief moments of glory, however. As one reporter put it, "The Alabama 'Million Dollar' Band put on a show which was worth the price of admission."

1960 Bluebonnet Bowl Game

Alabama 3　　Texas 3

In days of Sington, Thomas, and Wade,
Bama's grid fame was known far and wide;
But in '54 there came a plague,
And the Big Red was more ebb than Tide.

Eight wins in four years was hard to take,
The alumni were tearing their hair;
At times the games were more like a wake,
So they took their lament to ol' Bear.

This season the Tide came in with a roar,
Rolled past eight of 10 foes;
And now they're in a bowl once more,
A tribute to football, a la hard nose.

His pre-game talk with his "little boys,"
For the second Bluebonnet battle
Will be: "I want to hear some noise,
When you're out there herding cattle."

—Tommy Thompson

There is no great glory in a tie, especially if the game is 60 minutes of knock 'em-sock 'em, bruise-producing football as played by the University of Alabama and the University of Texas in a 3-3 standoff in the 1960 Bluebonnet Bowl on December 17 at Houston, Texas.

But when the road Alabama traveled to receive an invitation to Houston is considered, there is considerable honor in the deadlock. Courage bought the Crimson Tide its ticket to the Bluebonnet Bowl.

One display of such courage by Alabama during the regular season makes a much better story than the one the Crimson Tide wrote in playing the Longhorns even-steven at Houston.

The scene was Grant Field in Atlanta. Favored Georgia Tech led Alabama, 15-0, at halftime and Yellow Jackets fans were whooping and shouting—and throwing bottles—in uncontrollable joy.

Alabama won the game, 16-15, when Richard O'Dell kicked a 24-yard field goal on the final play of the game. The Crimson Tide went on to pick up two more victories for an 8-1-1 regular season record—the best for an Alabama team since 1945—and a trip to the Bluebonnet Bowl.

Paul Bryant, the Alabama head coach then as he is now, remembers that comeback afternoon in Atlanta as the day his Crimson Tide players found they were made of something special.

In his book, *Bear*, Bryant says, "I'll never forget the 1960 Georgia Tech game, not if I live three lifetimes. If it wasn't the greatest comeback I've ever seen, it was certainly the greatest I've been involved in.

"We were down, 15-0, at the half...When we came in I didn't know what to do or to say. You have to have a plan, but I was fresh out. If we were down 6-0, I was going to really get after them, make them look me in the eye, but I wasn't prepared for this. I knew they expected me to blow up, rant and rave, and chew some tails. But if I did I was afraid we'd lose by 50.

"So I went the other way. The first thing I said was, 'Where are the Cokes?'

"And I walked around, patting 'em on the back and clapping my hands. I said, 'Damn, this is great. Now they'll see what kind of mamas and papas we've got. They'll see what we've got in us.'"

Alabama had plenty inside. The Crimson Tide defense clamped down on the Georgia Tech offense, and the offense, led by quarterback Bobby Skelton, went to work. It was 15-13 Georgia Tech, with 3 minutes, 21 seconds left to play and Alabama had the ball on its own 20 yard line.

Versatile and agile Richard (Digger) O'Dell.

Two first downs put the ball at the Alabama 40. Skelton passed 18 yards to Bill Battle to the Georgia Tech 42. On fourth down, Skelton passed to Norbie Ronsonet for a first down on the 32. With 32 seconds left, Skelton passed to Butch Wilson, who ran to the 6.

Time was running out quickly and on the Alabama sideline, Bryant was hurrying O'Dell, a sophomore who had only attempted and missed two field goals all year, into the game.

Skelton held the ball, O'Dell kicked it wobbly, and referee John Lynch called it good as time ran out. Bryant's reaction when he saw the ball go over the crossbar? "I couldn't believe it."

Tommy Brooker, the regular Alabama kicker, was sidelined with a knee injury that day. He was with the team in Atlanta, however, and recalled an embarrassing situation.

"I probably could have attempted that field goal," Brooker said, "but my leg had me slowed so much I couldn't get on the field in time. There were only eight seconds on the clock when the team lined up.

"But I have always been given credit for kicking the field goal anyway. You see, I was No. 81 and O'Dell was No. 87. The radio announcer misread the numbers and told everybody listening that I kicked the game-winner.

"Well, when we got back to Tuscaloosa, I was swamped with beautiful women at the airport. I was the hero, although I kept telling people I didn't kick the ball. O'Dell, on the other hand, was walking all alone in the shadows.

"When people finally found out the truth, they had a pep rally and screamed, 'We want O'Dell! We want O'Dell!' He refused to come out and meet them."

Brooker got his chance to bask in genuine glory two weeks later when he kicked a 22-yard field goal to defeat cross-state rival Auburn, 3-0. He later kicked the field goal which allowed Alabama to tie Texas in the Bluebonnet Bowl and went on to become an outstanding kicker with the Kansas City Chiefs of the National Football League.

"The kick against Auburn was a big highlight in my football career," Brooker said. "I was still hurt, so I went on the field without any shoulder pads, knee pads, or anything.

"Our defense did a job on them that day. They had that great kicker, Ed Dyas, and everybody said he would beat us with field goals if they got inside our 40 yard line. They only

Tommy Brooker kicks field goal.

Some members of 1961 national championship team relax before game.

made it past the 40 one time all day."

Alabama accepted the Bluebonnet Bowl bid immediately following the victory over Auburn.

Alabama entered the game as a slim favorite to defeat a Texas team which had compiled a 7-3 record. But the Longhorns, coached by Darrell Royal, were much larger than the Crimson Tide. Leon Fuller, whom Bryant called "the best overall player on our team," weighed only 160 pounds.

"We liked quick players in those days," Bryant said, "and quick ones happened to come in small packages."

Since Bryant had coached four years at Texas A&M before taking the job at Alabama, the Bluebonnet Bowl was a homecoming of sorts for him. His appearance back in Texas created more fireworks than the impending battle between the Crimson Tide and Longhorns.

"It is true that Alabama will play Texas in the Bluebonnet Bowl come Saturday, but a fan who reads the pages of Lone Star State newspapers—and particularly those in the Houston area—gets the idea that a bunch of Texans are more concerned about Coach Paul Bryant's postseason homecoming," wrote Charles Land in the *Tuscaloosa News*.

"History has recorded Bryant's almost startling revival of Texas A&M football fortunes, along with his three-year job here at Alabama and the successes of the years before he headed for the Brazos.

"One thing is certain—the Southwest has never gotten over the big man...."

Bryant was mobbed by reporters every place he went in Houston during game week. The questions asked of him were at times pointed: "Why were Tampa and Furman (easy victories of 34-6 and 51-0, respectively) on your schedule this year?" they asked. "Because I put them there," Bryant answered. "In 10 years those wins will look just as big as wins over Auburn and Georgia Tech."

There was also a terrific cat-and-mouse game between Bryant and Royal during the week.

"On this particular night, I feel like all the Alabama players are 14 feet tall," Royal said the night before the game. "I'd like to brag a little bit and say we have some more speed in the backfield, but I can't say that tonight. Alabama is much quicker and those kids of Bryant will hit you like a ton of bricks."

Bryant quickly got in his jabs in the psychological battle—"Our kids have done a tremendous job of preparing themselves, but I still think we'll have to play over our heads to win. I think they have a little better football team than we have."

Both were obviously wrong. Brooker kicked his field goal in the second quarter and Texas' Dan Petty matched it with a 20-yard kick with 3½ minutes left in the game.

There was plenty of suspense and controversy, however.

The game ended with Petty attempting a 35-yard field goal

with no time left on the clock. He got his chance to win the game when pass interference was called on the Alabama secondary on the previous play. (A game cannot end on a penalty play.) Petty missed the attempt, wide to the left.

Alabama had been crying foul since late in the first quarter, when Skelton claimed he scored a touchdown on a third-down run from the Texas three yard line. Fullback Billy Richardson was stopped on the fourth-down play, so the Crimson Tide walked away from the opportunity without scoring.

"I was in there," Skelton said then and still says. "I had chalk all over my jersey when I got up."

Brooker contends the same. "I know Bobby scored on the play," he said. "He had chalk from the goal line on his stomach and there is no way he could have gotten it there without going into the end zone.

"To this day, I think we got robbed in that game. We didn't play very well, but I still think we got a bad deal."

Royal says, what the heck, no harm was done—"Son of a gun, it ended just like it began."

1962 Sugar Bowl Game

Alabama 10   Arkansas 3

A wall of Red blocked the goal,
Opponents got 25 points, all told.
A rolling Tide moved up the field,
Many a touchdown, plenty of thrills.

Alabama was the team they cheered,
For 1961 was a special kind of year;
Tuscaloosa shone in a bright Crimson sun,
The Bear had a bunch named No. 1.

—Larry Parker

"I could name so many favorite players on that team. Mike Fracchia, Billy Neighbors, Pat Trammell, Lee Roy Jordan, Jimmy Sharpe, Richard Williamson, Billy Richardson, Ray Abbruzzese, Bill Rice, Bill Battle, Charley Pell, Darwin Holt, Tommy Brooker, Cotton Clark—they played like it was a sin to give up a point."—Paul (Bear) Bryant.

Genuine, never-to-waver leaders are difficult to find on a college football team, but in 1961 the University of Alabama was blessed with several—names which have become synonymous with the word "championship" in the Crimson Tide vocabulary.

For in that year Alabama produced a team which captured a modern-day national championship by easily winning all of its 11 games, including a 10-3 victory over powerful Arkansas in the 1962 Sugar Bowl game. The players who made up that championship team were the first freshmen Bryant had at Alabama when he returned to coach the Crimson Tide in 1958.

"In 1961 we had the best team in college football," Bryant remembered. "We had 16 or 17 players, the nut of the team, and all 16 or 17 were leaders."

The leader among leaders was Trammell, the 6-foot-2, 205-pound quarterback who made All-American. Since the day he arrived at Alabama after a standout prep career at Scottsboro (Alabama) High School, he was the man out front for the Crimson Tide. During the championship season, he quarterbacked the Alabama offense to 297 points in 11 games—the mighty Crimson Tide defense gave up a meager 25 points—and took control of the team when it started floundering in games or in practice.

"Trammell was the bell cow of the whole outfit," Bryant recalls. "You'll have to forgive me for getting sentimental, but Pat Trammell was the favorite person of my entire life.

"As a quarterback, he had no ability. He couldn't do anything but win. He was not a great runner, but he scored touchdowns. He didn't pass with great style, but he completed them. As a leader, I have never had another like him.

"The players rallied around him like little puppies. He could make them jump out a window to win. We didn't have any bad practices when he was here because he wouldn't let it happen."

Players remember Trammell in much the same manner. Richardson, the tiny Alabama halfback nicknamed "Little Bitty Billy With The Big Heart" and a standout three years for the Crimson Tide, admits having minor differences with Trammell, but respect remained intact.

"Pat was an outstanding person and a brilliant guy," Richardson said. "He almost had a photographic memory and was our general on the field. Coach Bryant thought so much of him that he had the authority to actually send people off the field during a game.

"Pat was rough and liked to scrap. But he liked practical jokes, too. He was some kind of leader.

"Coach Bryant and Trammell spent so much time together that their thoughts paralleled. Coach would be thinking of a play on the sideline and Pat would be calling it in the huddle."

Trammell became a doctor after he was graduated from Alabama, but in 1968 he was struck by a rare form of cancer.

Bryant stayed at his side until he died at age 28.

"When Pat told me he had cancer, my stomach turned over," Bryant said. "If I had been standing up I'd probably have dropped to my knees. Pat's funeral was the most moving I've ever been to. He was everything known to man. I still miss him."

If Trammell was the "bell cow" on the 1961 Alabama team, he had quite a herd working toward a championship with him. Neighbors, a hard-nosed tackle, and Jordan, a devastating linebacker (they both went on to illustrious pro careers), joined the quarterback on just about every All-American team. Fracchia, a leaping fullback, and Brooker, a steady tight end and placekicker, made all-Southeastern Conference.

Perhaps Auburn head coach Ralph (Shug) Jordan, a stout Alabama rival, best described the play of the Crimson Tide when he said, "It is a helmet-busting, hell-for-leather, gang-tackling game we play in the Southeastern Conference. Since Bear Bryant came to Alabama, it's the only game that can win."

Alabama played the game better than anybody in the country in 1961. The road to the championship and what was written about it included:

ATHENS, Ga.—A powerful University of Alabama football team, flashing more offense than a Bryant-coached Alabama team has ever shown, plus the usual Bryant-styled defense, completely smashed an outmanned Georgia Bulldog team here Saturday afternoon in Sanford Stadium, 32-6.

MOBILE, Ala.—Alabama's sputtering Crimson Tide defeated Tulane's stubborn Greenies, 9-0, Saturday night on breaks. The Tide failed to add to its national stature in the lackluster contest.

NASHVILLE, Tenn.—Old Warhorse Pat Trammell marked Alabama's most impressive offensive battle in years with his best performance ever here Saturday night as unbeaten, untied Alabama relentlessly battered down previously perfect Vanderbilt, 35-6.

TUSCALOOSA, Ala.—The man who came to pass, North Carolina State's Roman Gabriel, passed and passed this beautiful October Saturday afternoon and when the figurers moved in to figure, the noble Roman was found wanting. A red-shirted warrior, quietly efficient Pat

Pat Trammell: talent, courage, and respect.

Trammell, had overshadowed the vaunted sharpshooter and Alabama had fashioned a 26-7 victory.

BIRMINGHAM, Ala.—Coach Bear Bryant called Alabama's crushing 34-3 victory over Tennessee here yesterday "the best football game we've ever played."

HOUSTON, Tex.—Pat Trammell and Alabama's rawhidey defense put another great effort together here Saturday night as Paul Bryant's unbeaten Crimson Tide wrapped up victory No. 6 from a very reluctant and homecoming Houston, 17-0.

TUSCALOOSA, Ala.—Alabama's defense, as alert and staunch as ever, provided the openings and the Crimson Tide whipped Mississippi State, 24-0, in the rain Saturday.

TUSCALOOSA, Ala.—Alabama had a terrible day... making PATs. Old Bear just must do something about it for the Crimson Tide failed to convert after five touchdowns against Richmond. Imagine such a catastrophe: of course, with a far-away look in their eyes the Tidesmen managed to take Richmond, 66-0, anyhow, Saturday before 28,000 at Denny Stadium.

BIRMINGHAM, Ala.—Second-ranked Alabama, cooly masterminded by quarterback Pat Trammell, broke up a defensive dogfight with two long scoring drives Saturday to topple Georgia Tech, 10-0, before 53,000 fans.

BIRMINGHAM, Ala.—National championships are won on the football field, not in Monday morning bull sessions. Alabama probably claimed one here Saturday by soundly whipping rival Auburn, 34-0, to wrap up an undefeated, untied regular season.

So it was on to the Sugar Bowl for the most powerful Alabama football team in many a moon, possibly ever. The Crimson Tide was so talented in 1961 that the Rose Bowl considered breaking its tie with the Pacific Eight and Big Ten Conferences so it could invite Alabama back to Pasadena.

The thought died, however, and national champion Alabama accepted a trip to New Orleans to face the Razorbacks, who were 8-2 and ranked eighth in the nation.

Bryant took Alabama to Biloxi, Mississippi, for Sugar Bowl practice sessions. Workouts there were viewed by many fans, curious types who wanted to be able to say they saw the "best in the land" practice. The Crimson Tide rolled into New Orleans on December 30 and found the place covered up with Razorback fans.

The Hogs found The Bear, too.

"I checked in the hotel with my grandchildren," Bryant recalls. "I got a suite up on the sixth floor and directly across from my room, some Arkansas students had a suite.

"When they saw me, they started raising hell like you haven't ever heard, so I just invited them over. They came in and visited with us and I made a deal with them. I told them they could come over anytime they wanted, if they'd just do

131

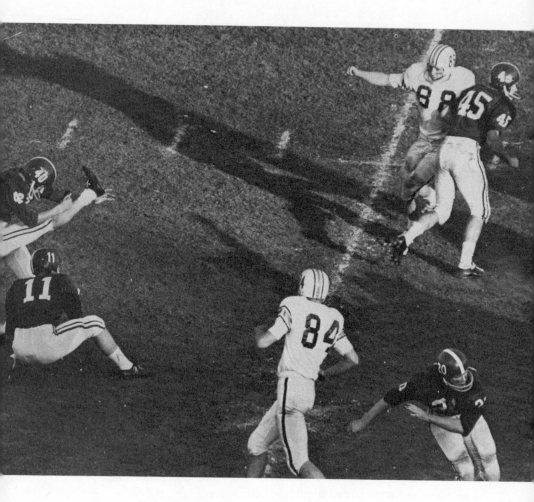

Four field goals by Tim Davis won for Alabama.

one thing—be quiet and stop hollering that damn 'Sooie! Sooie! Sooie!' business.

"And you know, they stuck with it and we had a real good little thing going there."

Alabama and Bryant had a better thing going in the game, although the Crimson Tide had to hold its breath at the end to escape with the victory.

Trammell got Alabama on the scoreboard in the first quarter when he ran 12 yards over tackle for a touchdown. Tim Davis, who later was an Alabama hero in the 1964 Sugar Bowl

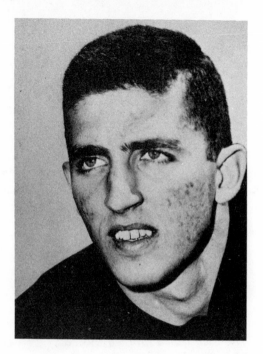

Tim Davis, outstanding kicker.

game, kicked the extra point for a 7-0 Crimson Tide lead. Davis kicked a 32-yard field goal in the second quarter for a 10-0 Alabama lead.

Mickey Cissell got the Razorbacks their points by kicking a 23-yard field goal in the third quarter. Late in the game, Arkansas All-American halfback Lance Alworth had a touchdown pass trickle off his fingertips that might have tied the game.

Bryant was a proud man. "Regardless of who was coaching them, they still would have been a great team," he said. "I said early in the season that they were the nicest, even the sissiest, bunch I'd ever had. I think they read it, because later on they got unfriendly."

1963 Orange Bowl Game

Alabama 17   Oklahoma 0

Friends said he was country,
The Bear called him hardnosed;
When he whipped up on opponents,
They said, "Well, that's the way it goes."

Lee Roy came from a little town,
He came only to Excel;
At 'Bama, he was an All-America,
Running backs just called him hell.

Lee Roy, the linebacker,
Mighty and mean No. 54;
When he struck his licks,
Oklahoma was screaming, "No, please, no more."

—Tommy Scarbrough

Lee Roy Jordan, college and professional linebacker de-
luxe, calls it "one of his greatest thrills" in a football career
which saw him travel from tiny Excel in South Alabama to the
University of Alabama at Tuscaloosa, and on to Dallas and a
Super Bowl championship in the play-for-pay National Football
League.

The "it" in question is the 1963 Orange Bowl game won
by Alabama, 17-0, over a strong Big Eight Conference champion
Oklahoma.

It was an all-winning afternoon under sunny Miami skies

One of Alabama's greatest and most durable linemen, Lee Roy Jordan.

for Jordan the day the Crimson Tide walloped Oklahoma. As captain of the team, he won the pregame coin toss by then-President John F. Kennedy. During the game he was credited with 24 tackles on enemy Sooners and was named Most Valuable Player. And as winning captain, he won a date with the Orange Bowl Festival queen.

"The Orange Bowl win over Oklahoma was a tremendous highlight of my football career," said Jordan, who retired from his duties as an all-pro linebacker with the Dallas Cowboys after the 1976 season. "I have been fortunate enough to play in some big games—the Super Bowls, the conference championships with Dallas, and many important battles for Alabama—but that Orange Bowl win over Oklahoma has to be among my biggest thrills. It was my best football game as a collegian."

Jordan and Alabama performed admirably against Oklahoma. The convincing victory put the wraps on a 10-1 year for the Crimson Tide, the only loss coming to Georgia Tech, 7-6, ending an Alabama streak of 26 games without defeat. (Texas tied the Crimson Tide, 3-3, in the 1960 Bluebonnet Bowl.)

With teammates like All-Southeastern Conference picks halfback Cotton Clark, end Richard Williamson, quarterback Joe Namath, and others like ends Bill Battle and Richard O'Dell, linemen Charley Pell and Jimmy Sharpe, and backs Butch Wilson and Eddie Versprille, Jordan was not the only outstanding player on the 1963 Orange Bowl championship squad.

But on that Orange Bowl afternoon, he was the player most noticed—by fans, coaches, and players. Alabama head coach Paul Bryant was so impressed by the defensive performance turned in by his linebacker that he said, "If they stay between the sidelines, Lee Roy will tackle them."

Jordan looks back without boasting.

"Sure, I was pleased with my effort that day," Jordan says, "but I think I was credited with a little more than I actually accomplished. I did have some big plays, however, the kind which help win games.

"It was just a great victory for what I think was a good, sound football team—a small, but very close team."

Bryant describes his 1962 squad with less flair, but to the point—"We had a great football team."

Alabama was rated a three-point favorite over the 8-2 Sooners coached by close Bryant friend, Bud Wilkinson. The

Paul (Bear) Bryant congratulates Lee Roy Jordan.

Joe Namath on his way to fortune and fame.

game was billed as a defensive struggle, but Alabama exploded in an early offensive outburst which sent Oklahoma reeling.

Namath, just a sophomore who Bryant was saying had the potential to become his greatest quarterback ever, fired a 25-yard touchdown pass to Williamson in the first quarter and Tim Davis kicked the extra point for a 7-0 lead. Clark ran untouched around left end for a 15-yard touchdown in the second quarter, with Davis again kicking the extra point for a 14-0 advantage at halftime. Davis kicked a 19-yard field goal in the third quarter to push the final margin to 17-0.

Oklahoma never got on track offensively as Alabama defenders swarmed the Sooners. The Sooners did get inside the Alabama 10 yard line twice, but both times Jordan squarely smacked fullback Jim Grisham and he fumbled, ending Oklahoma hopes for a score.

The headline in the *Miami Herald* on January 2 summed up the affair—"It's Ala-BAM! Over Sooners; Kennedy Sees 17-0 Crusher." The story under that headline, written by Gene Miller, told the details:

In magnificent sun and orange-perfumed air, President John F. Kennedy and 73,379 other Orange Bowl spectators Tuesday saw the Crimson Tide of Alabama blub-blub-blub over Oklahoma, 17-0.

Even though Charles Wilkinson, the "Bud" who runs the President's Physical Fitness Program, left the green-dyed lawn visibly shaking his head, it was a great day for spectacles. All kinds.

A cheerleader burst into tears for the President, a shotgun barrage frightened the bejabbers out of the Secret Service, the queen took a tranquilizer, and the Bowl people passed out apples instead of oranges.

President Kennedy, perhaps cheering for Oklahoma with a little more "vigah," evened things up by inviting Alabama cheerleader Martha Campbell up to his red-carpeted 50-yard-line box.

"Come up," said the President.

Martha, 19, nodding dumbly, found herself escorted by police. Suddenly she began to weep big, happy tears.

"Hello," said the President. "Your team is doing mighty well, isn't it?"

And that's precisely when Martha began to blubber like a baby. A speech major, she was absolutely speechless.

"I couldn't even remember my name," Martha bawled happily four minutes later.

She recovered in time to pose for photographers, blissfully allowing a feather-bottomed Oklahoma injun to pretend to scalp her flaming red hair.

President Kennedy arrived at the stadium 10 minutes before kickoff and stopped by the Oklahoma dressing room to wish the Sooners luck before taking his seat among fans. His failure to pay tribute to Alabama players before the game—or after, for that matter—gave the Crimson Tide a psychological lift.

"The President being there was a great break for us,"

Bryant said, looking back on the game, "because he visited their dressing room. I'm sure Bud didn't want that, but I sure didn't mind."

Jordan remembers, too. "When he went to their dressing room and didn't bother to come visit us, it gave us a little added incentive," Jordan said. "It was a little spur-of-the-moment psychological edge, just before kickoff.

"But President Kennedy being there added a lot to the game. He was a big Oklahoma and a big Bud Wilkinson fan, but more importantly, he was a great man. It was a tremendous thrill playing in front of him."

The game had its other serious moments. One came the night before kickoff when an Alabama fan found an Oklahoma playbook and presented it to Bryant.

"The playbook incident provided a little bit of a flareup before the game," Bryant said. "One of my friends, Julian Lackey, found a game plan in the bar at the motel and gave it to me. Well, it had one of their big stars' name on it—one Bud had some trouble with—so we thought it might have been his.

"It was the darndest looking notebook I ever saw. It had all kinds of crazy formations in it and some sounds that I knew Bud used. I didn't know what to do, because I knew it was planted for us—at least I felt like it was—to make us waste a lot of time. I prayed over it all day.

"We were supposed to go to a movie the night before the game, so I talked to Lee Roy and asked him what he thought. 'I hate to take up your time,' I told Lee Roy. 'We could be going over that thing three or four hours.' And he gave me my answer, 'Well, Coach, let's go over it.'

"We were staying at the Seaview Hotel and couldn't get a room, so Lee Roy and I went across the street to the ballroom at the Americana and spent three hours saying, 'If they do this, if they do that,' and they had a bunch of crazy stuff in there.

"As it was, the only way they hurt us during the game was with a quick lineup and that wasn't in the notebook."

Jordan discounts the value Alabama received from the notebook and says the Crimson Tide was well prepared for the game without it.

"I don't know if we got a great deal of benefit from it," Jordan said. "We were ready to play, regardless. Coach Bryant always had us prepared. He usually covered everything a team had done for the past 20 years."

There was humor in the game, too, involving defensive ends Pell and O'Dell, Jordan, Bryant, an authoritative official, and an Oklahoma player.

"Oklahoma had a halfback who gave away some of their plays with his stance in the backfield," Bryant said, "and Pell and O'Dell—we called him Digger O'Dell—worked up a little key to help our defense. Pell would holler, 'Look out, Digger! Look out, Digger!' and that was a warning the play was coming toward O'Dell.

"Well, Oklahoma had a black player playing across from Pell and when Pell hollered at O'Dell, the official kept getting on him. I didn't know about it until halftime when Lee Roy came up to me and said, 'Coach, Pell's gonna get thrown out of the game.'

"I said, 'Thrown out...what the hell?' And Lee Roy said, 'Well, Coach, the official thinks he's calling that boy a nigger and all he's doing is hollering at Digger.'

"So I went to the official...and Pell, too, and tried to get that changed. And, uh, anyway, it was a real fine game."

And what about the date Lee Roy won with Orange Bowl Festival queen Virginia Jasper?

"Well, I don't like to say a whole lot about that," Jordan said, "but that was part of the package the winner got and she did have a good set of equipment."

1964 Sugar Bowl Game

Alabama 12   Mississippi 7

Come rain, snow, sleet, or Mississippi,
Alabama had its job to do;
Just because Joe was in the stands,
That didn't mean the Tide would lose.

Sloan quarterbacked under cloudy skies,
Tim Davis cranked up his golden toe;
'Bama's defense refused to yield,
And few people remembered Bad Joe.

—Jim Fullington

False prophets are a dime a dozen. Take the case of a sportswriter who made an off-the-cuff, tongue-in-cheek statement while relaxing in New Orleans four days before the 1964 Sugar Bowl football game.

"Alabama has about as much chance of beating Mississippi as it has a chance of snowing in New Orleans on New Year's Eve," the writer stated.

Well, it snowed...and Alabama beat favored Mississippi, 12-7, in a shocking upset of its Southeastern Conference friend and neighbor.

It took four field goals—a Sugar Bowl record—by Tim Davis, a bending but never breaking defense, and steady guidance by a nervous quarterback named Steve Sloan to lock up the Alabama victory that cloudy, cold January 1.

Mississippi was the conference champion and considered

mighty. Alabama had an 8-2 regular season record and was about as unsettled as a swarm of bees being burned out of their nest.

The big thing which had people wondering about Alabama chances against the Rebels was the much-publicized Joe Namath suspension. Without its ace quarterback who was suspended from the team before the final regular-season game because of training infractions, the Crimson Tide was given about as much chance of winning as there was a chance of it snowing in New Orleans.

"That victory in the Sugar Bowl was one of the greatest, greatest games that has ever been won," says Alabama head coach Paul Bryant, while looking back on the events leading up to the contest. "Under the circumstances, I don't see how we won it. It was a terrific football game won by a bunch of dedicated kids."

Alabama's two losses during the season were by a combined total of six points, with both games proving unusual. First came a 10-6 loss to Florida, the only defeat Bryant has suffered in Denny Stadium at Tuscaloosa since becoming the Alabama coach in 1958. Then came a 10-8 loss to Auburn, the first for Alabama after four consecutive victories over its rival.

Nine days after the loss to Auburn, Bryant announced the suspension of Namath, the junior from Beaver Falls, Pennsylvania, who was being called the greatest passer in Alabama history. But long before the suspension, Namath had been the subject of rumors concerning his off-the-field behavior. Each one had proved false, but Namath was back in the spotlight after the Auburn game because he had fumbled the ball when the Crimson Tide appeared headed for a touchdown.

The Miami game had been moved to two weeks after the Auburn game because of the death of President Kennedy, after being scheduled two weeks before the game with the cross-state rivals. The break in action prompted horseplay among players.

In making his bombshell announcement, Bryant said he was suspending Namath "because of an infraction of training rules this past weekend."

In the *Birmingham News*, Benny Marshall, a sportswriter close to the situation, explained the suspension in a series he wrote on Namath six years after it happened.

"It was not a series of incidents, as some gossips had it," Marshall wrote. "It was one, reported to Bryant. Namath and

Joe Namath talks it over with Alabama players.

some other players had been drinking. The person who brought the report named only Namath. Joe would take the rap. The others have never been named. At least one was a star on the team.

"Bryant had been hearing rumors, too. He asked his assistant coaches. The violation was news to them, they said. Finally Bryant went to the dormitory dining room. Namath was there. He came to the coach's table, as quarterbacks are encouraged to do.

"From there, they went to the privacy of Bryant's room at the dormitory, and now was the time to ask Namath. The answer of Alabama's scrupulously honest quarterback was, 'It's true,' and Bryant said, 'You are suspended from the team. Get in touch with Coach (Sam) Bailey and he'll help you find a place to stay. You can't live in the dorm. If you come back, that's up to you this spring.'"

When Bryant told Namath of his suspension, none of the other Alabama coaches or players knew about it. The head coach called a meeting and informed his assistant coaches and all of them except Bebe Stallings disagreed with Bryant. All except Stallings, who had played for Bryant at Texas A&M, pleaded for leniency. But Stallings said, "If it had been me, as a player, you'd have fired me, Coach."

Bryant thought the matter over for about two hours in the privacy of his office, then called in the assistant coaches and Namath to inform them that the suspension stood.

Namath returned to the team the following spring and led the Crimson Tide to a national championship, before going on to lead the New York Jets to a Super Bowl championship as a professional.

Namath has since said the suspension was "one of the best things that has ever happened to me." But at the time, it was not pleasant for Namath or the Alabama team. With Sloan and Jack Hurlbut at quarterback, the Crimson Tide was unimpressive in defeating lowly Miami, 17-12, and looked like a wounded bird flying toward New Orleans and its Sugar Bowl date with Mississippi.

But after the Miami game, which Bryant said Alabama "won without really beating anybody," the team pulled itself together.

"The loss of Namath was a blow to us," said Paul Crane, a sophomore center at the time and now an assistant coach at Alabama, "but we knew Coach Bryant was doing the right thing.

"Anyway, we have never had a one-man team at Alabama, so we retained our confidence. Namath's acceptance of it had a lot to do with helping us regroup."

Bryant took the team to Mobile to prepare for the game, where he dropped another bombshell by announcing that Sloan, an inexperienced sophomore, would open at quarterback against rugged Mississippi.

"Actually, I didn't think we had a chance to win the game after we had disciplined Namath," Bryant said. "I had no idea we could ever win.

"Hurlbut was a senior and great kid, but I didn't think he could win the game offensively, so I decided to use him on defense, where I knew he could help the team.

"Anyway, five or six days before the game, I announced Sloan would be the quarterback. I wanted both Hurlbut and Sloan to know what was happening. I thought that would be the best way to handle it, plus I didn't want Sloan to be nervous when we got to New Orleans."

The plan worked well, except for one thing. Sloan was plenty nervous.

"When Coach Bryant announced that I would be the quarterback, I was surprised," said Sloan, who is now a successful head coach at Ole Miss. "And you know how I found out? I read it in the paper. Yeah, that was some way to find out I would start, but there are some people who have ways of doing things that should never be questioned. Coach Bryant is one of those people and it seems his ways seem to always work out."

Sloan admits to being nervous right up until game time, but says his anxiety vanished when he took the field. "I was one excited person," said Sloan, who later led Alabama to a national championship in 1965. "But I really didn't play a very good game. It was just a thrill to know I didn't do anything to keep us from losing."

Sloan did have a major mishap during the game. He went the wrong way while running an option play and pitched the ball to an official, while his running back teammates circled the other end.

"I'm just glad the official didn't catch the ball," Sloan said.

Davis was the real hero in the Alabama victory. He kicked field goals of 31, 46, 22, and 48 yards to put the Crimson Tide

Cool under pressure, Steve Sloan.

points on the scoreboard. He was named Most Valuable Player in the game and his 48-yard kick was the longest in bowl history.

Alabama led 3-0 after one quarter, 9-0 at halftime, and 12-0 after three quarters. Ole Miss got its touchdown in the fourth period and threatened several other times, only to be beaten back by a gallant Alabama defense.

Bryant, though pessimistic about Alabama chances a week before the game, was not totally surprised when his team won.

"We had a dinner the night before the game," Bryant said, "and I got to watching our kids and somehow I got to thinking we could beat Mississippi. After dinner, I had a little talk with them and told them, 'You know, I think we're gonna beat those people now, at least I think you're gonna beat 'em.' And by golly, I honestly believe our kids thought all along they were going to win that game."

Steve Sloan passes with excellent protection.

1965 Orange Bowl Game

Texas 21   Alabama 17

Inches from glory, Joe fell,
'Cause only the officials could tell.
Texas was the winner that Miami night,
Though 'Bama put up quite a fight.

The national champs fell victim,
To a mighty Longhorn stampede;
The winner left in happiness,
Clutching its oft-challenged lead.

—Mark Maddox

Steve Bowman went to the well three times and never found water. Joe Namath tried once, also to no avail.

But when the lights had been turned out at the Orange Bowl on the night of January 1, 1965, both Bowman and Namath walked away with thirsts quenched.

Bowman, a University of Alabama fullback, was tickled silly over the football game he had played that night, despite the fact the Crimson Tide had the glitter from its national championship season dimmed by a 21-17 defeat at the hands of Texas.

Namath, who brilliantly quarterbacked an Alabama comeback which fell just shy of victory, exited Miami $400,000 richer. He signed a professional contract with the New York Jets immediately after the contest—the highest-paid contract ever at that time—and has become one of the greatest passers in professional history.

Steve Bowman looks for running room.

It was the first Orange Bowl game staged at night, enabling the festival to put on one of the most staggering halftime shows in collegiate football history.

The game was just as earth-shaking from the standpoint of dramatic endings. Alabama, victimized by a big-play Texas offense, trailed 21-7 at halftime, but Namath—playing on a gimpy knee in relief of starting quarterback Steve Sloan—passed the Crimson Tide back into contention. Ray Perkins caught a 20-yard touchdown pass from Namath in the third quarter and David Ray kicked the extra point to make it 21-14. Ray kicked a 26-yard field goal in the fourth quarter to cut the margin to 21-17.

Then came the dramatics. With less than seven minutes left in the game, Alabama had the ball and a first down at the Texas six yard line. Bowman ran to the two yard line on the first play, then to the one on the next. It was third down and the Crimson Tide needed one yard for the lead. Bowman tried again, making only one foot. Namath then attempted to sneak into the end zone on fourth down. There was a human mass of red-shirted Alabama players and white-shirted Texas players on the goal line. The pile subsided slowly. The officials took a look at Namath and he was on the ground, inches from a touchdown.

End of dramatics, end of game. But memories linger....

"That game was something," Bowman remembers, "the best football game I've ever been in. I completely enjoyed playing it.

"Sure, some of the glamour was taken off because we lost as national champions. But it was a good, hardnosed football game and anybody who has ever played the game knows it was one to cherish forever.

"From a fan standpoint, it was a pleaser. The game had everything—exciting plays, surprises, emotion...everything."

Emotion! The thoughts of those who played in the spine-tingling contest. The thoughts of Bowman as Alabama surged, plunged, and failed?

"When we had the ball on the six yard line, I thought we would win the game for sure," Bowman said. "There was little said in the huddle. There was a feeling of excitement and calmness at the same time.

"When I made it to the two, I felt even more confident. After all, we had three tries to make two yards. But they knew what was coming on the next play. It was a wedge play and we

Alabama warms up under watchful eyes.

had run it all year. They just stood up and muscled us. I still thought we would score. When I ran on third down, they were even more determined to stop us. I lunged for the end zone, but Tommy Nobis, their All-American fullback, stopped me.

"When we got in the huddle on fourth down, I told Joe to run the ball over tackle, but he didn't hear me. There was a lot of talking going on by both teams. They were setting a defense and we were trying to get a play together. Then suddenly, it was quiet. Everybody knew the game was coming down to one play.

"Before Joe tried the sneak, I still thought we would get the touchdown. But we just didn't do what it took to win. The officials say they stopped us and that's what counts. If we had done our jobs, there would have been no question."

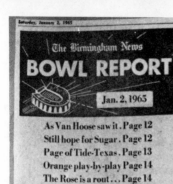

The Birmingham News
BOWL REPORT
Jan. 2, 1965

★ ★ ★ ★ ★ ★ ★ ★ ★ ★ ★ ★

Bear's question:

'Can Joe play?' Whole dang country knows!

BY BENNY MARSHALL
News sports editor

MIAMI, Jan. 2—The flipping of the half-dollar, the introduction of the players, the rendition of the National Anthem, the fireworks, the scalping of the tickets and all other pre-game ritual had been seen to.

There had been a slight rain, following an afternoon downpour, but now the national half gone away in mist until a halftime redial for showing Ernie Seiler's beautiful floats.

A warm wind blew tugging at suspender skirts and banners, and things. The night was alive with anticipation, loaded with promise.

The minute before the kickoff had come to the Orange Bowl. The players ran to take their places and the roar of the multitude swelled to greet them. This is the time that somehow you always must remember. Great noise, quieting to a murmur, then the storm. That's the way football games begin, all of them.

— The decision

ON THE ALABAMA SIDE of the field, Paul Bryant had slid his raincoat and his sport jacket and replaced his checked hat with an old Alabama baseball cap. Sartorial splendor had been sacrificed to the urgency of the heat and comfort.

Now, he tossed alongside Jim Goostree, the fine Crimson Tide trainer, and Alabama's coach had a question, just around the . . .

"Can Joe play?" Bryant asked.

"He can," said Goostree. "He can play."

And that's when the decision was made which sent Namath to the battle before the first quarter was finished and kept him there through the long and steaming night.

— In epic

HOW JOE PLAYED and the way he played, with one team try, and finally looking for mastery from eyes blued with pain, made an epic for the history of the Orange Bowl last night.

This was the night when Alabama's riotous luck champions couldn't make it all the way, because they fell too far behind, but the young man from the once Felix Pa., now near becomes pro football's richest quarterback with the New York Jets, reached inside himself and gave Alabama every ounce there in the Orange Bowl that was lost.

Joe Namath paid, in full measure, for all Alabama football has given him in the last brave performance that none could have dreamed of Monday when his only knee buckled beneath him and they led him from practice, hurting, apparently all done.

Turn to Page 13, Column 1

'The arm' unlimbers

Tide magnificent, inches short
Atop a pile of might-have-beens: Texas

Touchdown

Between two defending Longhorns, Ray Perkins pulls in a throw from Namath at the two and falls across the goal line

A fine win, but—

No. 1 not for Texas, that's past—Royal

BY ALF VAN HOOSE
Assistant sports editor

MIAMI, Fla., Jan 2— said, about to claim any national championship for his Texas Longhorns who whipped Alabama, 21-17, Friday night in maybe the greatest Orange Bowl of them all.

A Texas writer had sort of spurred the Steers, asking Longhorn coach to boast a No. 1 claim to a jubilant dressing room but Royal balked.

"I feel the noise star about that," Royal said, "and I did not rate him (before No. 1 Texas went forth to compete No. 1 Navy in the Cotton Bowl.)

"THEY CLOSE, the poll after that 10th game. We won a last-fourth Alabama was it this year.

"I wasn't going to be much my back our trophy if we got it. Last year, and I don't believe Alabama is going to as perfect as theirs this year."

"But, as for having the No. 1 much, oh, that was another matter."

"And I don't think you can feel anything but elated," Royal added.

me of greatest— If THIS ONE, this most extravant which had being snatched from his dedicated Longhorn, had to be, Royal admitted, "one of our greatest wins."

But Royal didn't get much choice to speak at Texas heroes. Nearly all questions answered his tactics, Joe Namath, the usual aggressive 'spot' player of all-time.

And Royal didn't do anything but please the TIDE QUARTERback from Beaver Falls, Pa., who hatted more than 71,000 Orange Bowl witnesses into nervous wrecks, winners and losers alike.

THE BEST college quarterback he'd ever seen? "don't like to play plays ern," Royal replied. "It's true, star.

"But I'll say this: Namath's among the greatest I've seen. He tried all sorts of defenses against everybody.

"Ernie Koy had one of his better nights on offense," Royal would say. "And both (Marv) Kristynik and (Jim) Hudson did a fine job of quarterbacking.

Kristynik proved a gambler attack which Koy led with a 100 Texas in its back, including 79 and one-yard touchdown runs.

Hudson was chief Texas quantum upsetter, for killing that being a disaster TD both to and George Sauer.

"SAUER was a perfect game, and made a great catch," Royal defeated. And Hudson really did it some.

Those 21 points Texas won out surprised its much, and Royal admitted it.

"I heard Alabama might - I know, it particularly if Namath played much," he said.

Turn to Page 15, Column 1

Touchdown

Ernie Koy's in with third Texas TD

★ ★ ★ ★ ★ ★ ★

Steer-Tide chart

RUSHING

Each wins a half, Longhorns' is larger

BY BENNY MARSHALL News sports editor

MIAMI, Jan 2—It was Alabama's turn today to taste the special game of might-have-beens as Texans and television sponsors beamed big and bright about things that happened Friday night in the 31st Orange Bowl.

Texas had a 21 to 17 victory over the national champion Crimson Tide to take back its range country.

The TV people couldn't wait to check the ratings on a dream, no suspense-laden that Alfred Hitchcock could have envied the script. Nobody went to sleep on the first major bowl game ever played at night.

For Alabama, Coach Paul Bryant said it of all. "We had a great 1964. That wasn't much of a way to start 1965.

Losing has become easy as popular at Alabama since Bryant came to be the coach in 1958.

Pain not eased

THE FACT that it took the unhappiest first half ever . . .

and the queens and the hand-maidens to come in another Orange Bowl halftime spectacular.

Alabama took charge of the second half, its defense answering every Texas rout . . .

. . . that it kept the Namath . . . his offense without having . . . . . . a come-from-behind lead so, it went would have eclipsed anything the Tide did . . . in . . .

Turn to Page 15, Column 1

Statistics

	ALABAMA	TEXAS
First downs	19	15
Rushing yardage	48	222
Passing yardage	206	101
Passes	20-44	6-11
Passes int'p'd by	1	2
Punts	5-42	8-36
Fumbles lost	1	0
Yards penalized	30	32

NO TD SIGNAL, JUST UNCERTAINTY

MIAMI, Jan. 2—You'll head to squawk aloud if from the University of Alabama's football fans do, but if the television cameras were focused on far Namath and some of his friends, you'll know how they felt about one play in Friday night's Orange Bowl loss to Texas.

It was fourth down. The Tide less than a yard away from a touchdown which probably would have won.

The clock showed less than seven minutes to play.

Namath took the final shot himself, and straight ahead, presently, was hurled under the mass, and indecision was apparent among the officials.

Finally, one of the Texas boys on the field relayed the verdict.

Alabama had not got its touchdown.

But the reason the officials waited, said one who was there:

"One official said it was a touchdown. Two others came running over and said 'are you sure?' And they talk it form out of it.

"There was never a touchdown signal given, however."—BENNY MARSHALL

Texas won, or did...?

Except in the record books, there will remain a question. Did Namath make a touchdown on the much-publicized sneak?

In the hotel lobby the morning after the game, Namath looked squarely at Alabama head coach Paul Bryant and said, "I made it, Coach. I scored on that play."

Bryant, who viewed the play from the sidelines, patted Namath on the head and said, "I couldn't see well enough to determine if you made it or not. The officials must have seen the ball. They were closer than I was."

Now Bryant puts his appraisal of the play in more clear terms—"We didn't deserve to win after failing in four cracks from the six. When something means that much to you, you should push people out of there far enough to remove all doubt."

Bowman, who was directly behind Namath as the quarterback attempted to score, said, "I'm prejudiced, but I will always believe Joe scored. He got the ball over the goal line, before they pushed him back."

Nobis, the great Texas linebacker who went on to have an illustrious professional career with the Atlanta Falcons, looks back on the play and sees it from a different viewpoint.

"Of course, he wasn't over the goal line," said Nobis, now a public relations man with the Falcons. "Joe got up and raised cane with the officials, and I admit it was close enough to call either way. But he did not score. He squirmed on the ground with the ball after he was stopped.

"No, we didn't know what kind of plays they were going to come at us with down near the goal, but looking back I am not too sure they had good play selection. Of course, we were ready for just about anything, because we had been in situations like that before.

"And in that game, we knew stopping Alabama was plenty important. We knew it would probably determine the outcome of the game. Heck, that whole game was something, the most exciting one I ever played in during my football career."

Alabama concluded a magnificent season in the Orange Bowl. The Crimson Tide breezed to its national title with victories over Georgia (31-3), Tulane (36-6), Vanderbilt (24-0), North Carolina State (21-0), Tennessee (19-8), Florida (17-14), Mississippi State (23-6), Louisiana State (17-9), Georgia Tech (24-7), and Auburn (21-14).

Bryant put it best after the loss to Texas. "We had a great,

155

great 1964, but this is a heckuva way to start 1965."

The Orange Bowl was viewed by 72,647 fans, including Billy Graham, Richard Nixon, Bebe Rebozo, Jackie Gleason, and a Japanese princess who was watching her first game.

Of all the talented players on the field that night, Namath is the one most will remember.

"He is among the greatest quarterbacks I've ever seen," said Texas head coach Darrell Royal. "How many passes did he complete? Eighteen? And we tried all sorts of defenses to stop him. He is one fantastic player. We just couldn't slow him down."

But Texas did manage to stop him once—inches from a possible Alabama victory.

1966 Orange Bowl Game

Alabama 39   Nebraska 28

Faith is the substance of things hoped for, the evidence of things not seen. —Hebrews 11:1

Big hearts can move mountains.

Miracles can happen.

If there are any doubters, lend an ear to the story of Johnny Calvert.

For the record, on January 1, 1966, Calvert stood 5-foot-11 and weighed 178 pounds. He played offensive guard that night for the University of Alabama against Nebraska in the Orange Bowl game.

Walt Barnes and Tony Jetter were defensive linemen for Nebraska. They weighed 250 and 230 pounds, respectively, and Calvert had the responsibility of looking the big Cornhuskers in the face and blocking them well enough so that Crimson Tide running backs would have room to operate. On some offensive plays, he attacked Barnes, an All-American, and on others he charged at Jetter.

Johnny Big Heart did quite a job on both, as did his comparable-in-size-and-challenges teammates. Alabama, an underdog at kickoff, won the game, 39-28, in a wild offensive show.

The miracle was not victory alone but rather what the win brought Alabama for the second consecutive year—a national championship. The Crimson Tide woke up in Miami the day of the game ranked as the fourth best team in America. When Alabama players went to sleep that night—or near daylight the next morning, as stories have it—they were No. 1.

For the first time, national championship ballots were passed out after bowl games that year and on a wacky New Year's Day of football, No. 1 Michigan State lost to UCLA in the Rose Bowl, No. 2 Arkansas lost to Louisiana State in the Cotton Bowl, and No. 4 Alabama beat No. 3 Nebraska.

Therefore, the Crimson Tide, a team which had fought an uphill battle all year after a disputed 18-17 loss to Georgia in the first game of the 1965 season, was named best in the land. Few people questioned the ranking.

It was another David—Goliath story at Miami. Tiny Alabama, a team with a mission, put its rock directly between the eyes of the giant. In three months, the Crimson Tide rose from last in the Southeastern Conference to first in the country with a 9-1-1 record.

The men who did the job on Nebraska:

Ends: Ray Perkins, Dennis Homan, Richard Brewer, Wayne Cook, Don Shankles, Charles Harris, Creed Gilmer, Ben McLeod, Vernon Newbill, and Tommy Tolleson.

Tackles: Jerry Duncan, Louis Thompson, Cecil Dowdy, Nathan Rustin, John Sullivan, John Sides, Richard Cole.

Guards: John Calvert, Billy Johnson, Bruce Stephens, Willie Stewart, Tommy Somerville, Allen Harpole, T. J. Morris, Byrd Williams, and Terry Kilgore.

Centers: Paul Crane and Jimmy Carroll.

Backs: Steve Sloan, Steve Bowman, Bud Moore, Gene Raburn, John Reitz, Kenny Stabler, John Mosley, Frank Canterbury, Les Kelley, Dickie Bean, David Ray, Bobby Johns, Steve Davis, Kent Busbee, Eddie Propst, Jimmy Israel, William Hobson, Wayne Trimble, David Chatwood, and David Bedwell.

They were small. They were quick. And....

"We believed in ourselves," said Calvert, "and that was our secret to beating Nebraska in the Orange Bowl. We all had that feeling. We went to Miami thinking we were going to beat 'em and I attribute that feeling to Coach (Paul) Bryant. He had faith in us and when he has faith, it kind of grows on you.

"Coach told us after the Georgia loss that he thought we could go on and become a great team and we put our minds to doing just that. Our team had a lot of heart and when we got the chance to play Nebraska, we were determined to make the best of it.

"Sure, we were a little bunch, but we were a team which

158

John Calvert, a standout guard.

played well together. We were given a challenge and we met it."

The big challenge against Nebraska rested with the offensive line, a group of men who looked more like the backfield the big, strong Cornhuskers put on the field against Alabama. Although Bryant, a master of psych, never said anything to his offensive line concerning its importance in the game, Calvert says the Crimson Tide coach did pull a bit of low-key trickery to get them ready to play.

"When they had picture day in Miami before the game, Coach Bryant posed with everybody except us guys on the offensive line," Calvert said. "He said he didn't want to get his picture taken 'with these small guys, because they're gonna get the hell beat out of them' during the game.

"After he said that, we started talking to each other and decided, 'Well, we'll show that so-and-so he doesn't know what he's talking about.'

"I tell you one thing; we didn't have a player in Miami who thought we would lose. There was no doubt in our minds."

By halftime in the game, few people among the huge crowd watching in the Orange Bowl or millions more watching on television doubted the Crimson Tide. Alabama had played 30 splendid minutes and led the previously unbeaten (10-0) Cornhuskers, 24-7.

The Crimson Tide got another shot in the arm at halftime, although it was not needed.

"Coach Bryant came walking in at halftime and told us Michigan State had been beaten in the Rose Bowl," said Homan, a sophomore pass receiver who was to go on to make All-American as a senior. "Well, we had already heard Arkansas had lost, so that was all we needed.

"It was almost unbelievable. There we were beating Nebraska and only 30 minutes away from a possible national championship. It was a shocking thing."

Shock and disbelief became contented realization in the second half. Led by remarkable Sloan passes in the first half, Alabama went to a ground attack in the second half for 15 more points. Nebraska scored 21 points in the final 30 minutes, but never challenged.

Alf Van Hoose, writing in the *Birmingham News*, summed it up the following day: "Alabama's magnificent little men—stars all—shot down Orange Bowl records like meteors here Saturday night and might have bagged a third national championship in five years by lambasting gigantic Nebraska, 39-28.

"If the No. 4-ranked Tide isn't voted a second straight U.S. crown after this spectacular show, a proud, bubbling Paul Bryant ought to appeal to a higher court, national opinion.

"Bama would win there for sure, starting with the 72,647 witnesses who saw Bryant's lightweight fighters live in the flesh—plus millions more who saw it on countrywide, prime-time TV.

"Grand Steve Sloan led the Crimsons to the surprise of no one. He also paced the record assault, principally by completing a new-high 20 passes for a new-high 296 yards.

"The 185-pound senior quarterback from Cleveland, Tennessee, also guided a Crimson offense which netted 518 yards, also a fresh standard for the bowl which has lately been the world's greatest.

"Alabama's dedicated men in red, giving away 35 pounds per man up front, blew open this wild affair with a 17-point blitz in the second quarter—after Nebraska squared an early 7-0 Bama takeoff."

Bryant was overjoyed after the game, quickly pacing around the Alabama dressing room hugging his players. He called his team the best offensive unit he had ever coached.

"I'm proud, I'm happy, I'm overjoyed at the way this football team performed," Bryant said. "I don't have a vote for No.

Dennis Homan, receiver deluxe, with his coach.

1, but I wish I did."

Nebraska head coach Bob Devaney did not have a vote either, but he voiced an opinion—"Alabama is outstanding. As far as I'm concerned, they have the best football team in the country."

Bryant became a prophet when bowl pairings were made that year. He outlined a plan which worked.

"I put in on the board for the players," Bryant said, "charting how it would happen. UCLA would upset Michigan State, LSU would upset Arkansas, and we would play Nebraska for all the marbles. It wouldn't happen again in a million years, but that's exactly the way it went.

"That night at the Orange Bowl, I took Steve Sloan aside and said, 'Steve, we're not going to win the national championship by lucking out, 7-6, or something. We have to win big. I don't care where you are on the field or what the score is, I want you to play like you're behind."

Sloan, the most valuable player in the game, remembers entering the game with confidence—in himself and his teammates. "We were an experienced football team with a bunch of seniors who were real close," he said. "I was never a real confident player at Alabama, but I had confidence in our team. I knew those little guys up front on offense would do an outstanding job."

It rained in Tuscaloosa the Monday following the Alabama conquest of Nebraska, but Crimson Tide loyals were not dampened by the water as they waited for THE WORD. It came in early evening—the Crimson Tide had been voted No. 1, Michigan State No. 2, Arkansas No. 3, UCLA No. 4, and Nebraska No. 5.

By winning its third national championship, Alabama had permanent possession of the trophy the Associated Press awards its champion each year. A wild celebration was held on campus. Governor George Wallace addressed the Alabama students by phone from Montgomery. Bryant did the same from the Senior Bowl game at Mobile.

And Johnny Calvert looked at his ring finger and dreamed. "Getting that championship ring meant more to me than anything in the world," Calvert said 11 years after the Orange Bowl game. "You just don't see many people walking around wearing them. I didn't letter in 1964 when we won the championship and every time I saw one of those who did wearing that ring, I

162

"Snake" Stabler unleashes pass.

almost cried. I wanted one badly.

"Maybe everybody felt like I did and maybe that's the reason we let Nebraska have it. I never got tired in that game. I wanted the championship.

"We had busted our tails and sweated all year for the chance to win the title and the thought never left my mind the entire game. It simply boiled down to whoever it meant the most to.

"And, you know, I think the championship meant more to Alabama."

1967 Sugar Bowl Game

Alabama 34   Nebraska 7

Notre Dame plays politics,
Alabama plays football;
In your heart you know, we're No. 1.

—Author unknown

Dennis Homan is not the kind of guy to carry a grudge. He is quick to forgive.

But forget? No, sir. Homan remembers the 1966 college football season as well as he recalls his name. Most of the other players on the University of Alabama team that year do, too.

That Crimson Tide team was fantastic, possibly the best Alabama has ever put on the field. The squad had four All-Americans—defensive halfback Bobby Johns, tackles Richard Cole and Cecil Dowdy, and end Ray Perkins—plus All-Southeastern Conference selections guard Johnny Calvert and defensive halfback Dicky Thompson.

It was the kind of team any school would want when in defense of two consecutive national championships, which Alabama was in 1966. It was the kind of squad which would be a betting favorite to make it three national titles in a row.

But another national championship did not come to Alabama. Not because the 1966 team failed to deserve one, but simply because the voters failed to cast ballots in favor of the Crimson Tide.

"We were the only unbeaten and untied team in the country and probably one of the best teams to ever play the collegiate game," Homan said, "but they gave the championship

164

trophy to Notre Dame. To this day, that is the most disappointing thing that has ever happened to me in football.

"I am convinced the only reason we were not named champions is because Alabama had won the title in 1964 and 1965. Coach (Paul) Bryant thought we were champions, we thought we deserved to be champions, and Nebraska thought we should be named champion.

"There is no doubt in my mind that we were the best team in the country. I think a lot of politics went into the voting. It has been a long time, but I will never forget the disappointment."

Had Alabama taken its case to court in 1966, it would have had plenty of evidence to back up its claim to the No. 1 spot. During the regular season, the Crimson Tide piled up 267 points and allowed only 37 in defeating Louisiana Tech, Mississippi, Clemson, Tennessee, Vanderbilt, Mississippi State, Louisiana State, South Carolina, Southern Mississippi, and Auburn.

Then, before a packed house in the Sugar Bowl at New Orleans and a live television audience, Alabama celebrated the second day of January 1967 by putting on one of the greatest exhibitions of football in Crimson Tide history while destroying Nebraska, 34-7.

Notre Dame was named national champion with a 9-0-1 record. Michigan State was second at 9-0-1. Those two teams played to a 10-10 tie and Notre Dame was heavily criticized for running out the clock rather than trying long passes in an effort to win that game.

Notre Dame and Michigan State stayed home during bowl season, the champion Irish refusing to accept a bid and Michigan State banned from the Rose Bowl because it had been there the year before.

Bryant, who has called his 1966 team "a great, great team, full of talent and want-to," cried "foul" when his team was not awarded the championship and maintains the same feeling now. In his book, *Bear*, the Crimson Tide head coach is outspoken about the matter.

"The 1966 team should have won the national championship because it was undefeated and untied and the best team in the country that year," Bryant said in his book. "But I suppose by then the voters were tired of seeing us up there and hearing Bryant brag on his quick little boys.

"The 1966 team was the best I ever had and got done in

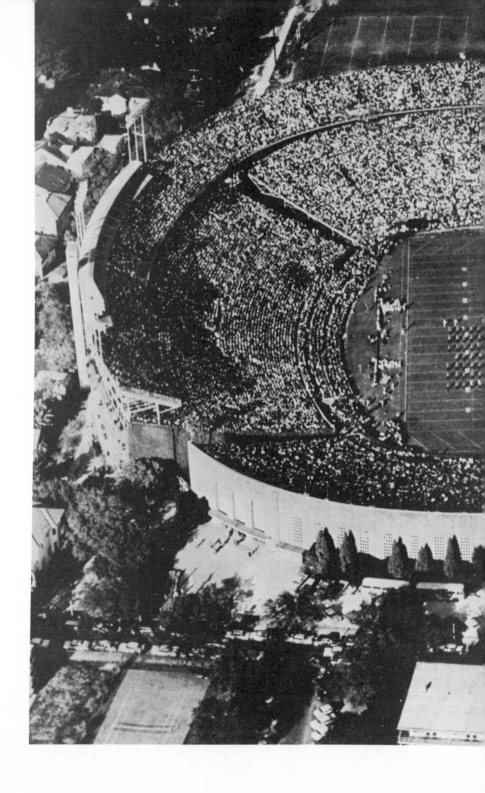

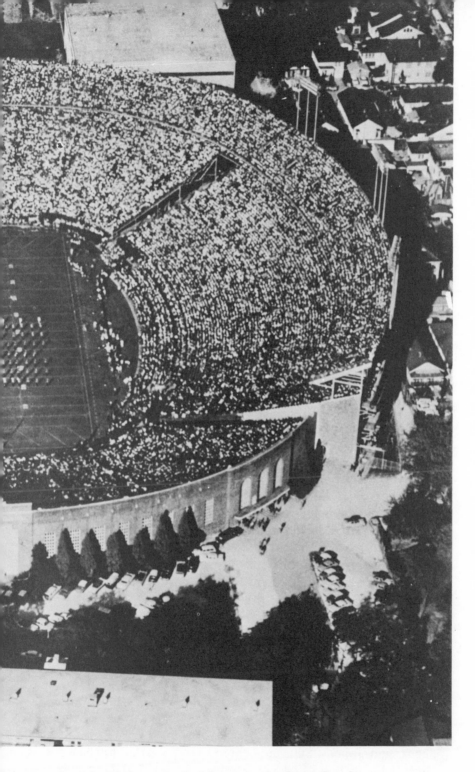

A packed house watched Bama in the Sugar Bowl.

by the ballot box....That's my prejudiced opinion, of course. The final vote went to Notre Dame, but I wish we could have played them or Michigan State that year."

Alabama was an explosive team in search of the title. Still small and quick as in the two previous championship seasons, the Crimson Tide swarmed on defense and hit quickly on offense.

Frustrated by the fact it was ranked third behind Notre Dame and Michigan State, Alabama entered the final regular-season game against Auburn with one more chance to prove its worth to voters. The score was tied at zero for 24 minutes; then, boom! Alabama exploded for 17 points in six minutes and went on to win, 31-0.

At halftime of the Auburn game, the telephone rang in the press box at Legion Field in Birmingham. Charles O. Finley, the owner of the Oakland A's baseball team, was calling after watching the first 30 minutes of action on television.

"Alabama looks mighty good in California," Finley said. "I vote for Alabama No. 1."

Alabama fans carried signs at the Auburn tussle which said, "Notre Dame plays politics, 'Bama plays football: In your heart you know we're No. 1."

Benny Marshall, writing in the *Birmingham News*, described the Alabama victory over Auburn:

"For a quarter and a half on a frigid Saturday afternoon 67,000 here and millions across the country could wonder if Alabama was No. 1, even at Legion Field in Birmingham, Alabama.

"Then after Auburn's gallant Tigers fired and fell back, the only college football team in the United States with a perfect record for 1966 spent the rest of the day demonstrating just how convincingly it had won most of the rest.

"This Alabama, third to go through a season unbeaten and untied for Paul Bryant, is a will-o-the-wisp which often has given the appearance of going nowhere. Suddenly the scoreboard says that they have already been."

They had all tried the players in red—ends Perkins, Wayne Cook, Charlie Harris, and Mike Ford; tackles Byrd Williams, Dowdy, Louis Thompson, and Cole; guards Calvert, Bruce Stephens, and Johnny Sullivan; center Jimmy Carroll; linebackers Mike Hall and Bob Childs; quarterback Kenny Stabler; running backs Les Kelley and David Chatwood; flanker Homan; and de-

From left to right for Alabama are Eddie Bo Rogers, Mike Hall, and Mike Ford.

fensive backs Johns, Donnie Sutton, Johnny Mosley, and Wayne Owen—but to no avail. The voters spoke.

After Auburn, only 9-1 and sixth-ranked Nebraska remained. For Alabama, the Sugar Bowl game was a chance to take out its frustrations. For Nebraska, it was a chance for revenge, after a 39-28 loss to the Crimson Tide in the Orange

Bowl one year earlier.

"Frankly, I was more than a little worried entering the Sugar Bowl game," Homan said. "We were going good and had plenty of confidence, but I knew Nebraska would be like a swarm of hornets after the way we had beaten them the year before.

"And there was some pressure, too. The championship was gone, but we were still playing to show people a few things. It was like the game was for all the apples. We were down to the nitty-gritty. We wanted to show the nation something."

Some show it was. What was thought to be a classic re-match turned into a mismatch.

Alabama struck quickly, Stabler passing 45 yards to Per-kins on the first play of the game to the Nebraska 27 yard line. Seven plays later, Kelley scored a touchdown and the rout was in progress.

Alabama led, 17-0, after one quarter and 24-0 at halftime. Kelley, Stabler, Wayne Trimble, and Perkins scored touchdowns and Steve Davis kicked four extra points and two field goals, from 30 and 40 yards. Stabler completed 12 of 17 passes for 218 yards.

Sportswriters heaped praise on the Crimson Tide.

"It was over almost before Nebraska's Cornhuskers knew what had hit them," wrote Marshall. "The beginning was the ending.

"There they were, the mighty men from Lincoln lined up on an ice soggy Sugar Bowl field made in order for making mincemeat of little, quick Alabama.

"This was the moment of revenge the Cornhuskers had forecast with growing confidence as the long, wet week before the game headed to its climax. Now they'd get even for the Orange Bowl.

"THEN the tornado hit, the explosion exploded, the roof fell in."

Charles Land of the *Tuscaloosa News* wrote, "Maybe it isn't the Alabama quickness that makes the Crimson Tide so great.

"Maybe it isn't the pride, either, or the intense prepara-tion.

"Maybe Alabama is just stubborn.

"The Crimson Tide of Paul William Bryant just keeps re-fusing to believe any claims that it isn't the best college football

The "Snake," Kenny Stabler.

team in the nation."

Bob Devaney, the Nebraska coach who was obviously frustrated after his second straight sound whipping at the hands of Alabama, gave 27-point conquering Crimson Tidesmen the ultimate compliment—"They are better than the score indicates. Alabama is the best football team I have ever seen."

Sports Illustrated, the weekly magazine, ran its "best and worst of the bowls" feature and lauded Alabama: Best Team, Alabama; Best Offense, Alabama; Best Strategy, Alabama; Best Player, Stabler of Alabama; Best Receiver, Perkins of Alabama; Best Defender, Johns of Alabama; Best Blocker, Dowdy of Alabama; Best Kicker, Davis of Alabama. Perkins, Dowdy, Stabler

Johns, Carroll, Thompson, Harris, and Childs were named to the *Sports Illustrated* All-Bowl team.

The magazine also added another category—Last Laugh—and awarded it to Bryant, the coach of an Alabama team which had a less-than-glorious distinction....

Unbeaten, Untied, and Uncrowned.

1968 Cotton Bowl Game
Texas A&M 20   Alabama 16

The teacher stood ready,
To discipline the child;
But when class was dismissed,
The Cotton Bowl was going wild.

Bryant, the master, was beaten,
Bebes, the scholar, was the man;
Alabama fell to Texas' Aggies,
As Stallings stood paddle in hand.

The meeting took place in the Baker Hotel in Dallas, Texas, on December 28, 1967. No introductions were needed. Paul William (Bear) Bryant, the head coach at the University of Alabama, was well acquainted with Gene (Bebes) Stallings, his football peer at Texas A&M University.

Bryant had coached Stallings when Bryant was the coach at Texas A&M and had hired Stallings as an Alabama assistant coach, a position Stallings held until 1964 when he left the Crimson Tide to become head coach at Texas A&M.

Suddenly, they were opponents—coaching their respective teams in the 1968 Cotton Bowl Game. The teacher—pupil matchup received much publicity.

Bryant was established. He had already won three national championships since becoming the Alabama coach in 1958 and his Crimson Tide teams had an overall 76-7-4 record in the 1960s, by far the best of any school in the nation. Alabama carried an 8-1-1 record into the Cotton Bowl.

Stallings, on the other hand, was trying to make a name for himself. He was young—32—and his Texas A&M team had posted an unimpressive 6-4 record during the regular season, although it did win the Southwest Conference championship.

When they met for their pregame press conference that afternoon, they were a picture of contrasts. Stallings wore a dirty, sweat-stained coaching cap, the bill low on his forehead much like the way Bryant wore his when on the practice field. He also wore a maroon jacket, muddy khaki britches, and high-top laced hunting boots.

As Stallings chatted with writers, Bryant entered wearing charcoal slacks, a checked blue sports coat, white shirt, charcoal tie with blue stripes, and alligator shoes.

When he spotted Stallings, Bryant stopped, backed up a step, and mumbled something about "the old dingy cap" the Texas A&M coach was wearing. "I absolutely refuse to have my picture taken with somebody that looks like an ol' Arab," Bryant said with a chuckle.

"I thought the least Stallings could do is not come up here in his work clothes," Bryant continued, slapping his protege on the knee.

"You taught me to work," Stallings retaliated. "I can party after the game."

The verbal fun continued with both Bryant and Stallings passing out compliments to each other and the opposing teams.

"If I had my choice, I'd prefer playing Alabama and Coach Bryant," Stallings said. "I like the relationships involved, but if I was looking for someone I had a chance to beat, I can think of a lot of other folks....Yeah, I'd like to beat him."

Bryant came back quickly, "Bebes thinks I'm a soft touch. Heck, I'm glad we're playing Texas A&M. Half of his staff—practically all—I've been associated with as player or coach....I'd walk from here to Birmingham to beat him."

The meeting was fun, but on January 1 at 4 p.m. on a muddy Cotton Bowl football field, Bryant and Stallings picked up their swords and went to war.

The kid won. Texas A&M beat Alabama, 20-16, much to the delight of most of the 71,000 pro-Texas fans who braved inclement weather to watch the game in a chilly Cotton Bowl Stadium.

It was not one of the best efforts Alabama had given Bryant since he became the head coach of the Crimson Tide. He was not pleased, but as always, was a gentleman. After the game, he walked to midfield, smiled broadly at Stallings, and picked up the Texas A&M coach and gave him a hug.

"Congratulations, old boy. That was a fine win for you," Bryant told Stallings at their postgame meeting.

"Thank you, Coach," Stallings said. "We were very fortunate."

Bryant surprised Stallings later by appearing in the Texas A&M dressing room. "I don't want to see you," Bryant told Stallings, who was breaking away from sportswriters to greet his former coach. "I want to see some of your players."

Bryant then went around the dressing room offering congratulations to Texas A&M players.

It had not been a good day for Alabama. The Crimson Tide scored first, but Texas A&M tied the game, 7-7, at the end of the first quarter. Alabama went ahead, 10-7, early in the second quarter, but Texas A&M scored to take a 13-10 lead at halftime. In the third quarter, Texas A&M stretched its lead to 20-10, before Alabama scored late in the period to make it 20-16.

Alabama challenged time and again in the fourth quarter but could not score, the final charge halted with 12 seconds left in the game when a Kenny Stabler pass was intercepted by Curly Hallman, a native Alabamian who is now an assistant coach on the Crimson Tide staff.

"I had no idea they were going to beat us," Bryant says, looking back on the Texas A&M upset victory. "We had the best football team, but Stallings just did a better job coaching than I did.

"We didn't play very well and I felt badly about it, but after the game I hugged Stallings because he had played for us at Texas A&M. It was a big moment for him and he was happy.

"We were on our way down that year. We weren't quite as good as we had been and didn't have as many players. But when we went out to play the Aggies, we should have won the football game."

Dennis Homan, a senior pass receiver on the 1967 Alabama team and an All-American selection, remembers the loss. "I feel like we had a better team than they did," Homan said, "but we didn't on that particular day. We were not ready to play. I think some of us had something on our minds instead of football."

The defeat at the hands of Texas A&M ended an

up-and-down season for an Alabama team which figured to do much better than the final 8-2-1 record the Crimson Tide put in the books. It was the worst Alabama record since 1958, the first year Bryant returned as coach.

Entering the 1967 regular season, Alabama had won 17 games in a row and was favored to win another Southeastern Conference championship. The preseason Associated Press poll tabbed the Crimson Tide as the second best team in the country behind Notre Dame.

But Alabama was experiencing internal problems entering the season, although they were not visible on the surface. Stabler, the All-American quarterback who had led the Crimson Tide to an 11-0 record in 1966, was suspended from the team during the off-season because he was experiencing academic difficulties. Bryant, who three years earlier had suspended another star quarterback, Joe Namath, because of training infractions, decided to let Stabler rejoin the team. The announcement was made on August 17, a little over a month before Alabama opened the season against Florida State.

"Alabama's chances for a fourth national football championship shot up Thursday when Bryant permitted ace quarterback Kenny (Snake) Stabler to rejoin the squad," an Associated Press story said.

In making the announcement, Bryant said, "Kenny will be permitted to rejoin the football squad for all practices beginning September 1. Ken has assured me that he will adhere to the academic regulations of the university and will pursue his degree until he graduates. I feel he is worthy of another chance."

So Stabler was back with his talented left arm, along with other All-American candidates guard Bruce Stephens, end Mike Ford, and linebacker Bob Childs. All was assumed fine and dandy in the Alabama camp and it was taken for granted the Crimson Tide was ready for another banner year.

The bomb dropped quickly, however. On September 23, Florida State, considered a patsy opener for Alabama, fought the Crimson Tide to a 37-37 tie at Birmingham. In tying Alabama, the Seminoles scored as many points as the Crimson Tide had allowed 10 opponents in 1966.

After three victories—over Southern Mississippi, Mississippi, and Vanderbilt—Alabama tasted defeat for the first time in 21 games, losing 24-13 to eventual Southeastern Conference champion Tennessee. With a 3-1-1 record after five unimpressive performances, the Crimson Tide was at a low ebb.

Bryant was not totally discouraged, however. "I imagine everybody will write us off," Bryant said after the Tennessee defeat, "that is, everybody except me. We are going to keep working to develop a better defense and running attack."

The defense came. Alabama allowed only 19 points in the remaining five regular-season games, victories over Clemson (13-10), Mississippi State (13-0), Louisiana State (7-6), South Carolina (17-0), and Auburn (7-3).

Stabler, who would later go on to lead the Oakland Raiders to a Super Bowl championship in 1977 and become the most valuable player in the National Football League, made one of his greatest plays as a collegian in the victory over Auburn. He ran 47 yards for the winning touchdown in the fourth quarter on a muddy, rainy day at Legion Field Stadium at Birmingham.

Sportswriter Benny Marshall of the *Birmingham News* described the game in the following manner.

"The rain had come early, riding in on the great gusts of wind, and the lights looked down on an eerie scene at Legion Field, a swamp on the west side of Birmingham where Auburn and Alabama played football Saturday.

"Did 71,200 sit under the sea of umbrellas? That was the crowd announced for Alabama-Auburn, but who could have told?

"It was the fourth quarter and Kenny Stabler stood in the middle of the muck in the middle of Legion Field, and at this moment, this was Auburn's football game because John Riley had kicked a 38-yard field goal in the third quarter, and because Auburn had been master of a day which grew darker and wetter and windier.

"Eleven minutes, a little more, to play and the Crimson Tide was at Auburn's 47 because Tommy Lunceford didn't get a punt away when the snap from center came low.

"They sloshed from the huddle and the Tigers were dug in again as Stabler looked them over and made his voice heard above the multitude to call the ball from Terry Kilgore at center.

"Stabler had it and he was sliding down the line of scrimmage, running the option play again. He looked for a trailing back to pitch to, looked again, and surely he was waiting too long. The defense had the wide men. Stabler, almost reluctantly

Kenny Stabler, victorious over Auburn and rain.

it seemed, turned to the job himself."

History records the rest. Stabler slipped, sputtered, dodged, and snaked his way in front of the Alabama bench and on into the end zone to earn Alabama its victory.

When Alabama fans roared in delight and cheered the victorious Crimson Tide, an unlikely figure stood among them. The man was Gene (Bebes) Stallings, an Alabama loyal who would later become a conquerer.

1968 Gator Bowl Game

Missouri 35   Alabama 10

I've got a tiger by the tail,
It's plain to see;
And I won't be much,
When she gets through with me.

—Buck Owens

"They beat us every way known to man—out-everythinged us. We would have been better off if I had planned a quarterback sneak every play and quick-kicked every now and then. Sure, we respected them, but we didn't expect anybody to run up and down the field like they were playing a barber's college.

"We were pretty fortunate. They deserved to beat us more than they did. We were fortunate we didn't have any more injuries the way they knocked us around.

"I thought we were still in the ball game going into the fourth quarter, but they scored a touchdown and took it to us. After that, they toyed with us like children.

"They were blocking and running well—like they were out to practice early. They were better prepared for us than we were for them and I mean that as a compliment to Coach Dan Devine and his people.

"No, I don't remember getting embarrassed like that before at Alabama.

"No, I can't think of anything that pleased me about us.

"They just wanted to win more than we did.

181

"It was all Missouri and it wasn't much of a game."

Paul William (Bear) Bryant, head football coach at the University of Alabama, has a reputation for being a man who calls a spade a spade, a heart a heart, and a sound thrashing a sound thrashing. He was in true form when he made the above remarks in the dressing room after the Gator Bowl game on December 28, 1968.

Missouri beat Alabama, 35-10. The loss came in the first Gator Bowl appearance for Alabama and was the worst bowl defeat a Crimson Tide team had suffered. The margin of defeat was also the worst for a Bryant-coached Alabama team in 11 seasons.

It was not a pretty day for Crimson Tide football. Alabama had minus-45 yards running in the game and only 23 yards total offense. The Crimson Tide managed only six first downs. Missouri, on the other hand, racked up 21 first downs and 402 yards total offense, all running.

The strangest thing about the game—it seemed almost like a miracle—is the fact that Alabama still had a chance to win with 12 minutes remaining to be played and the Crimson Tide trailing, 14-10.

But the massacre became a reality in the final quarter when Missouri scored 21 points and rendered Alabama helpless.

The most often-asked question after the game was what had happened to the proud Alabama defense which had led the Crimson Tide to an 8-2 regular-season record?

Charley Thornton, sports information director at the time and now an assistant athletic director at Alabama, probably handled the rash of questions better than anybody. He wore a small sign on his coat lapel which said, "If you're a friend, don't ask."

Mike Hall, an All-American linebacker who saw a brilliant Alabama career—and an even more sparkling senior season—end in misfortune against Missouri, has not escaped the question with as much ease. At Alabama, victories are cherished, losses are forever remembered.

"I don't look back at the Gator Bowl as a nightmare," said Hall, a native of Tarrant, Alabama, now living in Jasper. "Sure, we would have liked to have won, but we got beat by a good team. It was a good experience.

"We thought we could win the game, so the score surprised me. And so did Missouri. They did some things offensively

Hard-nosed linebacker Mike Hall.

which we didn't expect. They had a good ball club with a big fullback who ran through us like he owned us.

"I don't think we were prepared for the game as well as we were for some we played while I was at Alabama. There was a different attitude, but I still contend our defense played better than the score indicates. We were in the game until they broke loose in the fourth quarter."

The Gator Bowl, one of the so-called minor bowls, was something new to Hall and his teammates. His sophomore season, the Crimson Tide played in the Sugar Bowl and his junior season, Alabama played in the Cotton Bowl.

"It was a different kind of trip for us," Hall said, "and the coaches approached it from a different standpoint. We went to Jacksonville a couple of days before the game and treated the bowl game like a regular-season game.

183

"When we went to the Sugar Bowl, we were in New Orleans for almost a week and enjoyed Christmas together. We had a good time and were entertained as a group. The same thing happened at the Cotton Bowl.

"About the only thing we did as a team at Jacksonville was eat a couple of meals together. It was a different kind of arrangement."

The regular season leading to the Gator Bowl bid was more *barely* than *bear*-ly for Alabama. The Crimson Tide barely got past most of its opponents in winning eight games, yet barely came out on the short end of the two it lost.

Victories came over Virginia Tech (14-7), Southern Mississippi (17-14), Vanderbilt (31-7), Clemson (21-14), Mississippi State (20-13), Louisiana State (16-7), Miami (14-6), and Auburn (24-16). The losses were to Mississippi (10-8) and Tennessee (10-9).

Alabama spurned the opportunity for a short field goal to try for a second-quarter touchdown which failed against Mississippi and Tennessee kicked a 54-yard field goal against the Crimson Tide which helped the Vols to their margin of victory.

"We just didn't have as many quality football players in 1968 as we had in previous years," Bryant said. But the players Alabama had were scrappers and became known as the Cardiac Kids, because they pulled off victories at the final gun and fell to defeat in the same manner.

The victory over Auburn was the highlight of the year. It was the fifth straight win for the Crimson Tide over its bitter rival.

For Hall, it is a more pleasant day to remember. He played his most impressive game for Alabama against Auburn, making 16 tackles, intercepting two passes, breaking up three tackles, making a key block as a tight end on a touchdown run, and scoring a touchdown as a tight end by catching a five-yard pass from sophomore quarterback Scott Hunter.

"If Hall is not an All-American, there are no All-Americans," Bryant said after the game.

Praise for the Alabama linebacker who signed a professional contract with the New York Jets did not end there. He was the main subject of every newspaper story after the game.

"Mike Hall magnificently found the greatness so often predicted for him, and his Alabama teammates fell right in step and beat stubborn, ambitious Auburn, 24-16, here Saturday after-

Bear and Shug meet after annual Alabama versus Auburn shoot-out.

noon," wrote Charles Land in the *Tuscaloosa News*. "It was a fitting climax to a great Hall day, the kind Alabama coach Paul Bryant said he needed to make it a great season. Hall was simply terrific."

Hall, a fierce competitor and leader, was team spokesman for Alabama in the Auburn game. After his performance, he was awarded the game ball but gave it to Dr. Pat Trammell, the former Alabama quarterback who was dying in his fight against cancer.

"We functioned well as a team against Auburn, about as well as we had all year," Hall said. "The offense moved the ball well and the defense continued to do a good job. We were a pretty good football team that day."

The victory over Auburn was the best Alabama effort of the season and it impressed Henry Dartigalongue, president of the Gator Bowl Association. He watched the game in Legion Field at Birmingham, after watching Missouri conclude a 7-3 regular season by losing to Kansas, 21-19, one week earlier, and proceeded to make one of the worst predictions of his life.

"Both Alabama and Missouri have strong defensive football teams," Dartigalongue said. "We think this will prove to be the best game in the history of the Gator Bowl."

Alabama loyals try their best to forget the Gator Bowl defeat and nobody has a harder time doing so than Assistant Athletic Director Thornton. He has an unusual souvenir.

"They gave us a watch at the banquet after the game," Thornton said, "and it has kind of haunted me since. After we left Jacksonville, Doris (his wife) and I went to the Sugar Bowl at New Orleans to watch Georgia and Arkansas play.

"While we were in New Orleans, I looked down at my watch and it had stopped running. And guess what time it was?

"Thirty-five to ten."

1969 Liberty Bowl Game

Colorado 47   Alabama 33

"You can't roller skate in a buffalo herd."—Roger Miller.

Alvin Samples was stunned and appreciative.

He had reason to feel both ways. After all, how many football players are honored for their offensive efforts without playing a single down on offense?

It happened to Samples, a University of Alabama All-American guard in 1969. He was named the most outstanding offensive lineman for the Crimson Tide in the Liberty Bowl game at Memphis, Tennessee, on December 13, 1969. He played linebacker in the wild and wooly offensive contest won by Colorado, 47-33.

"It was a complete surprise," Samples said eight years after the Liberty Bowl. "Receiving that award was startling, to say the least. When they called my name at the banquet, I was stunned.

"But I was proud, too, and I am still proud of winning that award. I sure as the devil wasn't about to give it back to 'em either. It wasn't a mistake. They meant to give it to me."

The outstanding player awards in the Liberty Bowl were voted by members of the press covering the game. Samples, a tremendous blocker as a junior and again as a senior during the 1969 regular season, was moved to defense in an effort to plug up gaping holes which had plagued the Crimson Tide during a 6-4 campaign.

"I guess the voters were trying to say something to me," Samples said. "You know, something like, 'Alvin, we knew you

187

would have done a good job on offense if you had been in there.' To this day, I'm very thankful for those who voted."

Nothing that happened at the Liberty Bowl banquet should have come as a surprise, for it ended one of the craziest, zaniest days of football in history. The game, which featured enough offensive fireworks to light most of the sky over West Tennessee, was a delight to fans—those sitting in the stadium and millions more watching on nationwide television.

"Colorado, a Yankee Doodle Dandy come to town, showered Memorial Stadium with football fireworks yesterday afternoon and burned gutty little Alabama, 47-33, in the 11th Liberty Bowl game. A record 50,042 fans cheered the windy but radiant football day into the sunset," wrote Kyle Griffin, a Memphis sportswriter. "It was a great game to watch."

The Liberty Bowl, which has developed into one of the finest of all the postseason shows, looks back on the Colorado victory over Alabama and calls it the game which propelled it to its current stature. It was definitely an attention-catcher. Eleven touchdowns were scored in the game, by way of running, passing, and kickoff returning. There was a field goal, eight extra-point kicks, and a safety.

Colorado, big and powerful runners, jumped to a 10-0 lead at the end of the first quarter, then made it 17-0 early in the second quarter. Alabama rallied to cut the margin to 17-13 midway through the second quarter. Colorado pushed it to 24-13; then Alabama scored a touchdown to make it 24-19. Colorado ran the ensuing kickoff 91 yards for a touchdown and went to the dressing room at halftime with an amazing 31-19 lead.

The two teams had scored 40 points in the second quarter, the most ever for one period in a bowl game.

Given up for dead at intermission, Alabama gallantly fought back in the third quarter with 14 points and grabbed the lead, 33-31, at the end of the period. Sixteen points by the Buffaloes in the fourth quarter—the final nine coming late in the game when Alabama was forced to gamble on offense—put the finishing touches on the Crimson Tide.

When the game ended, Big Eight Conference representative Colorado did exercises in the end zone as score-drunk fans watched in dismay.

"Two things really embarrassed me." said Coach Bryant. "When they ran that kickoff back for a touchdown after we struggled so hard to score just before halftime and when they

All-American guard Alvin Samples.

went down to the end zone and worked out after the game. They acted like we didn't give them a good workout and I don't guess we did.

"Colorado was big and we couldn't block them. They caught us with a team which could score points, but we had very little defense, very little kicking, and very little of everything else it takes to win football games."

Samples is more profound in his analysis of the game—"It was one of the most exciting things I've ever been involved in and we lost it."

The Liberty Bowl loss to Colorado was not the only unusual game the Crimson Tide played during a season which produced the worst record for Alabama since 1958, Bryant's first year as head coach.

Alabama defeated Mississippi, 33-32, in a nationally televised game the third week of the season when Scott Hunter outdueled Archie Manning in a battle between passing quarterbacks. It remains one of the most exciting games in collegiate history.

One week after the victory over Ole Miss, Alabama was defeated by Vanderbilt, 14-10, a decision which shocked the football world. It was the first victory for the Commodores over Alabama since 1956 and the last to date.

Auburn ended five years of frustration against Alabama by defeating the Crimson Tide, 49-26, on the final weekend of the regular season. Auburn was led by Pat Sullivan, a sophomore quarterback who went on to win the Heisman Trophy as a senior.

Alabama also lost to Tennessee (41-14) and to Louisiana State (20-15). The Crimson Tide picked up victories over Virginia Tech (17-13), Southern Mississippi (63-14), Clemson (38-13), Mississippi State (23-19), and Miami (42-6), in addition to its thrilling win over Ole Miss.

"Our entire season depended on our defense and it never jelled," said Samples as he looked back on the disastrous year. "We had a good offense, but our defense never came up to par.

"We got off to a good enough start by winning our first three games, but we started going downhill after that loss to Vanderbilt.

"Every championship team gets breaks, no matter how good it is. The breaks never came our way in 1969. We never materialized. It just wasn't a good year for us."

By the time the regular season was over, Alabama was thankful for the chance to play in a bowl game. The Crimson Tide had played in 10 straight postseason games and was anxious to extend the streak. In an interview with Alf Van Hoose of the *Birmingham News* a few days before the Liberty Bowl game, Bryant talked about the importance of the game his Crimson Tide was to play.

190

Alvin Samples with Coach Jimmy Sharpe.

"We need to win a football game," Bryant said. "Ordinarily, at Alabama, bowl games are rewards for jobs well done. This one is different. We can't approach it as we have.

"We can't be frolicking around. The only singing I want to hear is in the dressing room after the game.

"It's a big game for me all right—every game is—but for the school and players it's bigger, particularly the senior players. We coaches get paid, win or lose.

"But our seniors need to win. They've been on two losing bowl teams (against Texas A&M in the Cotton Bowl and Missouri in the Gator Bowl). They lost to Auburn for the first time in six years.

"They haven't won a bowl game. They are entitled to a better record than I have caused them to have."

Bryant was critical of himself after Alabama lost four games during the regular season. After the loss to Colorado in the Liberty Bowl, he started talking about resigning. Bryant went to Dr. David Mathews, president of the university, and urged him to start looking for a suitable replacement and to take an extensive look at the condition of the Alabama athletic program.

Although Bryant attempted to deal with Mathews quietly, the story leaked and remained a hot question until Mathews issued a statement on January 8, 1970. The coach was staying.

"I have asked Coach Bryant to take that responsibility (that of coaching Alabama in the 1970s) and he has accepted," Mathews told Van Hoose for publication in the *Birmingham News*.

"I'm more delighted than I can express it that he has accepted, that the university can look forward to Coach Bryant's continued athletic leadership.

"At the same time, it is Coach Bryant's feeling that we should begin to look toward that time when there must be new leadership of the football program, and start to groom new leaders.

"We have just completed a very, very hard look at our football program, and, again let me say, it was Coach Bryant's recommendation that we do it.

"We are very proud of that program. It has brought great honor to the university. It will, we feel confident, continue to do so."

The same week that Mathews made his announcement that Bryant would stay as coach, Samples was soothing the wounds of the Liberty Bowl loss by playing an outstanding game in the Senior Bowl at Mobile. It was there, among the best senior players in the country, that Samples found a basic truth about Alabama football.

"I was feeling kind of bad about the year we had," Samples said, "because Alabama had such a great reputation and tradition. Shoot, if you don't win 'em all, you've had a bad year.

"Well, I was talking to this player from up North and he asked, 'Hey, Samples, what kind of year did you guys have at Alabama?' I told him it was a bad one, 6-4 during the regular season and a bowl loss to Colorado. He just shook his head,

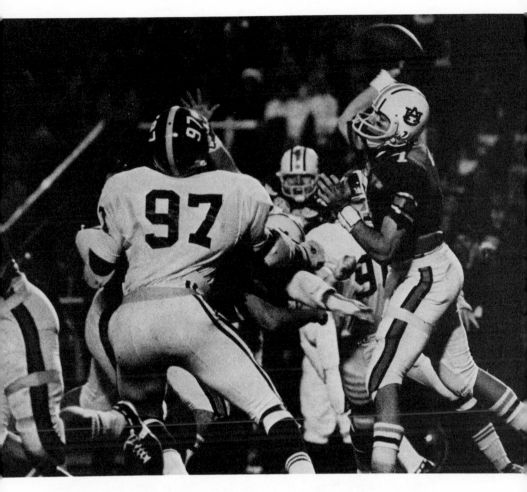

Defense throttles Heisman Trophy winner Pat Sullivan of Auburn, but not very often.

laughed, and said, 'Six-four, what in the world is wrong with that?'

"That guy just couldn't understand that we have a different set of standards at Alabama."

1970 Astro-Bluebonnet Bowl Game

Alabama 24   Oklahoma 24

'Bama was down,
The Tide was troubled;
Ten losses in two years.

But hold the phone,
The end of the struggle;
A tie at Houston...and cheers.

—Martha Cox

The object—as always in college football—was to win the game, but when the University of Alabama team went to Houston, Texas, to play Oklahoma in the 1970 Astro—Bluebonnet Bowl on December 31, Crimson Tide players went to have fun, too.

And why not? Alabama had missed out on a lot of good times during the regular season leading to the game. The Crimson Tide had played 11 games and lost 5 of them.

It marked the second consecutive year that Alabama had lost five games. Crimson Tide fans were restless, sportswriters across the nation were critical, and Alabama players were frustrated.

"What is wrong?" fans asked. "Alabama magic is a thing of the past," sportswriters wrote. "Let's play one more and get ready for next year," players declared.

But when Alabama had finished its business at Houston, where the Crimson Tide battled the Sooners to a 24-24 tie, fans were more subdued, writers more complimentary, and players more confident and looking to 1971 with renewed dedication.

Steve Higginbotham, a 177-pound junior defensive half-back who became All-Southeastern Conference as a senior, had a major hand in leading Alabama to its six victories in 1970. He remembers well the mood of Crimson Tide players as they prepared for the Astro—Bluebonnet Bowl match with Oklahoma.

"There wasn't much good going on that year for us," said

Little man with a big heart, Steve Higginbotham.

Higginbotham. "In fact, the bowl bid was about the only bright thing about the entire season. So when we got the invitation to go to Houston, we decided it was going to be a fun trip. And boy was it!

"It was different than most bowl trips. We were more relaxed and spent a lot of time with Oklahoma players before the game. I enjoyed every minute of it. They were quality people, as well as outstanding football players. We all had a terrific time.

"We played a decent game, too. It helped us forget the regular season we had played and made us more hungry for better things the next year."

Oklahoma football had dipped somewhat in 1970, too. The Sooners finished with a 7-4 regular-season record and were rated seven-point favorites over Alabama in the Astro—Bluebonnet Bowl.

Both Alabama and Oklahoma challenged for the national championship the next year with 11-1 records.

"You could sense something special about both Alabama and Oklahoma when they lined up to play in the Astrodome," said Kirk McNair, now University of Alabama sports information director, who accompanied the Crimson Tide on its trip to Houston. "Both teams had suffered through bad seasons, but both squads were blessed with talented young players. Somehow, you just got the feeling Alabama and Oklahoma were going to go on to bigger and better things quickly.

"And Alabama and Oklahoma were big names in football, so the Astro—Bluebonnet Bowl was happy to have both teams there. They really did a great job of entertaining. I think the players—everybody who went to Houston, really—had a great time."

When Astro—Bluebonnet Bowl officials tallied up gate receipts from the game, they were proud of the Alabama versus Oklahoma matchup. A standing room crowd of 53,812 watched the contest in the Astrodome, which had a seating capacity of 52,000. The game was televised nationally, too, adding to the revenue.

Those who watched—live or through television—were not disappointed. It was an exciting game and the outcome was not determined until the final play, when Alabama missed a field-goal attempt.

"We weren't a great team, but we had gotten better and

Oklahoma's Chuck Fairbanks greets Bryant after Astro-Blue-bonnet tie.

played well at Houston," remembers Coach Bryant. "Oklahoma ran up and down the field on us for awhile, because we didn't know much about stopping that wishbone offense they were running. But we held our own with them.

"Actually, I thought we had the game won a couple of times—once before they kicked a long field goal to tie it and again when we lined up to try that field goal at the end. We were down that year, so getting that tie meant a lot to us."

There was little defense in the game, although both teams made some important stops which probably earned them ties. There were 843 yards total offense in the game.

Oklahoma was led offensively by All-American halfback Greg Pruitt, an outstanding pro runner now; quarterback Joe Wylie; and kicker Bruce Derr, who had a field goal and three extra points. Alabama was led by halfback Johnny Musso, who had an outstanding junior season and was headed for an even

197

The Italian Stallion, Johnny Musso.

greater senior year; quarterback Scott Hunter; pass receiver David Bailey; and kicker Richard Ciemny, who kicked a field goal and three extra points, but had the unwanted distinction of missing the final field-goal attempt.

The game was tied, 7-7, after one quarter, Alabama scoring first on a four-yard pass from Hunter to tight end Randy Moore, and Oklahoma scoring on a two-yard run by Wylie.

Oklahoma scored two touchdowns in the second quarter—on electrifying runs of 58 and 25 yards by Pruitt—to take a 21-7 lead, but Hunter passed five yards to Bailey for a touchdown just before halftime to cut the Sooners' lead to 21-14 at intermission.

Ciemny kicked a 20-yard field goal for the only points of the third quarter—making the score 21-17—and the two teams were ready for a wild fourth quarter which had fans on the edges of their seats until the final gun.

With 7½ minutes left to play and Alabama facing a fourth down on the Oklahoma 25 yard line, Johnny Musso took a handoff from Hunter and started running to his right, as on an end sweep. But the left-handed halfback stopped, then passed to Hunter, who had caught the Oklahoma defense by surprise and was all alone. The Alabama quarterback sprinted into the end zone for a touchdown and a Crimson Tide lead, 24-21.

Steve Sloan, a former Alabama player who was an assistant coach at the time (he is now head coach at Texas Tech), called most of the offensive plays for Alabama against Oklahoma. "But I called that Musso pass play," Bryant says. "Steve didn't agree with me completely, but I was right that time."

The Alabama "trick-play" appeared to be a game-winner, but Oklahoma roared back and Derr kicked a 42-yard field goal with 59 seconds left in the game to tie it.

The Sooners, not satisfied with a tie, attempted an onside kickoff, but the ball went nowhere and Alabama had another chance with first down at the Oklahoma 40 yard line. Musso ran the ball 21 yards to the 19, Dave Brungard ran for 2 yards, and Hunter was thrown for a yard loss.

Alabama called time out with five seconds on the clock and Ciemny came on the field to attempt a 34-yard field goal. He missed badly, shanking the ball toward the corner of the end zone.

"I just missed it a mile," Ciemny said in the dressing room after the game. "I don't know why. I think I kept my eye on the ball, but I didn't hit it squarely.

"I kept telling myself it was just like an extra point. I said, 'Just kick it like an extra point.' I just blew it."

Ciemny, an outstanding kicker for two years after enrolling at Alabama from a junior college in his native Kansas, has taken the rap for the Crimson Tide tie with Oklahoma. Higginbotham does not agree with the criticism.

"I'm the kind of guy who never likes to look down on anybody," Higginbotham said, looking back on the missed shot at victory, "so I sure won't be critical of Richard. He missed it, sure, but we did a lot of other things which kept us from winning that night.

"I feel sorry for those kickers, anyway. They're out there only a few plays a game. They have one or two shots for glory. They either hit or they miss. They are always in pressure situations.

"How did I feel when he missed that field goal? Well, I imagine I cussed a little bit, but we had other chances to win the game going away."

If Alabama was unfortunate in tying Oklahoma, the Crimson Tide had to take some consolation in the fact it was fortunate just to be there. Six-five seasons rarely merit bowl consideration, especially when losses are overwhelming and inconsistency is a team trademark.

During the 1970 regular season, Alabama lost to Southern California (42-21), Mississippi (48-23), Tennessee (24-0), Louisiana State (14-9), and Auburn (33-28). The Crimson Tide scored victories over Virginia Tech (51-18), Florida (46-15), Vanderbilt (35-11), Houston (30-21), Mississippi State (35-6), and Miami (32-8).

Although short on talent and victories, the 1970 Alabama team lacked nothing when it came to excitement. The Crimson Tide played some heart-stopping games.

"Football Mania" is the way John Forney described Birmingham when coming on the air to broadcast the Alabama versus Southern Cal game. The Trojans won easily with fullback Sam Cunningham, a 225-pound black, rushing for more than 200 yards. "Cunningham did more for integration in the South than Martin Luther King ever dreamed," wrote one sportswriter covering the game.

Alabama was victimized by a pass-intercepting (eight times) Tennessee defense in its loss at Knoxville. It was the first shutout of an Alabama team since the 1959 Liberty Bowl. Late in the game, after several Tennessee interceptions, Bailey came to the huddle and jokingly told Hunter, "Scott, throw one to a linebacker and I'll see if I can catch it."

Higginbotham was the star in the victory over Houston, the first trip for Alabama to the Astrodome and the first game for the Crimson Tide indoors. He intercepted a pass and ran 80 yards for a touchdown in the final minutes as the Cougars appeared headed for a winning touchdown. That interception was probably the Alabama ticket back to Houston for the bowl game.

Alabama led Auburn, 17-0, after one quarter and appeared headed toward a convincing victory over the favored Tigers. But Pat Sullivan, the Heisman Trophy-winning quarterback, teamed with pass-catching star Terry Beasley as Auburn roared back to take a thrilling victory in one of the best Alabama-Auburn tussles on record. Musso rushed for more than 200 yards for Alabama in a grand performance.

"It was a season to remember, to say the least," Higginbotham said, "but most of us would just as soon forget. It was just one of those years where we lost, lost, and lost because we didn't have enough talent.

"Southern Cal was great and they started us off on the wrong foot. Beasley got Auburn its victory over us and that was one heckuva way for us to end the season. I'm just thankful we were fortunate enough to end the year by tying Oklahoma."

The Oklahoma game was one of the most important ever played by an Alabama team. Since that night, Alabama has compiled a 63-9 record and has been in serious contention for four national championships.

The weapon Alabama has used in compiling that impressive record is the wishbone offense, which Oklahoma introduced to the Crimson Tide at Houston.

"We were in the air about 20 minutes on the flight home when I looked at Coach Bryant," said McNair. "He had opened up his briefcase and was busy diagramming plays in the wishbone offense. He didn't quit until we landed in Tuscaloosa.

"I thought he was still trying to figure out ways of defensing the wishbone. In August of 1971 I found out differently."

1972 Orange Bowl Game

Nebraska 38   Alabama 6

Across the country they swept,
The men in red tough and ready;
In Los Angeles the Coliseum shook,
Yet Bama stood firm and steady.

On they marched in unbeaten glory,
Taking the SEC and the rest;
Then it was on to big Miami,
To decide the nation's best.

Nebraska won and was named champ,
Alabama never could get on track;
But in the Orange Bowl a warning was made,
Beware, The Bear is back.

—Author unknown

Jimmy Grammer is one of the guttiest players to ever pull on a red University of Alabama football jersey.

He lacked size, playing his senior season as a 200-pound center, but made up for smallness with a big heart and lightning-like quickness. He lacked an abundance of talent, but earned all-Southeastern Conference honors with sheer desire and hard work. He earned the respect of both teammates and opponents by leading silently and doing an outstanding job.

And like everybody else on the 1971 Alabama team, Grammer had a dream. It was a big one—a national champion-

Alabama center, Jimmy Grammer.

ship.

That dream crumbled on the night of January 1, 1972, when unbeaten, untied Nebraska defeated unbeaten, untied Alabama, 38-6, in the Orange Bowl game at Miami, Florida.

It was a nightmare affair for the Crimson Tide, which had battled back into the national spotlight by defeating 11 straight opponents to become the second-ranked team in the country, after 6-5 and 6-5-1 records in 1969 and 1970, respectively.

1972 Orange Bowl: colorful, but sorrowful.

For Grammer, a soft-spoken man who now coaches high school football, the nightmare continues. Time has erased the sleepless nights he experienced following the game, but years, days, hours, minutes, and seconds have not helped him forget Rich Glover.

Glover was a strong 234-pound All-American middle guard on the national championship Nebraska team which manhandled Alabama at Miami. He played his greatest game as a collegian—making 18 tackles and wrecking the Alabama offense—thus making Grammer, the man charged with blocking the powerful Cornhusker, his victim.

A record national television audience watched the game and several minutes of camera time were dedicated to the Grammer—Glover match in the middle. The little Alabama center did not look good that night and has heard about it since.

When things go bad for a football team, somebody usually takes more than his share of the blame. Grammer is that man for Alabama, when in reality it was a team loss, one which can be summed up in six words...Nebraska Was Too Powerful for Alabama.

"It's a funny feeling being completely overpowered by somebody," Grammer said, while looking back on the loss to Nebraska. "And that's exactly what Glover did to me that night at Miami. No excuses. He was super strong—the strongest man I ever played against—and he was smart and quick, too.

"I had heard an awful lot about Glover long before we were matched against Nebraska. I had seen him on TV and remember being amazed by the way he handled people, like that All-American center from Oklahoma. That guy didn't block Glover all day.

"I knew I was going to be in for a challenge in the Orange Bowl. But I had faced a lot of guys stronger than me and had been able to beat them with quickness.

"Glover was different, however. He turned out to be everything people said he was."

Nebraska turned out to be awesome, too, and turned what was expected to be the greatest game in collegiate history into a mismatch.

Bill Lumpkin, sports editor of the *Birmingham Post-Herald*, amply described the aftermath left by the game.

If someone had told the University of Alabama late Saturday that Nebraska showed up in the Orange Bowl a day early, the beaten young Tiders would have agreed whole-heartedly.

The Cornhuskers should have been playing in the Classic's arena Sunday, with the Miami Dolphins and the Baltimore Colts, in pro football's playoff to determine its championship.

Nebraska took care of the collegiate world's grid championship Saturday evening, turning what was billed as the game of the century into a 38-6 rout of a proud Alabama eleven.

It was the biggest margin of defeat the Crimson Tide has ever endured in a postseason contest and it was the widest point difference in defeat since Auburn spanked the Tide, 40-0, in the final regular-season game in 1957.

Both teams went into the kickoff undefeated and untied, Nebraska having a 22-game winning streak alive and Alabama 11 in a row. The Huskers were defending collegiate kings and ranked first in wire service polls. Alabama was the challenger, holding the No. 2 ranking.

But it wasn't Alabama's night. Before first quarter had ended, the Cornhuskers already had posted 14 points on the scoreboard, a lead that was to grow to 28-0 before intermission. The loss also left Alabama without a bowl win for five straight years. The last time the Crimsons brought home a classic trophy, incidentally, was after beating Nebraska, 34-7, in the 1967 Sugar Bowl.

But this was the bitterest of all. A national championship had been lost, a dream shattered. The Alabama dressing room was like a morgue. No one spoke. The young men sat around dressing in silence. There were few tears. When one did speak, it was in a low whisper.

It came as no surprise that Alabama players took the defeat hard, but the ease and suddenness with which they were beaten was shocking.

A fumbled punt snap gave Nebraska the ball on the Alabama 47 yard line late in the first quarter and halfback Jeff Kinney quickly ripped over tackle for the first touchdown. The point-after kick made it 7-0. Moments later, halfback Johnny Rodgers grabbed an Alabama punt and raced 77 yards for the second Nebraska touchdown, pushing the score to 14-0.

Alabama fumbled the kickoff and Nebraska recovered on the Crimson Tide 27 yard line. A few plays later, quarterback Jerry Tagge ran into the end zone and Nebraska led, 21-0.

Alabama fumbled again late in the second quarter, Nebraska recovering on the Crimson Tide four yard line. Gary Dixon scored for Nebraska and for all practical purposes, the game was over at halftime with the Cornhuskers leading 28-0.

Quarterback Terry Davis scored for Alabama in the third quarter, but Nebraska got a field goal in the third quarter and another touchdown in the fourth quarter to win going away.

Statistics on the game were reasonably close, with Alabama mistakes spelling Crimson Tide doom.

"I'm not sure that Nebraska team is not the greatest college team I've ever seen," says Coach Bryant. "They made us look bad in the Orange Bowl and I think we had a great team that year. I know we weren't as bad as they made us look.

"Nebraska was a solid team all the way—kicking, defense, offense, and everything. And they had Rodgers and Glover.

"Rodgers could beat a team almost by himself. You

couldn't contain him. He could beat you too many ways. I've never seen a man who could play as well as he did.

"Glover just ruined our entire attack. We even tried to put two men on him at times and that slowed us down someplace else.

"Anyway, they literally ate us and I was embarrassed by the half. I told our seniors at halftime that they just couldn't afford to walk away from a game like this, because they would always be remembered by their last one. And they put a lot into it during the second half. But honestly, that may be one game we gave up on before it ended."

Granted, things looked bad for Alabama after the game had ended, but according to Grammer, things were not rosy from a Crimson Tide standpoint before kickoff.

"I am not making excuses for us, because Nebraska deserved all they got by beating us," Grammer said. "But I will always feel one great factor in the outcome of the game was preparation.

"I'll always believe we weren't ready to play that night. Maybe if we could have played the game some other time, it might have been different. Nebraska might have beaten us, but I think we could have made it closer.

"You prepare the same for every game, no matter how big the stakes are and sometimes you get to kickoff and find you are not psychologically or mentally ready to play. We weren't ready that night in the Orange Bowl."

If Alabama was not mentally ready to play against Nebraska, the Crimson Tide lost a lot of momentum during the month between its last regular-season victory over Auburn and its trip to Miami. From a highly publicized opening win over Southern Cal, 17-10, to a season-ending victory over Auburn, 31-7, Alabama was a scalding hot football team.

Opponents fell like stormy raindrops—sure and with force. Other victims were Southern Mississippi (42-6), Florida (38-0), Mississippi (40-6), Vanderbilt (42-0), Tennessee (32-15), Houston (34-20), Mississippi State (41-10), Louisiana State (14-7), and Miami (31-3).

The Alabama surge back into national prominence took the football world by surprise. It was a family secret, from the change to the wishbone offense to a new era of dedication among players.

"I had been redshirted one year so I was in my fifth year

at Alabama," Grammer said, "and I could definitely feel a different attitude among everybody as we approached the 1971 season. Some of us guys were in summer school and all we talked about was football.

"We didn't know if we would have any more talent that year, but we sure were talking a lot about winning football games again. It was a refreshing feeling to know we were serious about winning again."

It was on the first day of fall practice that Bryant told the team he was changing offenses—chunking the passing game and going to the running wishbone attack. He told the team, "We are going to sink or swim with the wishbone."

"We didn't know anything about the wishbone, except that Oklahoma had used it on us in the Astro—Bluebonnet Bowl," Grammer said, "and we didn't have a lot of confidence in it. But when Coach Bryant said we would sink or swim with it, we got interested in learning in a hurry.

"We had confidence in the offense when we went to Los Angeles to play Southern Cal. Since they had wrecked us at Birmingham the year before, we knew that game was gonna tell the story on us. We knew the season was wrapped up in that game. If we lose, that's it. If we win, there is no telling how far we can go."

Alabama unleashed its stars on Southern Cal and left Los Angeles fans stunned. Johnny Musso, the great All-American halfback, ran like a wild man in the Los Angeles Coliseum. Terry Davis, the shifty little quarterback, directed the attack like a genius. John Hannah, now a great pro player, joined Grammer, Jim Krapf, Jimmy Rosser, and others in opening up big holes in the Trojan defense. Robin Parkhouse, Tom Surlas, Steve Higginbotham, Jeff Rouzie, Jeff Beard, John Mitchell, and others put forth gallant defensive efforts to hold off a fierce Southern Cal attack at the end.

Alabama was back and it was a memorable game for 6,000 Crimson Tide fans who traveled to Los Angeles, as it was for thousands more who listened to the game on radio. About 5,000 students swarmed the Alabama campus after the game and staged a wild celebration, which included a parade around the quadrangle housing Denny Chimes and an early-September victory swim in the fountain which decorates the lawn in front of the university's Administration Building.

"Paul (Bear) Bryant of Alabama, the world's best college

football coach, has reached the stage in his life where he'd like to get things done in a hurry, even if he does talk slow," wrote Bud Furillo in the *Los Angeles Herald-Examiner* the morning after the victory over Southern Cal.

"The Bear is getting high on hours, as his 58th birthday today makes clear. So he didn't mess around waiting long for his 200th coaching victory. Bear reached out and grabbed it from a USC football team favored by a dozen points."

The victory over Southern Cal was a sweet one for Alabama, but the one the Crimson Tide got over Auburn at the end of the year was sweeter, because it came on the greatest sports day in state history.

Both state schools were unbeaten and untied. Auburn was ranked fourth in the nation and headed for the Sugar Bowl against Oklahoma. Alabama was ranked second and looking toward Nebraska. Pat Sullivan, the Auburn quarterback, had been awarded the Heisman Trophy as the best collegiate player in the

Alabama 17, USC 10: John McKay walks with The Bear.

John Mitchell, a big plus for the Tide.

country. Musso had ranked fourth in the Heisman Trophy vote race and the "Italian Stallion" was entering his final regular-season game for Alabama.

Musso made it a brilliant swan song. The star running back, who now plays with the Chicago Bears of the National Football League, played against Auburn with a peculiar toe injury which limited his workout schedule before the game.

He was on crutches Monday, jogged for 20 minutes Tuesday and for 40 minutes Wednesday, alternated at half-speed with three other halfbacks at practice Thursday, and did not suit up for a pregame workout Friday.

On Saturday, as almost 73,000 fans watched in Legion Field at Birmingham and millions more watched through national television, Musso ran 33 times for 167 yards as Alabama broke from a 14-7 lead after three quarters to overwhelm Auburn.

"Another Alabama Crimson Tide rose to greatness Saturday," wrote Alf Van Hoose in the *Birmingham News*. "Millions saw it. Move over storied Rose Bowlers of fading memory, also three national champs of the 1960s. You've got company. Hail your peers—certainly your equals."

Then along came Glover, Rodgers, and Nebraska.

Victory rides common at Alabama: John Hannah signals No. 1.

1973 Cotton Bowl Game

Texas 17   Alabama 13

Punt, Bama, Punt!
We do not believe.

—An Auburn fan

Lightning does indeed strike twice in the same place.

And it is possible to kill two birds with one stone.

The Auburn University football team proved both points at the expense of an outstanding team from the University of Alabama in 1972.

Lightning struck twice on December 2, 1972, during the final minutes of an amazing Auburn victory over Alabama at Legion Field at Birmingham.

Alabama was seemingly in control of the contest—as was expected from a Crimson Tide team which had defeated 10 straight opponents that season. The lead was 16-3 and the Alabama defense had Auburn cuffed, convicted, and locked up.

"They can play this game for five years and Auburn will never score a touchdown," said a sportswriter from his seat in the press box as the game moved into its final nine minutes.

Three and one-half minutes later—with five and one-half minutes left to play in the game—72,386 fans saw the start of a miracle. Four minutes later—with 90 seconds left to play—they saw the miracle completed.

Auburn blocked two consecutive Alabama punts, returned them both for touchdowns, added two extra points, and defeated the Crimson Tide, 17-16.

Bill Newton, an Auburn linebacker, blocked the first punt and defensive halfback David Langner picked up the ball and ran 25 yards for the touchdown. Then, on a play which looked identical to the first one, Newton blocked the second punt and Langner picked up the ball and ran 20 yards for the touchdown.

Number 2-ranked Alabama, in search of the national championship, was dazed. Unscratched, the Crimson Tide had been beaten for the first time in a season which had seen Alabama perform like national championship teams the school had fielded in the past.

Less than one month later, on January 1, 1973, Alabama was beaten again, 17-13, by Texas in the Cotton Bowl game at Dallas.

"We didn't lose that game to Texas that day in the Cotton Bowl," said Bear Bryant. "We lost it up in Birmingham when Auburn blocked those two kicks to beat us. That loss to Auburn beat us against Texas.

"After Auburn, we didn't have any zip—we didn't have anything. I bet every guy on that team was sorry we even had to go out there and play in the Cotton Bowl. Auburn had already killed us off as far as our chances for the national championship went."

Thus two birds were killed with one stone, or two blocked kicks.

Jeff Blitz, a defensive halfback for Alabama in 1972, agrees with Bryant. And he remembers and talks about the Auburn game.

"The Auburn game was the biggest fluke in history," said Blitz, now an attorney in Montgomery. "At the time it happened, and now, it was a fluke.

"The whole thing happened so quickly. They blocked one, then, boom—they blocked another one. I was in a state of disbelief.

"The bad thing about the blocked kicks is you could sense the second one before it happened. There we were on the sidelines scurrying around and trying to make corrections after the first one and we were already forced to kick again. We just didn't have enough time for communication. We didn't have time to make corrections.

"But you know, after they blocked that second punt and took the lead, we still thought we could win. Time just ran out on us. We only had a minute and that wasn't enough time."

Jeff Blitz: no love for Auburn.

Blitz continues to hear about the blocked punts. "Those Auburn people don't have much to crow about, so they still crow about that game," he said. "I still see those bumper stickers which say, 'Punt, Bama, Punt.'"

He also remembers the Cotton Bowl game with Texas and admits Alabama suffered a mental breakdown after the loss to Auburn.

"We were so depressed after Auburn beat us that we just couldn't concentrate very well on our game with Texas," Blitz said. "The Auburn game is something special. You don't play it and forget it. You live with it the rest of your life.

"We wanted to go to the Cotton Bowl, but the importance wasn't there. It was exciting playing against a great team like Texas, but more than anything else, we played that one for pride. We wanted to heal the wounds from the Auburn game.

"But the Cotton Bowl was over before we got to Dallas. The championship was gone. We prepared ourselves, but it was tough getting mentally ready to play."

Losing to Auburn was painful enough for Alabama in 1972. Getting beaten by Texas was another bruising blow, especially since the Crimson Tide lost that "battle of the wishbone offenses" after leading by almost as wide a margin as it had against bitter rival Auburn.

Alabama led Texas, 10-0, after only one quarter and 13-3 at halftime. But the Longhorns of Coach Darrell Royal scored a touchdown in the third quarter and then another in the fourth quarter to win. The final touchdown by the Longhorns came late in the contest and its legality is still questioned by Crimson Tide loyals, including Bryant.

Greg Gantt, the Alabama punter who had his punts blocked against Auburn, kicked a 50-yard field goal the first time Alabama had the ball for a 3-0 Crimson Tide lead. It was the longest field goal in Cotton Bowl history.

Steve Wade intercepted a pass to set up the field goal, then intercepted another and ran 42 yards to the Texas 31 yard line to set up the first Alabama touchdown. Halfback Wilbur Jackson ran untouched around end on the first play after the interception for the touchdown. Bill Davis kicked the extra point and Alabama was off and running toward what looked to be a victory, 10-0.

Texas got a field goal by Billy Schott in the second quarter and Davis matched it from 30 yards eight seconds before halftime.

After a short Alabama punt, Texas drove 59 yards in 15 plays for its first touchdown. Quarterback Alan Lowry ran three yards for the score and Schott added the extra point. Suddenly, it was 13-10 and the Cotton Bowl had itself a fine game.

Alabama was stopped consistently by the Texas defense in the third quarter, but in the fourth quarter the Crimson Tide put together a nifty march downfield. Starting at its 20 yard line, Alabama drove to the Texas 34. But on first down, quarterback Terry Davis attempted a pass to Wayne Wheeler and it was intercepted in the Texas end zone.

Run-oriented Texas started passing and drove to the Alabama 34 yard line with 4½ minutes left in the game. From there, Lowry faked two handoffs and circled left end. He tightwalked the sidelines and ran for the game-winning touchdown. Schott kicked the extra point and Texas had its final margin of victory.

Television cameras showed Lowry might have stepped out of bounds on his touchdown gallop. Alabama filed no protest, however, and the Longhorn victory is locked in the record books.

"We played pretty well in the game," Bryant says looking back at the Cotton Bowl, "and I probably lost the game for us with stupid coaching.

"Against Auburn, I substituted too freely, because we were wearing them out and I should have left the first groups in there. They kicked that field goal on our second team.

"So when we got to Texas, I said I was gonna leave the first group out there and let 'em go 'til they died. That was a big mistake, because Texas was wearing us out in the fourth quarter.

"That's when they got that run of about 30 yards for the winning touchdown, the one where the guy stepped out of bounds. But I don't think that touchdown had anything to do with the final outcome. They had us beaten down and were carrying it to us. I think they would have beaten us anyway.

"We just didn't look like a team that wanted to win. We didn't look like a team it meant a lot to."

The two losses ending the 1972 season dampened—or downright ruined—a year in which Alabama fans rallied behind the "We Believe" slogan, meaning they believed the Crimson Tide was back as a national power. During the season leading up

216

Halfback Wilbur Jackson in a familiar scene.

to the failure down the stretch, Alabama gave fans reason to believe.

Except for a 17-10 win over Tennessee, Alabama was never seriously challenged before the Auburn game. Victories came easily over Duke (35-12), Kentucky (35-0), Vanderbilt (48-21), Georgia (25-7), Florida (24-7), Southern Mississippi (48-11), Mississippi State (58-14), Louisiana State (35-21), and Virginia Tech (52-13).

The conquest over Tennessee at Knoxville was about as miracle-like as the Auburn game. The Vols led Alabama, 10-3, with less than three minutes left in the game and the Crimson Tide had the ball 48 yards from the Tennessee end zone. But two minutes later, thanks to some heroics by quarterback Terry Davis, Alabama had a 17-10 lead.

The first touchdown came with Alabama covering 48 yards in three plays—a 14-yard Davis pass to Wheeler, a 32-yard run by fullback Steve Bisceglia, and a 2-yard run for the score by Jackson. Bill Davis tied the game with the extra-point kick.

Bryant was criticized for instructing his team to kick the extra point to tie the game, rather than go for the lead by running or passing for a two-point conversion. The pro-Tennessee crowd booed the Alabama coach.

But the Crimson Tide got the last laugh. Defensive end John Mitchell recovered a Tennessee fumble on the Vols' 22 yard line and Terry Davis circled right end on the first play for a touchdown. Bill Davis kicked the extra point for the final margin of victory.

Describing the game in the *Tuscaloosa News*, Delbert Reed wrote, "Alabama danced the last dance here Saturday, and it turned out to be the best one of the ball game for the third-ranked Crimson Tide.

"While Tennessee was striking up the band, unsaddling its horses, and calling its dogs, Alabama was still playing football, and to the horror of 60,000 Volunteer fans, bringing in a 17-10 victory.

"Coach Paul Bryant's Tiders tried on the slipper one last time, even as the clock struck midnight and the coach turned into a pumpkin, and the shoe finally fit.

"It was a fairy tale victory for the Tide, which crammed two touchdowns into Tennessee's end zone in 36 seconds of the final three minutes of the game to escape what appeared to be certain defeat.

A big smile from John Hannah.

"For Tennessee fans, it had to be a nightmare ending, but for the 12,000 Alabama fans on hand, it was something to behold as the Crimson Tide ran its season record to 6-0 and its regular-season win string to 17 games.

"Alabama was like the famed movie star: When it was bad, it was only good, but when it was good, it was very good."

Outside Neyland Stadium at Knoxville that day, an obviously drunk Tennessee fan staggered up to Bryant and said, "Bear, you may be good, but you're the luckiest S.O.B. I've ever seen."

Who had that rabbit's foot the afternoon Alabama played Auburn?

1973 Sugar Bowl Game

Notre Dame 24   Alabama 23

Let Old Conquests be forgot,
Bring on the Crimson Tide;
It doesn't matter who they are,
We'll make that old Bear hide.

With offense scoring touchdowns,
And D stopping them cold;
We'll run and block and tackle,
With the pride of the blue and gold.

The managers have sweated,
The coaching staff is game;
Let's go team, tomorrow night,
And win it for old Notre Dame.

So, hey 'Bama, lookout,
We're gonna give you the slip;
And win this Sugar Bowl,
And bring home the championship.

—Notre Dame managers

Sylvester Croom cried without shame. He was heartbroken, deep in a blue funk. The tears streamed down his cheeks and dropped from his chin onto his red football jersey. The big black man made no effort to hide them.

"Everybody cried that night, all of us," Croom said while

Happy afternoon for Sylvester Croom.

looking back on the bitter evening the University of Alabama football team experienced on December 31, 1973, at New Orleans. "It was very disappointing. We were on the verge of greatness and then it was over."

Alabama lost a national championship that night, dropping a 24-23 decision to Notre Dame in the Sugar Bowl game.

The game, witnessed by 85,643 fans on a windy, damp, and cold night in storied old Sugar Bowl Stadium, remains one of the greatest—if not the greatest—football contests in history.

How could it miss? Unbeaten Alabama, the mighty Crimson Tide, against unbeaten Notre Dame, the Fighting Irish, with the stakes stacked as high as possible—cashing in for a national championship. It was the first-ever meeting on the football field for the two schools with glory-dripping traditions.

When it was over—after 60 minutes of grade-A football—fans who viewed the game in person and a record national television audience were hailing it as the Second Battle of New Orleans.

"It was a big one," says Coach Bryant. "It was a game people had looked forward to for years.

"If you saw that game you had to believe you were seeing football the way it ought to be played, college, pro, or whatever. I understand people had heart attacks watching it, and one Alabama sportswriter (Herby Kirby of the *Birmingham Post-Herald*) died in the press box right after. We sure don't want football to be that exciting, but the comments I heard were mostly how good the game was for college football, having two fine teams with great traditions play to such a thrilling finish."

For Croom, an All-American center who now coaches at Alabama, the thrill of playing in the classic contest was there, but losing was not a happy way to end a senior season which had been perfect through 11 games.

"We had one of the best teams in Alabama history," Croom said, "and had we won over Notre Dame we would have ranked right up there with the truly great ones.

"It was almost like a movie—win the game and climax the year with the national championship. It was like a dream, the chance to be remembered alongside great Alabama players like Lee Roy Jordan and Joe Namath.

"But how many teams have achieved greatness without taking that final step? The final step always makes a team great and we didn't take it.

"It was a great game, one I will always remember. But it will also always be one which nags at me. We had put so much into getting the chance to win that national championship, then we lost it.

"I tell you, I have never been around another team like that one we had in 1973. We really put it together on the field and off the field; we enjoyed being around each other. Blacks, whites, the rich, the poor—there was some kind of togetherness.

"We had good players on that team, but we didn't have any stars. We all worked together as a team. And the beautiful thing about it was the way everybody contributed. Guys who never played—people like Pete Pappas—practiced with a purpose.

"We had a feeling in 1973 that's impossible to describe. And we accomplished so much. We came from behind to win at Kentucky, won in that scorching heat against Florida, beat Louisiana State to win the Southeastern Conference championship in a hard-hitting game, and whipped Auburn to pay them back for those two blocked punts the season before.

"Then we lose to Notre Dame. It was hard to take. And you know, I don't think the best team won in the Sugar Bowl. I'm not taking anything away from Notre Dame, but I still think we had a better team than they did."

Bryant, the legendary coach who has won more big games than he has lost, agrees with Croom. "I don't look at that Sugar Bowl game as a loss," he said. "I don't think we got beat by Notre Dame. Time just ran out on us."

Outside of Notre Dame players and their outstanding coach, Ara Parseghian, few people probably wanted the game to end. Those listening over the radio and watching on television were treated to an extravaganza of entertainment. When the final seconds ticked off the scoreboard clock, Sugar Bowl Stadium was rocking with wild enthusiasm.

Perhaps a Japanese writer watching his first football game summed it up best when he said, "I am not sure what was happening on the field, but I know it was something exciting and something good."

It was a topsy-turvy, free-wheeling game which saw the lead change hands about as many times as momentum swapped sides. And it was a hard-hitting affair, with gold-helmeted Notre Dame striking blows with power, only to have red-clad Alabama return the licks in equal numbers and with equal force.

Notre Dame led at every juncture—6-0 after one quarter, 14-10 at halftime, 21-17 after three quarters, and by one point at the end. But Alabama led, too—7-6, 17-14, and 23-21 with four minutes left in the game.

Notre Dame got its early lead when fullback Wayne Bullock ran 1 yard for a touchdown, after the Irish drove 64 yards in seven plays, led by three passes from quarterback Tom Clements to receiver Pete Demmerle for 59 yards.

Alabama, badly beaten in the first quarter, got its offense in gear in the second quarter and marched into the lead. Halfback Randy Billingsley ran six yards for the touchdown and Bill Davis kicked the extra point for a short-lived 7-6 Crimson Tide lead.

On the kickoff after the touchdown, Al Hunter ran 93 yards untouched for six more Notre Dame points and Clements passed to Demmerle for the two-point conversion and a 14-7 Irish lead. Davis kicked a 39-yard field goal later in the second quarter to cut the Notre Dame lead to 14-10 at halftime.

In the third quarter, Alabama drove 93 yards to regain the lead, with Wilbur Jackson running 5 yards for the touchdown. Davis kicked the extra point and the Crimson Tide led, 17-14.

Notre Dame charged back, however, and late in the third quarter, Eric Pennick ran 12 yards for a touchdown after the Irish recovered an Alabama fumble on the Crimson Tide 20 yard line. Bob Thomas kicked the extra point for a 21-17 Notre Dame lead.

Alabama recovered a Notre Dame fumble at the Irish 39 yard line early in the fourth quarter and scored a touchdown on a razzle-dazzle play. Quarterback Richard Todd handed the ball to halfback Mike Stock, who ran to his right, stopped, then passed the ball back to Todd. Todd ran 25 yards into the end zone. Davis missed the extra-point kick, which later proved fatal to Alabama victory hopes. It was 23-21.

Notre Dame drove from its 19 yard line to set up its winning points, which came on a 19-yard field goal by Thomas with four minutes left in the game.

Alabama made one more gallant shot, but Clements passed Notre Dame to victory by throwing 35 yards to tight end Ron Weber from the Irish three yard line on a crucial third-down play.

"Before they completed that gutsy little pass from their end zone, I thought we were going to win the game," Bryant said. "I figured we would make them punt, get the ball deep in their territory, and score at the end to win. But they fooled us by passing."

Notre Dame ran out the clock after the pass completion and walked away with the championship.

"Add another chapter to an already golden legend of Notre Dame football—and with it another national collegiate football championship," wrote George Sweeney after the contest.

"The national championship will be announced Thursday, when the Associated Press releases its final poll.

"But as far as the Fighting Irish are concerned, that title was won when it knocked off No. 1-ranked Alabama, 24-23, in the 40th Sugar Bowl Classic before a record 85,643 and millions more on TV last night.

"'I can't believe it,' said quarterback Tom Clements in a crowded Notre Dame locker room. 'I'll have to read the papers tomorrow to make sure this isn't all a dream.'"

Herby Kirby, the *Birmingham Post-Herald* writer who died

after writing his final game story, said, "Call it luck, call it a leprechaun, but the issue in the 40th annual Sugar Bowl Classic was settled here Monday night by a cool Notre Dame quarterback named Tom Clements, who dared to throw from his own end zone with only two minutes left in the game against No. 1-ranked Alabama."

Alf Van Hoose, writing in the *Birmingham News*, said, "For mighty Notre Dame, now college football's kingliest place, another national championship, a record sixth since official polling began in 1936.

"For Irish-reputation-challenging Alabama, now another long, long nine months of frustration, playing might-have-beens....The Tide's gallant go for a fourth U.S. crown in 15 years was shattered by a very fine football club, equally motivated.

"Defeat has a thousand faces. Alabama can count 'em all after losing one of the game's all-time classics Monday night, 24-23."

Defeat showed on all Alabama faces in the dressing room after the contest and the fact the Crimson Tide had already been crowned national champion by United Press International did little to ease the agony of losing the big one.

It had been an emotional night from the time Alabama and Notre Dame players appeared like gladiators in the same tunnel leading onto the playing field and the evening had capped an equally emotional month which saw the dream match receive an enormous amount of pre-kickoff publicity. And although the game had lived up to its billing, Alabama players were left wanting....

"One point away from the national championship," said Gary Rutledge, the Alabama quarterback who had brilliantly led the Crimson Tide through the regular season. "That's not a good feeling. And I think we were the better team."

"It's about to kill me," said Robin Cary, the Alabama defensive back who had broken up a tied game against Tennessee with a long punt return for a touchdown during the regular season. "We had the best team. We knew it and they knew it."

"Yes, it feels pretty bad to lose like that," said Mike Raines, an All-Southeastern Conference defensive tackle. "I could feel better about it if they were a better team, but we're better than they are."

"Notre Dame is a good football team, but we just got some

bad breaks," said Buddy Brown, the offensive guard who was named the best blocker in the Southeastern Conference in 1973. "No, heck no, they're not the best we played. But there's nothing much you can say when you get beat. Nothing I can say will change that."

Losing was something Alabama players were not used to handling in 1973, because they had put together an unbeaten regular season without serious threat of defeat. Victories came over California (66-0), Kentucky (28-14), Vanderbilt (44-0), Georgia (28-14), Florida (35-14), Tennessee (42-21), Virginia Tech (77-6), Mississippi State (35-0), Miami (43-13), Louisiana State (21-7), and Auburn (35-0).

There were anxious moments, however. Alabama trailed Kentucky at halftime, 14-0, but ran back the opening kickoff of the second half for a touchdown and won going away. Georgia, Florida, and Tennessee battled the Crimson Tide toughly for one half, before Alabama ran away with awesome displays in the final 30 minutes of each game.

According to Croom, Alabama was a loosey-goosey outfit throughout the year.

"We did some crazy things, some things no Alabama teams had attempted," Croom said, "and they helped us. We even sang on the bus the night before games and somebody was always joking around in some way.

"We were confident, no matter who we came up against. Maybe that confidence hurt us some against Notre Dame, because we tried to treat the Sugar Bowl like it was just another game. Maybe they were a little more emotional than we were at the start of the game. Maybe...."

In his book, *Bear*, Bryant heaped praise on his 1973 team. "By the time we got to Notre Dame in the Sugar Bowl, I about had myself convinced that it was the best offense I ever had, no matter what the formation," Bryant said. "I'd have said it was the best, period, but Notre Dame beat us and since we didn't win I can't call it the best anything."

The one-point loss to Notre Dame did not convince Bryant, although he did call the Fighting Irish "a truly great team." In the Alabama dressing room after the game, he said, "I wouldn't mind playing them again tomorrow. In fact, I'd like it."

Those who watched the game would have liked the chance to see it again, too.

1975 Orange Bowl Game

Notre Dame 13   Alabama 11

One point one year,
Two points the next;
Alabama was not beaten,
The Tide was hexed.

Notre Dame got the victories,
But not without two fights;
To hell with you Irish,
Just wait—one of these nights.

—B. B. Whitington

Jigsaw puzzles are pretty, but only after they have been pieced together. And they can be frustrating as the devil when a couple of pieces are missing.

So it was with the 1974 University of Alabama football team, a group of fun-loving, somewhat wacky individuals who molded together into a winning unit. When all the parts—or players, if you please—were working together, the Crimson Tide was outstanding.

Getting all the parts together was the problem at Alabama that year. During the entire regular season, the Crimson Tide football team looked like refugees from a Red Cross camp. Injuries plagued Alabama from start to finish.

When January 1, 1975, rolled around, however, Alabama found itself in the same situation it had been in the year before—unbeaten in 11 games, chasing a national championship, and looking eye-to-eye at Notre Dame in a bowl game.

Play it again, Sam. Alabama lost, 13-11, to the Fighting Irish in the Orange Bowl at Miami. One year earlier, unbeaten Notre Dame had defeated Alabama, 24-23, to win the national championship in the Sugar Bowl at New Orleans.

"Losing to Notre Dame the second time wasn't like rubbing salt into a wound," said Ronny Robertson, an All-Southeastern Conference linebacker as an Alabama senior in 1974, "but losing in the Orange Bowl was bad because I think we had a better team than they did. The first loss to Notre Dame just seems a little more bitter.

"We were in shock after losing the first one. We were more let down after losing in the Orange Bowl."

The defeat at Miami came at the end of one of the craziest Alabama regular seasons on record, which was produced by one of the zaniest groups ever to wear Crimson Tide uniforms.

Snakes were among the pets in the athletic dormitory. Mike Washington, a defensive halfback, and Ralph Stokes, an offensive halfback, led teammates on a hat-wearing binge—all types, shapes, and colors. Some players wore tennis shoes with their travel uniforms. Players went out in public wearing Halloween masks. Guard John Rogers kept records of practical jokes he pulled on teammates.

Robertson kept teammates and newspaper reporters in stitches with stories about his coach, Paul (Bear) Bryant. As a junior in 1973, Robertson walked into a Tuscaloosa hamburger establishment with shaving cream covering his entire head and ordered 17 to go.

"Oh yeah, we were a crazy bunch that season," Robertson said in looking back on his final year with the Crimson Tide, "but we had unity and I think that helped us overcome some bad circumstances to win. We were a bunch of individuals, really, a bunch of players who did their own thing off the field and played together in games.

"We had guys who laughed on the bus going to games and that was something unheard of at Alabama. And we had good-luck freaks who carried special charms in their pockets. That team was definitely made up of a bunch of nuts.

"I guess you could say we were less regimented than Alabama teams of the past and it took us some time to jell together into a winner. But when we got it going, I think we were a pretty good football team."

Linebacker Ronny Robertson.

Alabama opened its unbeaten season by defeating Maryland, 21-16; Southern Mississippi, 52-0; Vanderbilt, 23-10; Mississippi, 35-21; and Florida State, 8-7. After those five games, the Crimson Tide was ranked second nationally, but was lacking the zing associated with Alabama teams.

But the week after being scared to death by winless Florida State, Alabama defeated Tennessee, 28-6, and the Crimson Tide was on its way to another Southeastern Conference championship. In the final five weeks, Alabama defeated Texas Christian, 41-3; Mississippi State, 35-0; Louisiana State, 30-0; Miami, 28-7; and Auburn, 17-13.

"We played some big games," Robertson said. "We could have easily lost to Maryland and Vanderbilt and the win over Florida State was like a loss. The win over Tennessee at Knoxville was the turning point for us. We started believing in ourselves after that game and believed even more after beating LSU. Of course, beating Auburn is always important."

Against Maryland, Alabama jumped out front and held on for dear life. Decisive underdog Vanderbilt fell to a fourth-quarter Alabama charge. Mississippi led early, then fell back as Alabama took charge in the final 15 minutes.

And to this day, nobody is exactly sure how Alabama squeaked by Florida State. A 44-yard field goal with 33 seconds remaining in the game provided victory for the Crimson Tide, after it appeared the Seminoles would win their first game after 17 consecutive defeats.

In the *Tuscaloosa News*, sportswriter Steve Martin described the game: "Bucky Berrey spent most of Saturday afternoon as just another jersey on the Alabama sideline. But, history will record the brief seconds that Berrey was on the playing field at Denny Stadium against Florida State.

"The sophomore from Montgomery drilled home field goals of 44 and 36 yards yesterday, the last with 33 seconds left in the game to permit Alabama to escape fanatically inspired Florida State, 8-7.

"Berrey got the chance to be a hero when Florida State made a questionable gamble with 1:27 left in the game. Leading 7-3 with a fourth down on its own five-yard-line, punter Joe Downey gave the Tide two points when he deliberately ran out of the end zone to give Alabama a safety. That made it 7-5 and a field goal could win it. And did."

After the free kick following the safety, Alabama moved from the Florida State 48 yard line to the Seminoles' 16. Three plays later, Berrey kicked Alabama to victory.

Mike McKenzie, another *Tuscaloosa News* sportswriter, amply described the situation Alabama was in after its narrow victory over Florida State: "Alabama played like the No. 3 team in town," McKenzie said. "They were No. 2 in Denny Stadium."

After the game, Bryant was also critical of the team he coached. "We certainly lost stature in my eyes," Bryant said.

But a week later, everybody changed their minds about Alabama. The Crimson Tide was, well, the Crimson Tide again in defeating Tennessee.

"In a 28-6 win over Tennessee, Alabama did almost everything nicely," McKenzie wrote in his column. "Alabama was a sumo wrestler crinkling a beer can in his hand. Alabama was a bottle, and Tennessee's ship wound up inside with no way out. Alabama was a barber and Tennessee is wearing a crew-cut today."

Robertson told it like it was in the dressing room following the victory led by fourth-team quarterback Robert Fraley. "How...sweeeeet...it...is!" Robertson exclaimed.

Bryant jumped on the bandwagon, too. "I don't have a great deal to say," he began his postgame press conference, "because my limited vocabulary won't let me express how proud I am of our players and coaches. They did a great job in turning things around in one week."

So Alabama was turned in the right direction and moved that way the rest of the season...with a lot of help from unsung hero Jim Goostree, the Crimson Tide trainer who kept injury-riddled Alabama patched up enough to finish unbeaten.

Goostree was given the game ball after the win over Tennessee. He should have shared in the Southeastern Conference championship trophy Alabama received at the end of the year.

Exactly three years after Alabama players reported for practice to start the 1974 season, Goostree was reminded of the rash of injuries the Crimson Tide had overcome that year.

"The 1974 season was unusual from an injury standpoint," Goostree remembered. "We lost a lot of key people all season long, but those kids overcame the handicaps to win.

"We trainers play the same role every year. It starts with prevention of injury, but you can't help but get people hurt in football.

"When injuries happen, we try to invoke conservative treatment so we won't compound them. And we hope for a shortened recovery cycle, which is up to the injured player more than anybody else. Those kids in 1974 were motivated enough to overcome the injuries they sustained. They were champions."

In his desk in Memorial Coliseum, Goostree maintains records of all football injuries. The list he has for 1974 is longer than the rest.

In September, halfback Randy Billingslev, Robert Fraley, starting quarterback Gary Rutledge, tackle Neil Calloway, full-

231

back Johnny Davis, linebacker Conley Duncan, receiver Joe Dale Harris, and defensive back Mike Washington all were sidelined at least one week with injuries.

The Tide had many players to get injured in 1974, including linebacker Conley Duncan.

In October the list was made up of center Sylvester Croom, and George Pugh, Washington, quarterback Jack O'Rear, guard John Rogers, tackle Steve Patterson, end Mike Dubose, receiver Thad Flanagan, linebacker Woodrow Lowe, and halfback John LaBue.

In November, as Alabama went down the stretch, guard Jerry Washco, Harris, linebacker Greg Montgomery, and end Leroy Cook stood wounded on the sidelines.

"It got bad for awhile," Robertson said. "We were beaten up most of the year, but those injuries might have been a blessing because they helped us unite.

"It seemed like we would say the same thing in every team

By midseason 1974, among 15 or more injured Tide players was linebacker Woodrow Lowe.

meeting—'If we can get everybody well, we'll be okay.' I think it helped us pull together.

"Coach Bryant laid it on the line to us before we went to play Tennessee with our first two quarterbacks (Rutledge and Richard Todd) hurt. He told us we had lost so-and-so here and so-and-so there, so we'd just have to make up for it somewhere else. From then on, we did okay."

After Alabama wrapped up the season with its victory over Auburn, Bryant paid his troops an eloquent compliment.

"We might have the best team in the country when we play Notre Dame," Bryant said. "I doubt very seriously if there has ever been an undefeated team in a major conference that had as many injuries as we had. To come around and win the conference championship makes them something special."

Alabama opened practice confidently for the Orange Bowl encounter with Notre Dame and happy about the chance to get another shot at the Fighting Irish, who had crushed the Tide's national championship hopes in 1973.

"Revenge is our No. 1 shot in the arm," said Alan Pizzitola, a defensive halfback. "Losses are not easy to forget and Notre Dame gave us a bad one last year in the Sugar Bowl.

"I'm tired of hearing about it. Everywhere I go, people ask me the same thing, what are we going to do to Notre Dame in the Orange Bowl?

"This game with Notre Dame is something special. It borders on hate. I'm getting emotional about it."

So unbeaten Alabama went to work at Tuscaloosa, while 9-2 Notre Dame practiced for the Orange Bowl on Marco Polo Island off the coast of Florida. Both teams arrived at Miami two days before the game.

Pregame publicity centered around another Alabama bid for the national championship and also reported turmoil on a Notre Dame team which was attempting to win the last game Ara Parseghian would coach for the Irish.

Alabama fans politically cried, "We're No. 1." Notre Dame fans dipped into Irish tradition during the Knute Rockne years and coined their own rallying point—"Win One for Ara." As expected when Alabama and Notre Dame are matched, emotions reached high peaks.

"We had played the whole season hoping for another shot at Notre Dame," Robertson said. "We were emotional. I don't think we treated it like just another game. We were mentally up for it and I think that hurt us in the end. We were too tight when kickoff arrived."

Notre Dame took advantage of a fumbled punt recovery deep in Alabama territory in the first quarter to score a touchdown and the Crimson Tide played catchup the rest of the game. The final nail was driven into the Alabama coffin with 1½ minutes left when Notre Dame intercepted a Todd pass.

The Alabama dressing room was like a morgue after the contest. Players said little and when they talked, they whispered. It was the eighth consecutive year Alabama had played in a bowl game without tasting victory, and losing two in a row to Notre Dame made the long dry spell more painful.

Perhaps Lowe, a linebacker who played one of his finest games in the Orange Bowl that night, summed it up best when he said, "We just seem to have bad luck against Notre Dame."

1975 Sugar Bowl Game

Alabama 13   Penn State 6

Roses are red,
Violets are blue;
Sugar Bowls are sweet,
Winning is, too.

—Shelia McKenzie

You have to pay the dues if you want to join the club.

The University of Alabama football team learned that fact of life in 1975 when the Crimson Tide withdrew from its bank account time and again, before replenishing it in one history-making night.

On December 31, 1975, at New Orleans, Alabama won its first bowl game in nine appearances—after seven losses and a tie—by defeating Penn State, 13-6, in the 42nd annual Sugar Bowl classic. It was the first Sugar Bowl game staged indoors, played in the fabulous Superdome, and 75,212 fans watched the hard-hitting, near-brutal affair.

"This victory was a long time coming," said Bryant, the Alabama coach who had not won a bowl game since January 1, 1967, when unbeaten Alabama defeated Nebraska in the Sugar Bowl. "This is one of the greatest victories I have had."

While several thousand fans celebrated New Year's Eve by getting smashed on alcohol, Alabama capped an 11-1 season and locked up a No. 3 national ranking by getting drunk on Sugar. It was especially sweet for the Crimson Tide, for a number of reasons.

236

On August 13, only a few days before Alabama opened summer practice, Bryant dismissed eight players from the squad for disciplinary reasons. Ron Kuykendall and Joey Bolton were dismissed permanently, and end Leroy Cook, defensive back Wayne Rhodes, linebacker Conley Duncan, halfback John La-Bue, tackle Bobby Davis, and halfback Johnny Gunnels were demoted to no assigned status.

While announcing the dismissals, Bryant revealed a work program for the players at the Veterans Administration Hospital in Tuscaloosa. The dismissed players were required to work there the entire season.

"None of these players will be counted on until they have shown me beyond reasonable doubt they will do what they say," Bryant said. "They told me they would and I believe them."

Cook and Rhodes returned to the squad and made All-American, while Duncan earned All-Southeastern Conference honors and played a fantastic Sugar Bowl game.

On August 23, less than two weeks after practice started, Bryant announced that Alabama was filing suit against the National Collegiate Athletic Association in an effort to overturn squad-reduction measures the governing body had enacted as a cost-cutting measure. The impending court case, which Bryant and Alabama won before the decision was overturned by a higher court, took the coach from the practice field to the courtroom. But as he testified on the witness stand, Bryant had thoughts of football games.

"My objective is always the national championship," Bryant said during preseason practice, "so that means the next game is the biggest. I am only thinking about Missouri."

On September 8, Missouri dished out misery, defeating Alabama, 20-7, in the first game of the collegiate season at Birmingham. It was a stunning upset—Alabama had not lost a regular-season game in its last 22—and suddenly, what was expected to be another championship-contending Crimson Tide was looking more like a team from Slippery Rock or Losersville U.

"They gave us a good ol' country spanking," Bryant said after the opening loss. "I don't know how we'll all react to this, but I think I have an idea what our kids will do.

"If we have the kind of people I think we have, we'll try to work at it and improve. If we don't, it will be the longest season

237

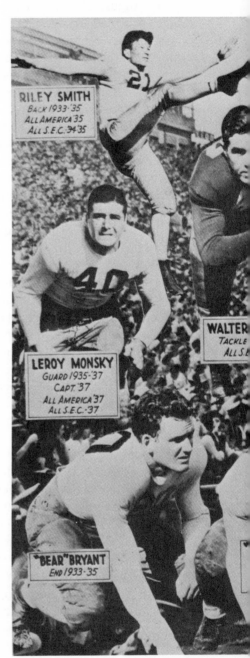

RILEY SMITH
BACK 1933-'35
ALL AMERICA '35
ALL S.E.C.-'34-'35

LEROY MONSKY
GUARD 1935-'37
CAPT. '37
ALL AMERICA '37
ALL S.E.C.-'37

WALTER
TACKLE
ALL S.E

"BEAR" BRYANT
END 1933-'35

JIMMIE NELSON
Back 1939-41
All America '41
All S.E.C. '40-41

"WU" WINSLETT
End 1924-'26
All America '26
All Sou. '26

JOHN MACK BROWN
Back 1923-25
All Sou. '24-25

"SHORTY" PROPST
Center 1922-'24

WHITE
4-36
CA '30
'36

DON WHITMIRE
Tackle 1941-42
All S.E.C. '42

RIGGS STEPHENSON
Back 1917-'20
All Sou. '20

labama's All-Time Second Football Team
Picked By Sports Fans In The Birmingham New-Age-Herald Poll

we've ever had around here."

After the opening loss, Alabama did more than work—it slaved! And things fell quickly into place.

Alabama defeated Clemson, 56-0, in its second game and opened the defense of its fourth consecutive conference championship by beating Vanderbilt, 40-7. By the end of the year, Alabama had wrapped up an unprecedented fifth straight conference championship, beating Mississippi (32-6), Washington (52-0), Tennessee (30-7), Texas Christian (45-0), Mississippi State (21-10), Louisiana State (23-10), Southern Mississippi (27-6), and Auburn (28-0).

After the victory over Auburn, which came in the last meeting between coaching rivals Bryant and Ralph (Shug) Jordan who retired after 25 years as coach at Auburn, Bryant praised his team for coming back after the shaky start and called the game one of the best the Crimson Tide had played.

"It is somewhat a sad note," Bryant said, "in that it was Coach Jordan's last game. I just wish he could have left here a little happier. I'm just sorry that we had one of our best games when we played him. I wish it could have been against somebody else."

Although things looked rosy for Alabama, Crimson Tide problems were not over by a long shot. First, Bryant was accused of ducking powerful Big Eight Conference representative Nebraska as a Sugar Bowl foe and personally matching his team against Penn State, which was 9-2 and Eastern champion. Then, after Alabama arrived at New Orleans for the Sugar Bowl, Bryant was forced to discipline 23 Crimson Tide players three days before the game.

For various reasons—shopping, snack-hunting, nightclub-hopping and others—the players missed the midnight curfew Bryant enacted when the team arrived in New Orleans. "I don't want to make a big deal of it, but I'm disappointed," Bryant said. "If we blow the game, I want their parents and people in their hometowns to know who missed curfew...and what I have to go through."

Bryant mumbled something about the last eight years—the bowl losses and tie—and announced the names of the players who had missed bed check.

On Monday before the game on Wednesday, seven players missed bed check. Seniors Ray Bolden, Jerry Brown, and Conley Duncan were among them. They were demoted from start-

240

Ray Bolden: Mr. Funny.

ing status, although Bolden and Duncan were first-time offenders. Bolden said he was in a teammate's room studying a Penn State scouting report, Duncan said he missed an interstate exit and was 12 minutes late, and Brown said he had his shirt and shoes off and was across the hall from his room.

Suddenly a smooth-flowing Crimson Tide had once again become a stormy tide and Alabama boosters were fearing another bowl defeat. The fears, as the record books will forever prove, were unfounded.

Bolden, a four-year starter from Tarrant who became one of the most efficient defensive backs ever at Alabama during his senior season, looks back on his final season in his typical half-serious, yet dead-serious manner.

His memories of the Sugar Bowl are not pleasant, except for the fact that Alabama won the game. Not only did Bolden not get to start in his final game, he got to perform on only three plays.

"The trip was great and they treated us nice," Bolden said. "The coaches gave us more freedom and let us do what we wanted to as long as we got back to the hotel on time. They didn't keep us closed in like the years before and I think that helped us win the game.

"But I'm still hacked off about the way I got in trouble down there, because I had never been in trouble of any kind before. It shook me up, then made me mad.

"I was in another player's room talking and going over Penn State plays when two coaches came in and told me I wasn't supposed to be there and to go back to my room. I was acting just like we had on all the other bowl trips, but I guess things were different this time because the boss (Bryant) was mad about the other 23 guys being out late earlier.

"The next night at supper, Coach Bryant said he wanted to talk to seven of us and that's when he told Brown, Duncan, and me that we weren't going to start the game. It shocked us, because it was like a shotgun trial. We couldn't say anything about it.

"I kept my mouth shut because I knew I would get to play a lot even if I didn't start. But when Brown and Duncan went into the game after only three or four minutes, I was left on the sidelines. I got to play three snaps of the ball in the first half and that was it.

"I still feel like I got singled out. It wasn't a very nice way to end a career, except for the fact that Mark Prudhomme, a good friend, played a great game starting in my place."

Bolden kept his mouth shut about the incident when Jim Lampley, an American Broadcasting Company sideline commentator who was aware of Alabama's curfew problems, queried him in front of a national television audience during the game.

"He asked if I had been playing and I said 'Nope,'" Bolden said. "Then he asked if I had any comment and I said 'Nope.' I didn't see any reason to say anything which might cast a bad light on our team."

With the disciplinary suspensions during the summer and the court case against the NCAA, Alabama had its share of publicity in 1975. The loss to Missouri magnified it.

Bolden remembers. "There was a lot of talk about drug arrests around campus that summer," he said, "and Coach Jack Rutledge (the resident coach at the athletic dorm) called a meeting and warned all of us players.

"When some of our players got caught, they brought it on themselves and they owe a lot to Coach Bryant for helping them get out of a bad situation.

"The drug thing didn't hurt the team as much as people think, because it just wasn't that big a deal. That kind of thing happens all over the country, so we just accepted it.

"It was another tough time for me, though, because my name got associated with it. It took about a month for me to get that straightened out, and I'm not so sure some of my friends and relatives understand now.

"The NCAA court case didn't hurt much at all, as far as preparation goes. The bad thing about the player-limit deal is that some deserving players didn't get to play much that year. Those of us who did play probably got more individual attention from coaches.

"The Missouri loss was just one of those things. They beat us and we just picked ourselves up and went back to work.

"There weren't many changes or rugged practices like people suspect. Things aren't done that way at Alabama. At Alabama, people expect you to win so there isn't a whole lot of excitement involved. You know, whooping it up and talking cocky like they do at Auburn and some other schools.

"At Alabama, you are taught to do your job and not make mistakes. If you do that, you'll win. So after Missouri, we just forgot the loss and went on with our 24-hour job of playing football.

"I think we had an exceptional group of players in 1975. We had a fun group and everybody got along well. There was never any friction. We just took things in stride and went on about our business."

If Alabama players were troubled, it did not show when they took the field against Penn State. Quarterback Richard Todd was named Most Valuable Player in the game after leading Alabama offensively, and the Crimson Tide defense played a super game, tackling and swarming with reckless abandon.

"Tide took a Todd-y for the body," was the headline in a New Orleans newspaper the day after the game, and the story written by Bill Bumgarner explained it.

"Threading his way through well-wishers, all of them from the opposition, Penn State coach Joe Paterno had eyes for only one person—the individual from Alabama who had laid waste to Penn State in the Sugar Bowl.

"When at last he spotted Richard Todd, the senior quarterback was about to take part in his three-millionth interview of the night, but he had time for Paterno's extended hand.

"'I want to congratulate you on a great game,' said the Nittany Lions' headmaster. When informed that Todd's immediate plans for the future centered around the upcoming Senior Bowl, Paterno quipped, 'I'd like to recommend you for that one. It's the least I can do since the Bear recommended me for this one.'

"Indeed, Bear Bryant had recommended Penn State, but his reward for that recommendation was a 60-minute session in an air-conditioned sweat box, before the eight-year Alabama bowl hex finally went asunder, thanks to a 13-6 win over the Nittany Lions.

"It was a night in which Todd, a figure his coach once called the best he'd ever had, showed the basis for that reasoning. He ripped the Nittany Lion defense to the tune of 210 yards through the air on 10 of 12 completions, that really should have been 11 of 12, as one long bomb was dropped."

Alabama scored its points on two field goals by Danny Ridgeway, 25 yards in the first quarter and 28 yards in the fourth quarter, and a 14-yard touchdown run by Mike Stock in the third quarter. Ridgeway kicked the extra point.

Penn State kicked two field goals, one in the third quarter and one in the fourth.

Alabama had the best defense in the nation against scoring, an average of six points per game during the 1975 season, and it lived up to its reputation against Penn State.

Duncan, the linebacker who did not start the game because of his violation of curfew rules, played one of his finest games as a Crimson Tide player. He made 11 tackles in the hard-hitting contest. He also walked away with quite a souvenir, his helmet which was cracked right between the number 57 on its side.

"I hit some dude hard and when I got up from the pile, my helmet was turned sideways on my head," Duncan remembered. "When I realized it was busted up, I knew it was time to get off the field."

Duncan was given another helmet ("it was about two sizes too small, but I didn't care," he said) and played the rest of the game. He left the Sugar Bowl that night clutching the broken helmet under his arm.

Fans at the Sugar Bowl that night gawked at the magnificent Superdome, a 52-acre bubble with seven views for spectators—the field and six screens which hang directly over midfield from the sprawling roof covering the arena.

Sugar Bowl MVP Richard Todd.

"It's more like we're headed for church than a football game, going into this place," said Jack Hicks, a former Alabama manager and now a high school football coach. He was just one of thousands of Alabama fans who walked into the Superdome to watch the Crimson Tide play Penn State.

Mike McKenzie described the evening from a fan's viewpoint in his *Tuscaloosa News* column:

A Sugar Bowl official before the game was jesting with a group of writers about the mammoth building which was the site of the game for the first time.

"Temperature at game time will be 72 degrees, with smoke and haze," he said. "Winds will be less than one mile per hour, from all directions...."

Many spectators were frustrated from being lost in the spreading aisles and ramps and escalators which branch throughout the $163,000,000 building. Ushers worked diligently to solve the problems. Order was maintained with few reported trouble spots beyond misdirections.

Parties carried on past kickoff deep within the outer regions of the arena in plush meeting rooms and suites, all furnished with television sets relaying the Sugar Bowl telecast.

The ABC showing was also aired on the six overhanging giant screens in the middle of the dome, complete with instant playbacks and commercial breaks. (Local businesses pay handsomely for short spots during timeout intervals...such as hamburger chains, a bank, a movie, and a Baptist Church.)

Many fans stuck around long, long after the game was over to wander the halls and go down to the field.

Taxis charged an inflated $1.50 per person rate to haul passengers the short six to eight blocks between Superdome and downtown hotels.

Among the more catchy fans' signs hanging around the complex decreed, "The Tide Just Can't Bear It In Bowls."

The sign proved wrong, of course, prompting one garrulous group of 'Bamans to break into chorus: "Penn State, Penn State, Penn Who? We could have chose Nebraska, but we chose you!"

Nebraska coach Tom Osborne and other Big Eight Conference spokesmen were uncomplimentary of Bryant after it was announced Alabama would play Penn State in the Sugar Bowl. But the Crimson Tide coach stuck to his opinion that Penn State was a good football team and worthy opponent.

As usual, the last laugh belonged to Bryant.

"I think we beat a great football team," Bryant says, looking back. "Anybody who didn't think Penn State was a good football team is an idiot or something.

"And I am tremendously proud of that Alabama team, because everybody contributed. I have never been around a team I have more respect for. When you get your brains beat out like we did against Missouri, then come back to win 11 straight, you have to have character."

Bryant showed character at the Sugar Bowl, too. He coached the game without wearing his houndstooth hat which has become one of his trademarks. "When I was small and living back in Arkansas, my mother taught me not to wear a hat indoors," Bryant said. "I remembered what she said."

Bryant remembered how to act as a winner in a bowl game, too.

1976 Liberty Bowl Game

Alabama 36   UCLA 6

It was cold as ice,
In old Memphis town;
And Alabama was ready,
To shoot UCLA down.

The Tide had limped,
Through a tough '76;
And the Bruins were taught,
Too many Bears don't mix.

Another win for 'Bama,
The famed Red and White;
Another chapter of glory,
On a warm, warm cold night.

–C. K. Briner

It was cold and windy at Memphis, Tennessee, the night the University of Alabama football team played UCLA on December 20 in the 1976 Liberty Bowl game. It was 23 degrees at kickoff, and the winds accompanying the frigid temperature pushed the chill factor to minus-zero degrees.

Paul (Bear) Bryant, the Alabama head coach, showed up that night looking like a cross between St. Nick and a foreman about to oversee winter work on the Alaskan Pipeline. The Crimson Tide boss was dressed in red, including the hood which covered his head so well that only his mouth, nose, and eyes were visible.

Bear was warm at Memphis as Alabama rolled.

249

"It was colder that night at Memphis than any I can remember for an Alabama football game," Bryant said. "I was dressed for it, but I imagine there were some uncomfortable people in that stadium."

Fans, almost 53,000 who braved the weather to watch the best matchup in Liberty Bowl history, were more than uncomfortable. They were downright miserable, as were cheerleaders, band members, officials, peanut salesmen, and newspaper reporters. Valley Forge was bitter, but George Washington would have probably shivered at Memphis.

Barry Krauss, on the other hand, was hot. He had a fire burning inside his body and the warmest flames were in his heart.

Krauss, an Alabama linebacker from the warm, sun-drenched town of Pompano Beach, Florida, was suffering from a bad case of dented pride when Alabama and UCLA squared off. He was too motivated to notice the weather. All he cared about was helping the Crimson Tide to victory, which he did, a surprising 36-6 win over the three-point-favored Bruins from southern California.

"I was totally psyched at kickoff," said Krauss, who was named Most Valuable Player in the game after making 18 tackles and intercepting a pass and returning it for a touchdown. "I could have run through a brick wall and not felt it.

"I admit it was cold. In fact, I had never been so cold in my life and my fingers even turned numb. But I never thought about the weather during the game. All I thought about was beating the devil out of UCLA.

"They thought we were just a bunch of old country boys from Alabama and we all wanted to show them we knew something about football. I think we proved our point."

Alabama entered the Liberty Bowl after failing to win the Southeastern Conference championship for the first time in six years. The Crimson Tide finished second to Georgia in the conference race and posted an 8-3 regular-season record.

UCLA had failed in its bid to win the Pacific Eight Conference championship, finishing with a 9-1-1 regular season after losing to Southern Cal and tying Ohio State. The Bruins were ranked sixth nationally, while Alabama was ranked 18th.

"You could sense the way UCLA felt about the game by the way they acted at Memphis," Krauss said. "They thought they had the game won before we went on the field.

"Those UCLA players walked around with cocky looks on their faces, acting like they were dissatisfied with playing us. You know, like they were thinking, 'Alabama? That's no big deal. After all, we're from the Pac Eight and they're just little guys from the SEC. We won't have any problem with them.'

"Well, that kind of attitude really got to us. It motivated us to give it to 'em. We liked the idea of being the underdog. It's like Coach 'Dude' Hennessey told us during practice for the game. He said UCLA would be bigger, quicker, smarter, and better than us, and if we won, we would have to do it with heart. That talk gave us a purpose.

"But you know what really fired me up for the game? It was that fireworks display the Liberty Bowl people put on just before kickoff. Wow! That was something. It jacked me up higher than the sky. I wish we could do that before every game."

Krauss, nicknamed "Space Kid" by his Alabama teammates, set the tempo for the game on the opening kickoff when he made a crushing tackle on the UCLA runner, bringing sighs of disbelief from the crowd. From that opening lick to the final play (which was viewed by only 12,000 fans in the stadium because the others left when Alabama made the game a runaway), the Crimson Tide was in command and easily marched to one of its most impressive bowl victories in history.

"I like to think that tackle on the opening kickoff set the mood for the game," Krauss said. "I think it got everybody on our team more fired up, because after that, we really jumped on them.

"I was a wild man on that kickoff. It was a solid hit, one that felt great. I don't even think that runner saw me coming. I had a full head of speed and crashed into him. He was surprised."

The entire UCLA team was surprised by halftime, because Alabama had a 24-0 lead and the outcome was no longer in question. The 24 first-half points by Alabama broke a Liberty Bowl record, the most previous in the first half being 21.

Alabama started its point parade slowly, but it quickly marched onward. The first three points came on a 37-yard field goal by Bucky Berrey the first time Alabama had the football. The Crimson Tide passed its way to the points, with quarterback Jeff Rutledge throwing to split end Ozzie Newsome.

On the fifth play after the ensuing Alabama kickoff, defen-

Split end Ozzie Newsome, one of Alabama's all-time great receivers.

Quarterback Jeff Rutledge looked toward the future.

sive tackle Charles Hannah deflected a UCLA pass, and Krauss intercepted the ball and ran 44 yards for a touchdown. Berrey added the extra point kick and the parade was on.

"That interception and the touchdown were great thrills," Krauss said. "I had intercepted one in the Notre Dame game earlier in the season and they just about ripped my head off before I got to run with the ball. Against UCLA, I got the ball and took off quickly. I wasn't about to let anybody tackle me."

Alabama scored again in two minutes, after Donnie Faust knocked the ball loose from kickoff return ace Wally Henry and Paul Harris recovered it on the UCLA 31. It took the Crimson Tide five plays to score, with fullback Johnny Davis running two yards for the touchdown. Berrey kicked the extra point and Alabama was on top, 17-0.

Tony Nathan, a halfback, passed 20 yards to quarterback Jack O'Rear for a touchdown in the second quarter and Berrey again kicked the extra point for the 24th Alabama point. The touchdown play was the same razzle-dazzle job the Crimson Tide had used in previous bowl games—the halfback passing to the quarterback after the quarterback had handed the ball to the halfback.

"When they called that play in the huddle, I didn't want to try it," said Nathan, who was named most valuable offensive player in the game after running for 67 yards on nine carries. "That play never did work in practice."

Berrey kicked two more field goals in the second half, from 25 and 28 yards, and fullback Rick Watson scored the final Alabama touchdown on a 1-yard run in the fourth quarter. Watson, one of few seniors on the Alabama team, called his own number on the touchdown play.

"I wanted to score in my last game," Watson said, "so when we got close, I turned to O'Rear in the huddle and said, 'Hey, Jack, remember I'm a senior.' He gave me the ball on the next play."

UCLA avoided a shutout late in the game by springing running back Theotis Brown on a 61-yard touchdown jaunt.

After the game, a tired Bryant met with the press and talked of pride and how it was the driving force on an Alabama team which had lost two of its first four games during the 1976 regular season.

"I doubt if I've ever been prouder of a team," Bryant said. "I am particularly proud of the seniors for coming back so tremendously from nothing in the early part of the season.

"I think we were a pretty good football team tonight and I think we beat a pretty good football team. I think we had a great effort from everyone.

"And I want to put one thing straight. I sure didn't pick our opponent for the Liberty Bowl (he has often been accused of matchmaking in bowl games). When I heard who we were playing I thought they meant the University of Central Louisiana. When I found out what UCLA really stood for, it almost scared me to death."

When asked if he was surprised by the final score, Bryant said, "Hell yes, weren't you?"

The week preceding the Liberty Bowl was marked by Bryant and youthful UCLA head coach Terry Donahue engaging in verbal jabs, each insisting his team to be the weaker. Bryant spoke about UCLA's powerful offense, while Donahue spoke about Alabama tradition and the awe he was experiencing coaching against a "legend" like Bryant.

Bryant again proved to be the king in the art of psych.

"The Bear is a sly old fox," wrote Roy Edwards in the *Memphis Commercial Appeal*. "Since his arrival in Memphis Friday, Paul (Bear) Bryant has been sweet-talking UCLA's Bruins. Too good, the Alabama Bear said. Too quick. Great coaching by Terry Donahue, he said.

"Then in the icy wind of Liberty Bowl Memorial Stadium, the Bear sprang his trap last night. He gave Donahue, the Bruins' first-year coach, a lesson from the master.

"Alabama won, 36-6, in a game that hardly was a contest to give the Bear his second straight bowl victory after eight consecutive postseason trips without one."

Donahue, a personable young man who captured the hearts of everyone he met, took the defeat in stride. He met Bryant at midfield after the game and said, "You gave us an old-fashioned butt-whipping and you know it. But I'd like a rematch some day, if we can arrange it."

Alabama players, though freezing by the time the game ended, were wild in celebration in the dressing room after the game. It had been a tough year for the Crimson Tide and the players were enjoying the sweet taste of a closing victory.

During the regular season, Alabama lost to Mississippi (10-7), Georgia (21-0), and Notre Dame (21-18). The Crimson Tide scored victories over Southern Methodist (56-3), Vander-

Memphis was cold, but Liberty Bowling Bama was hot.

bilt (42-14), Southern Mississippi (24-8), Tennessee (20-13), Louisville (24-3), Mississippi State (34-17), Louisiana State (28-17), and Auburn (38-7).

"This is the first time we all have put it together," said Bob Baumhower, a defensive tackle, after the Liberty Bowl victory. "We played as a team tonight, the way Alabama is supposed to play."

Other remarks on the Liberty Bowl Quotem Poll:

"It was like a consolation bowl to me, not in respect to playing Alabama and Bear Bryant, but any time you don't go to the Rose Bowl, it's a consolation game."—UCLA tackle Manu Tulasosopo.

"If Alabama had played the whole season like they played at the end and if we had played the whole season like we played in the beginning, we'd both have been playing for the national championship in bowl games."—UCLA end Rich Walker.

"This will happen in football. I've been on both sides. When you play Alabama, you can always get beat."—Georgia Tech head coach Pepper Rodgers.

"This is colder than Innsbruck. I never had to stand for three hours in weather like this."—Jim Lampley of ABC-TV.

"I wish I had been at the party UCLA players had the night before the game. It must have been something."—a Liberty Bowl fan.

"Maybe we were a little overconfident early in the year when we lost to Ole Miss and Georgia; I'm just not sure what the problem was. But we can't look back now. All we want to do now is celebrate this sweet victory."—Alabama defensive end Colenzo Hubbard.

And finally, Rutledge, the quarterback, as he looked toward the 1977 season and speculated as Crimson Tide players are expected to do—"The Liberty Bowl tonight, the national title next year."

1978 Sugar Bowl Game

Alabama 35   Ohio State 6

When you least expect it and your rear is unprotected,
You leave the heavy fighting to your son;
But when he has done it and you are sure he won it,
The Yankees vote the Irish No. 1.

Now that is the way I see it and I want Alabama to be it,
Looking down from the top is jolly fun;
So with unrelenting pride in the noble Crimson Tide,
I say ask Ole Miss who is No. 1.

—Alabama Jack
with no apologies

For a man who had just reached the end of another demanding football season, Paul (Bear) Bryant appeared extremely relaxed as he strolled about his Memorial Coliseum office. His face reflected satisfaction, which came as no surprise, because less than 24 hours earlier his University of Alabama team had scored one of the most impressive victories in a storied school history.

It happened at New Orleans, Louisiana, where in the Superdome on January 2, 1978, Alabama defeated Ohio State in the 44th annual Sugar Bowl game. The Crimson Tide, a meager one-point favorite at kickoff, did not barely slip by in that monumental first meeting between national powers, either. It won 35-6 in an awesome display of power which had Alabama fans hoping and praying for, and at least some expecting, a national championship.

259

Johnny Crow rambles for yardage against Buckeyes.

As Bryant rehashed the tremendous conquest in moments of obvious contentment, votes were being tabulated in both the Associated Press and United Press International polls, ballotings of sportswriters and coaches across the nation, respectively. About two hours later, when it was announced that Alabama had finished second to Notre Dame in both polls, Crimson Tide loyals went into rages of protest. The results brought bitter disappointment because Alabama had fought, clawed, and battled its way back into championship contention and, with an amazing twist of Lady Luck, appeared an obvious choice for the title.

Ranked third nationally entering the Sugar Bowl game, Alabama defeated No. 8 Ohio State with ease, while on a wacky day of bowl upsets No. 1 Texas fell to No. 5 Notre Dame (38-10) in the Cotton, No. 2 Oklahoma fell to No. 6 Arkansas (31-6) in the Orange, and No. 4 Michigan fell to No. 13 Washington (27-20) in the Rose.

As in 1965, when Alabama vaulted from fourth to first on bowl day, the Crimson Tide appeared ready to play the starring role in another fairy tale. It ended up playing the fateful part in a tragedy. The balloting was close, but Notre Dame won the championship, taking 37 first-place votes in the AP poll to 19 for Alabama and 15 for third-place Arkansas. The three teams—all 11-1 for the season—duplicated the finish in the UPI poll.

"I think Notre Dame is the only team which could have jumped over us," Bryant said. "I think we are as good as anybody in the country, but that's my opinion. Notre Dame winning the championship is the opinion of the other folks. Naturally I'm disappointed for our players and our staff, because they did an outstanding job this year. We came so far and did it against one of the toughest schedules in the country. But Notre Dame has our congratulations."

When Alabama used a wall-like defense and a down-to-earth gritty offense to whip Ohio State, it capped a newsworthy season which saw the Crimson Tide almost continuously whip adversity.

The problems started early—before Alabama embarked on a murderous schedule consisting of Mississippi, Nebraska, Vanderbilt, Georgia, Southern California, Tennessee, Louisville, Mississippi State, Louisiana State, Miami, and Auburn—and they lasted until the end—when voters scoffed at Crimson Tide success.

"I'm really proud of what our players accomplished this year," Bryant said after the Sugar Bowl victory. "They were mediocre early in the season because we had an ordinary defense, but they have since improved more than any team I've had. I think we have a great team. If you doubt it, line somebody else up against our players and see what happens.

"I don't know if we're the best team in the country, but I have one vote in the UPI poll and I'm voting for us. I really can't express how proud I am. Everybody associated with our program did a great job. Everybody worked hard to improve."

Ohio State is willing to testify that Alabama reached its announced goal, although the record books will forever disagree.

"Judging from what I saw today, Alabama should be ranked No. 1 in the country," said Ohio State head coach Woody Hayes. "They beat us every way a team can be beat."

The sometimes fiery and controversial Hayes was accurate in describing the aftermath left by the Sugar Bowl, for Alabama had the whip hand throughout the game viewed by 76,811, and the force with which the Crimson Tide used it grew as the game aged.

The contest was labeled a battle between the rugged defense of Big 10 Conference co-champion Ohio State and the explosive offensive magic of Southeastern Conference champion Alabama. It was no contest at all.

Alabama drove to the Ohio State 3 yard line on its first possession and did not score, but the Crimson Tide took the ball the second time and marched 76 yards in 10 plays for a touchdown.

Tony Nathan, the explosive junior halfback, dived over right guard from 1 yard out to score, but the big play of the drive was a 29-yard pass completion from quarterback Jeff Rutledge to split end Ozzie Newsome to the Ohio State 21 yard line. Roger Chapman kicked the extra point and Alabama led 7-0 with 11:31 left in the second quarter.

Alabama duplicated the 76-yard touchdown drive on its next possession, taking 11 plays to up its lead to 13-0. The touchdown came on a 27-yard pass from Rutledge to Bruce Bolton with 4:34 left in the second quarter.

Ohio State made its only real bid for momentum just before halftime, when the Buckeyes drove to a first down at the Alabama 11 yard line. But three plays gained only 6 yards and it was time for a gut check. On fourth down, Ohio State flanker Jim Harrell ran around right end and appeared headed for a touchdown. But Alabama defenders Wayne Hamilton, Ricky Tucker, and Don McNeal wrestled him out of bounds at the 3 yard line.

"That play probably won the game for us," Bryant said. "We had the upper hand, but that defensive effort helped us hold it."

Hamilton, the 6-foot-5, 230-pound sophomore end, agreed with his coach. "When we stopped them on the goal line I knew we were going to play a great defensive game," Hamilton said.

Alabama did.

The Crimson Tide marched 67 yards in 13 plays for a 21-0 lead, with Rutledge passing 3 yards to tight end Rick Neal for the touchdown, then to Nathan for a two-point conversion.

Ohio State cut the lead to 21-6 with a 38-yard touchdown

262

pass from quarterback Rod Gerald to Harrell, but Alabama took the ensuing kickoff and marched 84 yards in 14 plays for another touchdown. Freshman halfback Major Ogilvie dived over guard from 1 yard out for the score and Chapman kicked the extra point, giving the Crimson Tide a 28-6 lead with 6:30 left to play. Senior fullback Johnny Davis bulled over left guard from 7 yards out for the final Alabama touchdown and Chapman kicked the game to its final margin with 5:09 left to play.

The Alabama sideline was a picture of smiles, whoops, and hollers as the final seconds ticked off the scoreboard clocks, with Newsome sporting the brightest face.

"This is some way to end a career," said Newsome, the All-American receiver who is destined for many more great ones as a pro. "What a way to go out. And what about this team? We have a great bunch of guys on it and now, maybe, we'll get that championship we've dreamed about. It's not my decision, but I hope the voters will consider us. I think we proved today that we are the best team in America."

While Newsome gave the Alabama summation, his teammates echoed it—none more clearly than senior offensive guard David Sadler.

"Our kicking game won for us," said Sadler, "because we let it rip and kicked 'em in the butt. I tell you, we can beat anybody in the country when we play like we did today. It was a great effort by a bunch of guys who wanted to win. After watching this (the game was televised nationally by ABC) I don't see how anybody could possibly vote for anybody except us. We worked hard all year for the chance to be national champions and I think we proved our point."

Sadler's sidekick, senior offensive tackle Louis Green, played the game with pictures of Ohio State defensive linemen in his socks.

"I just wanted a reminder of what we were trying to do out there," Green said. "I wanted to put the pictures on my helmet, but I thought that might look trashy. As it worked out, nobody needed any more motivation than we already had. We did anything we wanted to do with Ohio State. I don't want to take anything away from them, because they were a hard-hitting team, but we handled them pretty well. We played an almost flawless game."

Rutledge, the junior quarterback, played his finest game for Alabama and was named winner of the Miller-Digby Award,

263

symbolic of the most valuable player in the game. He completed 8 of 11 passes for 109 yards, while playing only three quarters.

"This is a nice honor, but I'm not deserving of it by myself," Rutledge said when receiving the trophy. "This award should be torn up so every player on our team can have part of it."

The resounding victory was probably enough reward for Alabama players, but they received another one when Bryant reviewed the game.

"Our players played as hard and as well as they possibly could," said Bryant, who took his 19th Alabama team bowling. "It was a heckuva football game, too, played between two outstanding teams. There weren't many cracks on the field and there wasn't much room for error.

"This team will always have a special place in my heart, because we had some players who would do anything we asked of them. Most of them were not good enough to be named to all-star teams, but they won't be forgotten around my office. They overcame problems to get to the Sugar Bowl, then they beat a truly fine football team and beat it good."

When August rolled around and Alabama players started reporting for practice, most people thought the Crimson Tide would be an outstanding team. But a rash of injuries crept onto the scene—taking first-team quarterback Jack O'Rear with them—and doubts began surfacing.

Everybody knew Alabama would be able to score—and it did to the tune of over 30 points per game—but there were questions about the Crimson Tide defense which proved logical enough the second weekend of the season when Nebraska beat Alabama, 31-24, in a mild upset. Alabama players returned from Lincoln, Nebraska, undaunted, however.

"I know one thing," Sadler said after the loss. "We're a better team than we showed today. We'll come back, I'm sure of it."

Alabama did come back. It picked up its second win of the season at Vanderbilt, 24-12—to go with a first-game 34-13 decision over Ole Miss—and waltzed past Georgia (18-10), Southern Cal (21-20), Tennessee (24-10), Louisville (55-6), Mississippi State (37-7), LSU (24-3), Miami (36-0), and Auburn (48-21).

The win over Southern Cal at Los Angeles was the biggie, because Alabama beat the No. 1 team in the country. Bryant credited a lucky shirt with helping the Crimson Tide to victory,

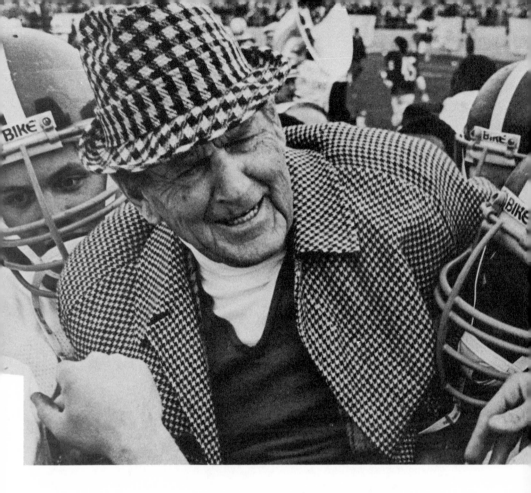

although a big heart did not hurt Alabama chances any.

"Let me tell you a little story about why, maybe, we won," Bryant said in a post-game interview. "I was getting ready to throw out some old clothes last summer when I came across this shirt (he was wearing it).

"I didn't think I'd ever wear it again—Marc (Tyson), who's my grandson, was there with me—and I'd already tossed it in the box when he came up to me.

"'Papa,' Mark said, 'isn't that the shirt you're wearing in this picture here?' He was holding a picture of me and John McKay (former Southern Cal coach) which was made after we had beaten them (17-10) in 1971.

"Marc, who's 14, said, 'Well, don't you think you ought to wear it this year? Maybe it'll bring you some more good luck.' He made me promise I'd wear it today and I'm telling you, I'm glad as hell he did."

The victory over Southern Cal was an Alabama spring-board back to national prominence, but the Crimson Tide was still having problems in the SEC. Those ended with the victory over LSU, when Alabama wrapped up its sixth conference championship in seven years and gained the automatic invitation to the Sugar Bowl.

The official invitation to the Sugar Bowl came a week before the game with Auburn. Ohio State was announced as the opponent—the Buckeyes had lost 14-6 to Michigan a week earlier in a showdown for a Rose Bowl invitation—setting up one of the most publicized games in collegiate history. Not only was Alabama going against Ohio State for the first time in history, but Bryant was going against Hayes, which meant a battle between the two winningest active coaches in the game.

Bryant added sweetness to an already Sugary matchup when he announced intentions of trying to break the all-time winning record held by Amos Alonzo Stagg. He made the announcement in early December, just after the victory over Auburn and in the heart of the recruiting season.

In 33 years as a head coach, Bryant has won 273 games and needs only 42 more to break the all-time winning record set by Stagg. He is third on the all-time list, 40 behind Glenn (Pop) Warner and well ahead of Hayes, who has 231 wins.

"Somebody has got to be the winningest coach ever and it might as well be me," Bryant said when announcing he was going to try for the thought-to-be-untouchable mark.

Then one day before the Sugar Bowl, he outlined how the timetable might work. "I'd like to coach 99 more years if I can make it that long," Bryant said. "Heck, I'm too old to start something new and too young to die. I want to coach as long as the Good Lord will let me and we keep winning."

The Bryant announcement was accepted nationwide—by fans, fellow coaches, and players. None was more vocal than former Arkansas head coach Frank Broyles.

"I think it is paramount to the future of college football that—if his health remains good—Coach Bryant set the record," Broyles said. "His doing it would be a tremendous boost to the sport. He is the only one who can ever do it, because of his tremendous dedication to and love of the game. Then, I'll say this: After he sets the new record, his will never be broken.

"Bear Bryant is an unselfish person. That's why he continues to coach and become an even larger legend than he already is. He has been more willing to give of himself and his talents than, maybe, the rest of us.

"The man was made to coach. He loves young people; loves working with them and helping them become fine young men and leaders. They just don't make men like Bear Bryant any more."

Before the Sugar Bowl, Ohio State fans challenged that observation. They showed up in New Orleans rallying behind Hayes and sporting eye-catching lapel buttons which said, "Woody Hayes: In all the world there is only one."

The Bear-versus-Woody matchup drew national exposure, with the sporting media calling it a battle between Bryant The Legend and Hayes The Institution. Both coaches shied away from the fanfare.

"Bear and I talked it over and we're not gonna play a down," Hayes said in Columbus, Ohio, the day before he took his Buckeyes to New Orleans.

"This Woody and Bear thing has gotten out of hand," Bryant said in Tuscaloosa while the Crimson Tide worked out.

Woody Hayes' face tells the story.

Another victorious ride for Alabama head coach Paul (Bear) Bryant.

"I'd rather talk about the players, because they will decide who wins and loses."

Then two days before the game—at a special joint press conference—Hayes and Bryant poked fun at one another.

Bryant hugged Hayes and said, "Woody, if you'll agree to it, I'm willing to stay in the dressing room during the game."

"Oh, no," Hayes replied. "I'm going to the sidelines. I want to see it."

Both played typical roles during the contest. Bryant was relatively calm, directing Alabama while standing between the 45 yard lines. He showed very little emotion until late in the game, when he clapped fervently as Alabama waltzed to victory.

Hayes was his normal fiery self. He threw his baseball cap onto the field when Alabama scored a touchdown, belted one of his players when the Crimson Tide made its goal-line stand, and slugged the goalpost as he walked to the dressing room at halftime.

When it was over, Bryant was a gracious and colorful winner.

"Our winning doesn't have anything to do with me being a better coach than Woody," Bryant said. "Woody is a great football coach....And I ain't bad."

1979 Sugar Bowl Game

Alabama 14   Penn State 7

Courage is but a word,
Its meaning hard to define;
But mighty Alabama displayed it,
On a Sugar Bowl goal line.

                               —O. M. Cummings III

A shade more than six minutes remained to be played in the 1979 Sugar Bowl when Marty Lyons, a defensive tackle from the University of Alabama, and Chuck Fusina, a quarterback from Penn State, stood over the football and chatted.

Alabama was ahead 14-7 and the ball was 10 inches from the Crimson Tide goal line. The sideline marker Fusina looked at said it was fourth down. A buzzing record crowd of 78,824, the most fans to ever witness a game in the Louisiana Superdome, was aware a showdown was at hand.

"How far do you have to go?" Lyons asked Fusina.

"Ten inches," Fusina answered.

"Then, you better pass," Lyons said.

Possibly stunned by such brash Crimson Tide confidence, Fusina went to the Penn State huddle and called his play, a crucial one he hoped would lift the unbeaten Nittany Lions to a national championship, certainly at least a tie in a war of a game against once-beaten Alabama.

Alabama defenders, Lyons anchoring, braced for the charge.

Instead of passing, as advised, Fusina handed the ball to his tailback, Mike Guman, who ran over tackle.

Crack! He was met head-on by linebacker Barry Krauss.

Boom! Krauss was joined in the attack by a host of red-shirted teammates, halfback Murray Legg and linebacker Rich Wingo leading.

Crunch! At the bottom of the pile was defensive tackle David Hannah, who had penetrated the Penn State backfield successfully enough to stymie the play before it got started.

An amazing goal line stand was history, left to be saluted by artists with their paintings, poets with their words, and vocalists with their songs.

And, to be remembered by Alabama fans forever as a measuring stick to Crimson Tide greatness in times of despair.

Alabama won the game 14-7 and two days later was named national champion by the Associated Press.

"I hit Guman head-to-head," said Krauss, a senior who won the Miller-Digby Trophy as most valuable player in the forty-fifth Sugar Bowl. "We were both above the top of the pile. It was a crunching lick. We both fell to the ground, me in pain with a pinched nerve in my neck, and Guman short of the goal line."

Lyons recalled the mood of Alabama before the "Gut Check" play.

"It was a mutual thing for all of us," Lyons said. "We grouped together and talked about the importance of stopping Penn State, how we had worked hard for the opportunity to win a national championship and how our chances had come down to one play.

"Somebody upstairs must have liked us, because it was tough down there. We went after it and Penn State went after it. We won the battle, in a way Alabama players are supposed to."

Defensive tackle Byron Braggs was at the bottom of the pile with Hannah. He recalls the ecstasy of the moment.

"When I heard the whistle blow, I looked at the scoreboard at the far end of the field," Braggs said. "Before the play, it had said fourth-and-one. Then, it said first-and-10. And, the score still said Alabama 14, Penn State 7. I was the happiest man on earth.

"Before the play, I was scared. I looked at the ball nestled against the goal line and said, 'Damn, that's close!' My legs were shivering.

"But, you know, I had a feeling we would stop them."

Having made two similar plays on the snaps previous, Alabama had reason to believe it could stop Penn State.

On the first play, a pass, defensive halfback Don McNeal tackled Penn State split end Scott Fitzkee at the one-yard line. He square-shouldered the receiver, or else his momentum would have carried him into the end zone for six points.

"It was a picture tackle, just like you would use in a clinic," said Bill Oliver, an Alabama assistant coach who became head coach at Tennessee-Chattanooga. "Had Don hit him a little off-center, he would have scored. It was a classic effort on his part."

On the second play, Penn State fullback Matt Suhey attempted to run over guard. Wingo hit him first, but received help from numerous teammates who threw the opposing player two yards back.

"I was fired up," Wingo said. "We all were. I was also proud to be a part of something like that. Those are the type tests that separate champions from losers."

Those efforts received applause from the winningest among living winners, Alabama coach Paul "Bear" Bryant. He recalls every block, every tackle, every emotional second that went into the making of that cherished Crimson Tide victory.

"We played superhuman football on defense," Bryant said. "I don't have a good enough vocabulary to tell you how proud I was of those players. They were put to a test and they passed it with flying colors. It was the finest defensive effort near the goal line I can recall.

"We peaked as a team when it mattered most. Our players came together and showed greatness. Everybody associated with Alabama football put a lot into that national championship. They gave an old coach a moment he'll never forget."

Bryant added Alabama won its fifth national championship under his direction the hard way, with "no soft touches" on the schedule.

Certainly, there were no sissy seconds in the game.

"It was an old-fashioned scratch, fight, and claw game, one we all enjoyed playing," said Allen Crumbley, an Alabama defensive halfback. "It was a tremendous challenge and we met it head-on.

"Nothing came cheap. It was a game that only the toughest team could win. I still tip my hat to Penn State, because we beat a super team. But I also tip my hat to Alabama, because we climbed to the top of the world beating them."

Penn State coach Joe Paterno, who saw his team lose for

Bear watched victory tally rise.

the first time in 20 games, agreed with Crumbley.

"It was a bang-bang-bang game," Paterno said. "Big plays were the difference, and Alabama made them. Alabama is a great team, a national champion team."

In a joyous Alabama dressing room after the game, Krauss and Lyons smiled on victory.

From Krauss: "We asked ourselves for a gut check and got one. When you are tired and hurting, that is all you can do. We wanted it badly. We had a lot to prove. Our goals were set high."

From Lyons: "It all speaks for itself, really. Those red jerseys mean a lot to all of us. Today, we did ourselves proud wearing them."

Alabama was not without offense in the game, gaining 299 yards, 208 running against a team that gave up only 54.5 yards per game during an 11-0 regular season.

The Crimson Tide got its points on two touchdowns—a 30-yard pass from quarterback Jeff Rutledge to split end Bruce

Alan McElroy demonstrated kicking skills.

Bolton, and an eight-yard run by halfback Major Ogilvie—and two extra point kicks by Alan McElroy.

Penn State scored its only touchdown on a 19-yard pass from Fusina to Fitzkee. Matt Barr kicked the extra point.

The Rutledge-to-Bolton pass broke a scoreless struggle just before halftime. The Fusina-to-Fitzkee pass tied the game. The run by Ogilvie with less than a minute remaining in the third quarter proved to be the difference.

Plus, it set up the defensive heroics.

Alabama, which lost a 24-14 decision to Southern Cal in September, ended the season with an 11-1 record and every national championship except the one given by coaches, United Press International. That title went to Southern Cal, which beat Michigan by seven points in the Rose Bowl.

"In my heart, I know we were the best team in the country at the end of the season," Lyons said.

"Yeah, I voted for us," said Bryant.

Alabama played what Bryant called "the toughest schedule

in school history" en route to its national championship. The Crimson Tide beat Nebraska 20-3, Missouri 38-20, Vanderbilt 51-28, Washington 20-17, Florida 23-12, Tennessee 30-17, Virginia Tech 35-0, Mississippi State 35-14, LSU 31-10, Auburn 34-16, and Penn State.

Alabama made its run after having pressure put on it in August, when the Associated Press announced the Crimson Tide was No. 1 in preseason polls.

"Being No. 1 is a goal we had already set for ourselves," said Tony Nathan, a halfback. "In other words, people believe what we already believe. Now, we have to prove it to ourselves."

That preseason logic from Nathan was supported by Wingo, who said, "I like being picked No. 1, because I know Coach Bryant will make us work to make that come true. He won't let us get complacent. He'll push us to make us champions."

Bryant broke out his verbal whip about a week into preseason practice. His players were wilting in the heat on Thomas Field. The coach was getting hot with anger on his observation tower. A whistle blew and players lined up for water.

Bryant took a megaphone in hand and addressed his squad:

"If it wasn't for days like this, we'd have 4,000 players out for football at Alabama. You might want to check yourselves and see what it means to you. Days like today make the difference between champions and also-rans."

About 90 minutes later, after a productive practice, Bryant explained his words:

"I guess today might have been a good thing. We all have to face reality at some point in our lives. We have to realize there's a big difference in boys playing football and football players.

"And, there are teams and there are football teams."

Two days before the opener at Birmingham with Nebraska, Bryant started breaking out in goosebumps.

"Yes, I'm excited about the season," Bryant said, "but I have mixed emotions. I'm looking forward to it because another year is here (he was only a week away from his sixty-fifth birthday), but I'm not looking forward to it from an age standpoint. This last summer moved by pretty darn fast.

"But I'm gonna try to enjoy this season. I think we have some people with class around here. Our players have punished

Halfback Tony Nathan in mid-game strategy session.

themselves in the heat."

A sellout crowd of 77,023 fans and a national television audience watched Alabama defeat Nebraska. Rutledge was named player of the game by ABC-TV. The performance was revenge for the senior quarterback, who a year earlier was ridiculed after throwing five interceptions in a loss at Nebraska.

"This game erases a lot of bad memories for me," Rutledge said.

Alabama fell behind Missouri 20-17 at Columbia, after leading 17-0, then came back to win impressively. The Crimson Tide rally in the second half was prompted by a blocked-punt touchdown, with defensive end E. J. Junior stopping the kick and linebacker Ricky Gilliland picking up the ball and running into the end zone.

Gilliland was greeted in the end zone by a black dog.

"That dog was just looking at me," Gilliland said. "I smiled at him and ran to the sidelines."

At halftime of that game, Bryant spoke magnificently.

"Coach Bryant made us come down off that cloud we'd been on," said Lyons. "He put it right to us. He made us aware that the No. 1 team in the country has no business letting anybody score 20 points on it. He made us aware of who we were and the tradition we were trying to uphold."

About 4,000 Alabama fans made the trip to Missouri. Among them was Buddy Slay of Birmingham.

"I've spent a lot of money following our Crimson Tide," said Slay. "But games like this one make it all worthwhile."

Such happiness turned to sorrow a week later at Birmingham, when Southern Cal came to conquer and did. The Trojans made Alabama look bad on national television.

"Most of the afternoon, it looked like a bunch of fine young men from Alabama playing against a football team," Bryant said. "We don't deserve the No. 1 ranking. But we might deserve it at the end of the year. If our players bounce back, I think we can have a great team. We're still in the hunt."

Yes, but Alabama fans were mad. The next week against Vanderbilt, they booed Rutledge during a game played on campus at Tuscaloosa. His teammates came to his defense.

"It's a sad feeling when you're out there playing your hearts out and your fans are booing in the stands," said Lyons. "I wanted to go up there and grab one of those fans and say, 'If you can do better, get down there on the field and prove it.' We'll come back and make them regret they every did that."

Alabama started its rally the following week at Seattle against Washington. Again, Bryant worked magic with his players, this time turning them toward the greatness expected from them. His words made an impact during a Friday night team meeting.

"Basically, Coach Bryant told us what a real football player is," said Rutledge. "He told us the importance of putting forth all we have. It was one of the best talks I've ever heard."

"He (Bryant) shared a lot with us," said Legg. "He told us about himself and the things he deems important in football and in life. Get the picture? There was a great man and a great football coach telling us private things about his life. When I went on the field, I didn't want to let him down. I think everybody felt that way.

"He told us that once the whistle blows to start a game, you have to be a killer on every play. He wasn't saying we should try to hurt an opponent, just that we needed to be ag-

277

gressive.

"That talk would have impressed anybody who heard it. It brought us closer together."

About 7,000 Alabama fans were there to watch the Crimson Tide grow up that day.

From that day forward, until the Sugar Bowl showdown, Alabama players honed their skills and developed huge hearts of stone that came in handy when Penn State came knocking at the goal line, only to be turned away.

1980 Sugar Bowl Game

Alabama 24   Arkansas 9

Auburn had reason to hope,
Arkansas played on a prayer;
Still, nobody could stop Bama,
And its growling man called "Bear."

—Brenda Thomas

When Wallace Wade coached football at the University of Alabama, he said, "Football players smelled like men."

But Wade, who led Alabama to its first postseason bowl game, the 1926 Rose Bowl, also said it was much easier to string out wins in his era than in this era of Coach Paul "Bear" Bryant.

"We had some hard-nosed, tough football players at Alabama during my years there," said Wade. "But everybody seems to have that type players now. That's why the record Alabama has produced in recent years is so fascinating.

"I'm proud of that winning streak we had in the 1920s, but, to be honest, it doesn't stack up very well against the one Alabama had in 1978, 1979, and 1980.

"To win that many in a row is phenomenal in this day and age of college football. It just goes to show the prestige Alabama enjoys in football. The tradition is better than that at any other school."

From the last game of 1924, a 33-0 victory over Georgia, to the last game of 1926, a 7-7 tie with Stanford in the 1927 Rose Bowl, Wade-coached Alabama won 20 consecutive games.

That streak stood as a school record until January 1, 1980, when Bryant-coached Alabama wrapped up a second consecutive national championship with a 24-9 victory over Arkansas in the Sugar Bowl.

Alabama stretched that winning string to 28 games in 1980, then saw it broken when Mississippi State claimed a startling 6-3 victory over the Crimson Tide at Jackson.

The 1979 season was indeed eventful for Alabama, which capped its perfect 12-game run by humiliating Arkansas at New Orleans. The Crimson Tide trailed Tennessee 17-0, but rallied to win, was frightened by Mississippi State, but won easily, and was stunned by Auburn, but scored a knockout punch under pressure.

By the time Alabama arrived in the Louisiana Superdome, it was so war-tested that its confidence bristled and its desire to overtake top-ranked Ohio State in national polls had reached a feverish pitch.

Before the game, Arkansas Coach Lou Holtz said, "We are about to play one of the greatest football names in history, possibly THE greatest."

After the game, Holtz said, "Alabama is a class football team. Alabama can get you so many ways—kicking, offense, and defense. I see no way anybody in the country can beat them.

"Is Alabama No. 1? Is the Pope a Catholic?"

It took help from third-ranked Southern California, which beat Ohio State in the Rose Bowl, but Alabama was indeed a consensus national champion after its victory over Arkansas. It was the sixth such title under Bryant for the Crimson Tide, which finished the year as the only unbeaten and untied team in the country.

Alabama annually shoots for No. 1, which had a couple of its most famous graduates thinking as they sat in the stands at New Orleans and watched their alma mater climb to the mountaintop again.

John Hannah, voted the best offensive lineman in the National Football League by his peers, played on an Alabama team in 1971 that went unbeaten during the regular season, then lost a national championship showdown game to Nebraska in the Orange Bowl.

"I was thinking about our loss to Nebraska as the clock ticked down to zero, locking up the Alabama win over Arkansas," Hannah said. "We wanted to be No. 1, too, so that loss leaves a bitter taste in my mouth.

"Winning 11 games and losing one is not a pleasant experience. There were several people from our 1971 Alabama team sitting near me at the game (Robin Parkhouse, John Rogers, Steve Williams, Jeff Blitz, and Mike Dean) and we all started talking about that (38-6) Orange Bowl loss.

"As the Sugar Bowl was winding down, we all mentioned how we'd like to have another shot at Nebraska. That's why that victory over Arkansas will forever be so meaningful to those guys who won it."

Ozzie Newsome, a standout tight end with the Cleveland Browns of the NFL, was a split end on an Alabama team in 1977. His team lost to Nebraska 31-24 early that season, then narrowly missed a national championship after a 38-6 victory over Ohio State in the Sugar Bowl.

"Alabama looks tops to me," Newsome said as he congratulated Crimson Tide players on the sidelines at New Orleans. "The memories this game brings to me!

"It's great that they will soon be No. 1, but it hurts me deep inside. I thought we deserved the championship, too. If only . . ."

Beating Arkansas, Alabama left few questions unanswered in the minds of those who vote in national championship polls. One such man was Bryant, who saw one of his Alabama teams go unbeaten and untied for the first time since an erroneously uncrowned Crimson Tide in 1966.

"I can't adequately tell you how proud I am of this group of Alabama players," Bryant said after the win over Arkansas. "They opened last year winning (14-7 over Penn State in the Sugar Bowl), won throughout the season, and opened a new year today winning.

"Sure I think it's more difficult for a team to win every game than it was in 1966. First, everybody in the world would rather beat Alabama more now than then. Second, everybody has outstanding talent now. This team has earned a special place in my heart.

"In fact, this is the greatest bunch of young men I've ever been associated with. They have displayed class and character all season. Over and over again, they have shown tremendous pride in themselves and winning.

"I said it before and will say it again, this team is made up of terrific people. I think we're the best team in the country. No, I know we are."

Bryant cherishes wins, no matter who the victim is, but he

expressed sentiment after the win over Arkansas. He is from that state, born near Fordyce, and much was made of the Razorbacks playing against a native son coach who once decided to attend Alabama instead of the state school from Fayetteville.

"I would have rather it been somebody else on the other side of the field," Bryant said, a smile surfacing on his face. "But I sure am glad they were the second best team in this one."

In the Alabama dressing room after the victory over Arkansas, junior halfbacks Billy Jackson and Major Ogilvie sat side-by-side, painting a picture that indicates patience is indeed a nice virtue. Before kickoff, nobody had reason to believe they would lead the Crimson Tide to victory.

But 77,486 fans would testify now that they did.

Out of the spotlight much of the regular season because of nagging leg injuries, Jackson and Ogilvie ran for 120 and 67 yards, respectively.

"If anybody watched the game, they can tell we beat them convincingly," said Ogilvie, who scored two touchdowns and had a 50-yard punt return to set up a field goal en route to the Miller-Digby Trophy as most outstanding player.

Ogilvie had missed much of the season because of a badly strained pelvic muscle, but he had played remarkably in the key games.

"We did everything we could to win the national championship," said Jackson, who made several crucial runs on Alabama scoring drives, but was beaten by Ogilvie 101/2 votes to 10 in balloting for most outstanding player honors.

Arkansas, a Southwest Conference co-champion which ended its season with a 10-2 record, got a field goal on its first possession for a 3-0 lead. But the Razorbacks were not stout enough to continue such an impressive start.

Alabama scored two first-quarter touchdowns and a second-quarter field goal for a 17-3 halftime lead.

Arkansas scored a touchdown on its first possession of the second half, cutting the lead to 17-9, but Alabama made a 98-yard touchdown drive in the fourth quarter to provide the final margin of victory.

"That last touchdown drive was a classic," said Bryant. "It came against a quality defense at a time when things were emotional and hard-fought on the field."

Alabama players smiled on the victory, because it came at

the end of a long comeback. The Crimson Tide had rededicated itself after a loss to Southern Cal early in the 1978 season.

"Before our loss to USC, there was enough pressure associated with Alabama football to bust a steel pipe," said defensive tackle Byron Braggs. "We didn't handle it very well. But that has since changed. This team has been loose all season. We had a mission and we finished it today with this win over Arkansas.

"We started climbing our way back to the top after losing to Southern Cal. We earned one national championship with our efforts last year (1979). Now, the whole world knows Alabama should be No. 1 by itself."

Arkansas quarterback Kevin Scanlon certainly knew. He sat slumped in the Razorbacks' dressing room and applauded the victors.

"Lord, they hit us," Scanlon said. "I know a couple of my pass receivers really got rocked. And, even when I got the ball off to one of them, somebody was always there to deck me.

"We've got a good team, but Alabama killed us. Anybody who doesn't vote them No. 1 is crazy."

Alabama began showing championship savvy long before it got to New Orleans to play in a put-up-or-shut up situation.

Tennessee led Alabama 17-0 in their third-Saturday-in-October meeting at Birmingham, but the Crimson Tide rallied to claim its sixth victory of the season. The dramatic contest came after victories over Georgia Tech 30-6, Baylor 45-0, Vanderbilt 66-3, Wichita State 38-0, and Florida 40-0, and it prompted serious analysis on the part of both coaches, Bryant and John Majors of Tennessee.

"We carried the fight to them early, but they brought it back to us in the second half," said Majors. "That is quite a football team we lost to today. Alabama showed power and poise."

From Bryant: "Our players did not seem too rattled at halftime (when they trailed 17-7). They knew what they had to do to win and did it. Overall, I was more than pleased with our effort. Our players showed a lot of pride.

"After watching the game, I know we're a good team. I have never seen a team make a comeback like that against Tennessee. It has happened at other places against other teams, but not against those Vols.

"I'm triple proud of our team for winning like that. The game showed them what can be done. I think it made us a football team. It is, by far, the best thing that could have happened to us."

Alabama was led by junior quarterback Don Jacobs, who subbed for senior starter Steadman Shealy.

"At halftime, we just talked about the things we had to do to win," said Jacobs. "Coach Bryant was real cool about it. He told us, 'I know you can do it and you know you can do it.' And, by golly, we did it. We went out in the second half and wore their pants off."

In the Tennessee dressing room, freshman guard Carlton Gunn said, "We won half the war, but Alabama claimed the victory. I guess that's what being No. 1 is about."

The victory over Tennessee is memorable for Alabama players, but a 31-7 victory over Virginia Tech the next week might have been as moving for their coach. It gave Bryant his two hundredth win at Alabama.

Against Mississippi State, a 24-7 victory, the Crimson Tide was sluggish. That is everybody except Shealy, who ran for 190 yards to replace Pat Trammell as the most productive running quarterback since World War II. Trammell, who led Alabama to its first national championship in 1961, ran for 143 yards in a 19-7 win over Tulane in 1959.

"Pat Trammell is one of the greatest people to ever play at Alabama," said Shealy. "The record means so much to me because of that."

Alabama slopped through the mud the next week to beat Louisiana State 3-0—Alan McElroy kicked the winning field goal at Baton Rouge—and the Crimson Tide intercepted five Miami passes in a 30-0 victory the next week, in the first game televised from Bryant-Denny Stadium on campus in Tuscaloosa.

Then came the showdown with the most hated of rivals, Auburn, and a bleak moment that turned bright.

Auburn led the top-ranked Crimson Tide 18-17 in the fourth quarter and had a grip on momentum. The ball was on the Alabama 18-yard line, when Shealy ran onto the field to engineer a brilliant series.

Seven plays later, Shealy ran around right end for a touchdown and Alabama, behind a tremendous offensive line, had scored a knockout heard around the nation.

"That was, without doubt, the most exciting drive of my career," Shealy said. "It meant everything. I really got emotional. Everybody did, and everything clicked.

"I'm not an emotional person, but when I went into that end zone for the touchdown, I couldn't help myself. I leaped into the air in a show of joy."

Jim Bunch was one of the several linemen who made instrumental blocks during the Alabama drive to everlasting glory.

"When adversity calls, a champion fights," said Bunch. "I knew we had 'em licked before the drive got under way. You could see that mirrored on our faces in the huddle. Frankly, I'm disappointed we didn't score on them again."

Bryant was willing to take the 25-18 final score and quit.

"I knew this team had class," Bryant said. "That drive proved it beyond doubt. It showed what our players are made of, what kind of parents they have. They are good folks. Our players are true champions."

At that time, Alabama was uncrowned, although 23 straight Southeastern Conference victories spoke for themselves.

It was on January 1 at New Orleans, that everybody fully realized the Crimson Tide was better than anybody else who played the game that year.

1981 Cotton Bowl Game

Alabama 30   Baylor 2

From Arkansas he came,
To join the Crimson Tide;
It was the birth of fame,
And a joyous Alabama ride.

The years have passed,
He has greeted many a sun;
But he lives in glory,
Soon to be No. 1.

—Edna Cox

His birthday came and went quietly as just another 13-hour shift at the office.

But 67-year-old Paul "Bear" Bryant, known as THE coach to University of Alabama football supporters, did find time to reflect on his life.

"I've had a full life in one respect, but I've had a one-track deal in another respect," Bryant said in the comforts of his office at Memorial Coliseum in Tuscaloosa. "Whether it has been good, I'll never know.

"My life has been so tied up in football, it has flown by. I wish it wasn't that way, but it has gone by mighty fast. Practice, recruiting, and games. There hasn't been anything except football.

"It has become a void, as it has to when your next minute, next hour, and next day all revolve around one thing.

"Frankly, I don't think that's good. It makes life pass mighty fast. You miss a lot of things you shouldn't miss and

Bear reflects on football career.

you do a lot of things you shouldn't do.

"When I look back, there are a lot of good things I wouldn't take anything for. But, still, you don't know if it's worth it or not. One thing I know that's worth it is the people I've been associated with. I've met and worked with really great folks.

"But I've never been able to associate myself closely with anybody, and that hurts. I've lived in a way that I've barely known my next door neighbors.

"Up to now, the whole thing has been football, football, and more football.

"I think anyone is wrong to get involved in one thing so completely. I've done that. You get to a point when 30 minutes after the last game, you start thinking about the next one. That's not all there is in life. It's ridiculous, I guess, but that's my way.

"Yep, it goes mighty fast. It's hard to believe I've been at it 40 years or more."

Bryant made those remarks on September 10, 1980. By nightfall on January 1, 1981, after his twenty-third Alabama team had beaten Baylor 30-2 in the Cotton Bowl, his overall record as a head coach was 306-79-16. That left him nine victories from becoming the winningest coach in history, eight from removing Glen "Pop" Warner from second place, and one more from unseating Amos Alonzo Stagg from the top position.

Alabama players from the 1980 season game him 10 victories in 12 games, the losses coming to Mississippi State 6-3, after 28 straight wins, and Notre Dame 7-0.

They also gave him one to remember, No. 300, as taken over Kentucky 45-0 on October 4.

There was not a triumphant ride to midfield on the shoulders of his players at Legion Field in Birmingham that day, nor a standing ovation from 78,200 fans who came to watch the third man in history scale the summit to No. 300.

There was not a loudly playing band. No drum rolls. No trumpet salutes. No smashing symbols.

Instead, Bryant crept into history books in a way reminiscent of his ambling walk, the head turned slightly to one side, and the feet shuffling.

"Coach Bryant told us he would have the score of the game painted on the ball we gave him and said he would put it in a trophy case on campus," said Tommy Wilcox, an Alabama sophomore safety who played an instrumental role in his coach accomplishing the feat. "He said that in 50 years, when we're all walking with canes, we can come back to Alabama, see that ball, and say we were the ones who put it there.

"But, you know, somebody else had to win all those other games. We just happened to be here today, in the right place at the right time."

Everything was just right for Bryant, too.

"I feel as good today as I did 10 years ago," Bryant said.

And, everybody smiled, including an Alabama placekicker named Peter Kim, a native of Korea who had heard about the greatness of the man.

"Yes, I've done my history," Kim said in the Alabama dressing room after kicking three field goals. "I know it takes a special man to win 300 games. The number itself speaks for his greatness."

Losing coach Fran Curci was not to be left out when it

came to applauding the man of the hour, man of the day, and football man of the century.

"Coach Bryant is a phenom . . . just to survive so long in this game. He is also a kind man. They beat us 45-0 today. He could have named the score, but chose to be nice. I appreciate that."

Kentucky defensive captain Tim Gooch was envious of the men dressed in red:

"When I was a kid, Coach Bryant was on top and Alabama was winning. It would have been an honor if they had come to get me. But at Alabama the great players keep coming."

And they keep giving their all for a coach who got victory No. 1 at Maryland; victory No. 50 at Kentucky; and victory Nos. 100, 150, 200, 250, and 300 at Alabama. He coached one year at Maryland, posting a 6-2-1 record; eight years at Kentucky, 60-23-5; four years at Texas A&M, 25-14-2; and in 1981 entered his twenty-fourth year at Alabama, 215-40-8.

Sammy Behr played on his only team at Maryland and scored the first touchdown for Bryant.

Fans showed support for Bryant.

"I've never met a finer gentleman or a greater coach than Paul Bryant," Behr said just before victory No. 300. "If you gave Coach Bryant a nickel as a player, he would give you a dollar in return. He is most deserving of every victory that has come his way.

"I'm proud of the chance to play for Coach Bryant, even if it was only one year (in 1945). And, I'm proud our team got him started toward such a remarkable record. I'm the more fortunate man, not him, because it was a great honor.

"For about an hour our first practice, Coach Bryant did nothing other than give us a lecture and demonstration on how to block and tackle. He took an active role, too, getting in there and mixing it up with us. He was a young man, only 32, a big man, and he had beautiful people working with him. He could also pass a mean lick.

"Coach Bryant was dedicated to fundamentals. In our first three games, we used only three plays. We worked on them tirelessly in practice and executed them pretty well in games.

"It was apparent after only that short period of time that he was a coach with special ability. I think Coach Bryant is so good that he could swap teams with most coaches and beat them in three weeks. He's a great coach and a great man. But he's a humble man, too. That adds to his greatness in football.

"The whole school was torn up about Coach Bryant leaving for Kentucky. He told the entire student body about it at an assembly on campus. He had spoiled us. We had a great (6-2-1) team that year and it was too bad he had to leave. The year before he arrived we won only one game. The year after he left, we dropped back to mediocrity.

"I begged Coach Bryant to take me with him to Kentucky, but he said, 'Sammy, I found you here and I have to leave you here.' I had one year with him and I'll always be thankful."

Bryant took a five-year plan for success with him to Kentucky. It included the importance of hard work.

"Have I ever worked harder than I did at Kentucky?" Bryant said before Alabama played the Wildcats in 1980. "No, and there has not been a coach since who worked so hard. Why did I go at it like that? Because I was trying to make a living and winning was the only way to do that."

Charles McClendon, the former Louisiana State coach and a friend of Bryant, was a player at Kentucky when the grizzly mentor directed that program.

"Fella, Coach Bryant did all the coaching back then, and he was tough," McClendon said. "He tried to do it all. Make that, he did do it all. He was all over the place. The man had so much energy, it was remarkable.

"His burning desire to win spilled over to his players. We respected him for what he was doing. There could have been some fear involved, but he gave us some great times."

Larry "Dude" Hennessey played under Bryant at Kentucky, then coached under him at Alabama.

"There is only one Coach Bryant," Hennessey said in 1980. "There will never be another coach like him. He was a master at Kentucky and still is now.

"As a coach, he has changed little through the years. He is a tireless worker and he believes in character. You have heard him talk about good mamas and papas? Well, he said those same things early in his career. He believes strongly that a kid has to do something worthwhile after his football days are over.

"Coach Bryant is always in charge. He knows how to handle the people who work for him. Consider how he dealt with Bob Gain, a big All-America tackle we had at Kentucky.

"Gain was raised in a coal-mining environment, grew up tough, and cared little about the discipline Coach Bryant demanded. One day, Coach Bryant got on him at practice and Gain said he was gonna beat Coach Bryant's tail. He popped off to us at the athletic dorm, and we all put down bets on the fight. Everybody was betting on the coach, so Gain got madder.

"So, we drove over to Coach Bryant's house and Gain went to the door. Coach Bryant answered his knock and said, 'Gain, what in the hell do you want?' And, Gain said, 'Uh, uh, Coach, I was just wondering if I could go home for Christmas break.'

"See what I mean? There is nobody else like him."

That description might be best confirmed by the ring Bryant wore as his team handed him victory No. 300. He has had champions, loves them, in fact, but he wore a diamond given him by his 1955 Texas A&M team that posted a 1-9 record.

"I'm proud of this ring and I'm proud of the men who gave it to me," Bryant said. "They won only one game (after going through preseason training at much-publicized Junction, Texas), but football meant a lot to them."

Bryant claimed victory No. 300 after much fanfare the

week before kickoff. He downplayed his individual accomplishment, speaking about players winning games, and worried that Kentucky might benefit from the hype.

Still, everybody got into the act. For instance, Joe Namath telephoned Bryant on Friday night before the game.

"We just chatted and I thoroughly enjoyed it," Bryant said.

What did the coach do on game day?

"I got up this morning, went to the bathroom, ate breakfast, went to the bathroom, went to a team meal, went to the bathroom, met with my quarterbacks, went to the bathroom, came to the stadium, walked around the field, went to the bathroom, and watched the game," Bryant said.

The victory over Kentucky, the fourth of the season for an Alabama team trying to win an unprecedented third straight national championship, was a high point in a somewhat disappointing year.

All was well until Mississippi State shocked the Crimson Tide at Jackson in game number eight. The Crimson Tide, which had defeated Georgia Tech, Mississippi, Vanderbilt, Kentucky, Rutgers, Tennessee, and Southern Mississippi—showing strong and weak signs along the way—put up a fight before falling to the Bulldogs.

In the last two minutes, Alabama marched, rather passed, its way to the Mississippi State three-yard line. But with a sellout crowd howling—"I never heard the signals," said Major Ogilvie, a senior running back—and the Bulldogs flexing, the Crimson Tide saw a last run toward possible victory end in a lost fumble.

Bryant went to the Mississippi State dressing room to congratulate the victors, who had won over Alabama for the first time since the year before Bryant returned to his alma mater as coach in 1958.

In the Alabama dressing room, meanwhile, Crimson Tide players cried and vowed to come back.

"The sun will shine again," said Byron Braggs, a senior defensive tackle, "but it won't be as pretty in Tuscaloosa tomorrow. We've done a lot of winning at Alabama, 28 in a row, so it's our turn to lose. We'll do it with class. That's the Alabama way."

While losing to Mississippi State hurt, Alabama still had hopes of a national championship. But those dreams were shattered two weeks later when Notre Dame beat the Crimson Tide on national television.

It was the fourth victory for the Fighting Irish over Alabama in as many meetings. The total difference in the two storied powers has been 13 points, Notre Dame winning by one, two, three, and seven.

Class prevailed in Birmingham.

"Gentlemen, I don't know what you think, but I think two of the greatest names in football history just played a great football game," said Dan Devine, the Notre Dame coach, who was three games away from retirement. "Alabama and Notre Dame are the epitome of excellence in college football. I'm proud to say I was a part of this day, a truly magnificent display of sports at its finest moment."

Two weeks later, Alabama regained its winning touch in an eighth consecutive victory over state rival Auburn. After that game, Bryant donned a cowboy hat—"This one is just like the one J. R. Ewing wears on 'Dallas' (the television show)," he said—and accepted an invitation to play Baylor in the Cotton Bowl.

Defensive skills led to Cotton Bowl victory.

Winning tradition returned to Alabama in Cotton Bowl action.

Cotton Bowl MVP Warren Lyles.

Tide rolled to victory again in Cotton Bowl.

Very little hoopla followed Alabama to Dallas—only a spattering of fans did likewise—but there was concern that the Crimson Tide, disappointed with the season, would not play well.

Those fears were put to rest, however, when Alabama put on a stunning defensive display and walloped the Southwest Conference champion Bears.

Baylor, 10-1 before kickoff, spoke of revenge in Dallas, a bid to erase memories of a 45-0 loss to Alabama during the 1979 regular season.

"We want to establish ourself as a national power in football," said Grant Teaff, the Baylor coach.

Alabama spoke of pride.

"We're playing for the continuation of Alabama tradition," said Braggs.

That mystique lives . . .

1982 Cotton Bowl Game

Texas 14   Alabama 12

The question seemed more absurd than the answer as Paul "Bear" Bryant contemplated and responded to a tough one during the spring of 1981. His smile indicated he was undaunted by the thought.

"No, I never think or worry about dying," Bryant said. "I'm not concerned with that at all. I probably should be concerned more about it. But I'm more interested right now in worrying about us winning football games, as well as helping our players become better people. You start thinking about death, or so I'm told, after you retire from whatever profession you're in. I know it's coming my way sometime. But. . . ."

On this morning the University of Alabama football coach was equally unconcerned about the publicized target of a number squarely in front of him—315.

He was nine victories short of becoming the winningest football coach in collegiate history. His team from that season was supposed to be the one to elevate him past Glenn (Pop) Warner and Amos Alonzo Stagg into first place.

"I never think about that record business until somebody mentions it," Bryant said that spring. "I refuse to discuss it because I'm afraid my players will think they're supposed to win for me instead of themselves. I've explained those concerns to them, but it's easy for them to get caught up in all that talk. I want this season to be as normal as the others we've had at Alabama. I want these players to win because of the same reasons our players have won for years, because of pride.

"My victories go way back, to my one year at Maryland, my eight years at Kentucky, my four years at Texas A&M, and my first

Bryant accepting President Reagan's congratulations.

twenty-three years at Alabama. You can't relate all of those wins to Alabama, so I want my players this season to forget about me and to accomplish things for themselves.

"That record business takes up a lot of time and distracts from our goal of winning a national championship this year."

Bryant was asked if he thought he would not reap satisfaction once he had won more games than any other collegiate coach.

"I'm sure that might be the case," he answered. "But what's important is that I'm thankful for what has already happened to me. I've been blessed by the good Lord more than anybody I know about. He has given me outstanding players to work with. I'm appreciative of the good things we've experienced here.

"Now comes this chance for me. I bet if you'd asked the folks at Lloyd's of London about this a decade ago, they'd have said there wasn't a chance for anybody to win as many games as Mr. Stagg did. But my players have put me in this position. It's them that should be publicized, not me. That's another reason I want this to be just another season at Alabama."

Bryant got his historic win, barely, when his team defeated intrastate rival Auburn in the final game of the regular season.

The normalcy he wanted never panned out, not from the first game on through a 14–12 loss to Texas in the Cotton Bowl. The Crimson Tide struggled much of the season with the pressure mounting, and the sixty-eight-year-old coach had to deal with numerous discipline problems among players.

Walter Lewis at work.

Without question, the highlight was a dramatic 28–17 victory over Auburn. With Alabama trailing in the fourth quarter, a lot of people wondered if the record conquest would come. But halfback Linnie Patrick made two dynamic runs in the fourth quarter and quarterback Walter Lewis passed crisply, and the game was won. Alabama had overcome a three-point Auburn lead with two touchdowns in a space of three minutes.

Once the victory was in hand, the accolades Bryant disliked poured in. President Ronald Reagan telephoned the Alabama dressing room at Legion Field from the White House. "Hello, Gipper," Bryant said to Reagan, who once played George Gipp in a movie about Knute Rockne of Notre Dame. With Crimson Tide players listening, the president called the accomplishment "a record all Americans can take pride in."

The following afternoon Reagan sent Bryant a taped message. It said, "America loves a winner, and the word *winner* is synonymous with Bear Bryant. You emphasize the mind, as well as the body. Your formula has worked. Our country salutes you. You are a living legend."

Living was the key for Bryant, according to a couple of his close friends, former Texas coach Darrell Royal and comedian Bob Hope.

"Bryant is just tougher than the rest of us," said Royal.

"I knew you would do it, Bear, even if you had to live better than everybody else," joked Hope.

Another person who was quick to congratulate Bryant was Eddie Robinson, the coach at Grambling. He later passed the former Alabama coach in 1985 to become the winningest collegiate coach, although many of his victories came against smaller programs.

"Everybody should be pleased with his record," said Robinson who had 297 victories when Bryant got number 315. "We Americans are hung up on records, but this is one that should be applauded by everybody. Amos Alonzo Stagg held it a long time."

Bryant seemed less impressed by his accomplishment than most people. He celebrated by eating bread and onions dipped in milk at his house in Tuscaloosa, with carryout fish and chicken on the side, then listened to a game on the radio with his grandson Marc Tyson.

Bryant discovered how much the game meant to his players while reading the newspapers.

"In the fourth quarter, with Auburn leading us, we kept talking in the huddle," said Benny Perrin, a defensive halfback. "We kept saying, 'Hey, we have to have this one. This is number 315. Coach Bryant is counting on us.' It had been a heavy burden. The time had come to end it."

After the game Auburn coach Pat Dye met Bryant at midfield to shake hands. "I'm proud for you," he beamed.

"I'm proud of you," Bryant responded to Dye, one of his former assistant coaches at Alabama.

It was definitely a rich moment in college football, in more ways than one, according to former Alabama middle guard Warren Lyles. "I'd been poor all my life," said Lyles, "but I felt like somebody had given me a million dollars after that game. Make that two million. I was one of those seniors. You talk about a proud man. That was me that day.

It stands to reason the Cotton Bowl game against Texas was a bit anticlimactic for Alabama, although the Crimson Tide went to Dallas with an outside chance of winning another national championship. But those slim chances went up in smoke in the fourth quarter, when Texas scored all of its points to win the game in dramatic fashion. Clemson won the national championship, with former Alabama star lineman Danny Ford coaching.

Texas, 10-1-1, finished second in the nation, after improving its overall record against the Crimson Tide to a surprising 7-0-1.

Alabama finished seventh in the nation.

The team Texas defeated in the Cotton Bowl—in the process denying Alabama the chance to win its seventh bowl game in seven

Alabama and Texas at the Sugar Bowl.

years, which would have been a record—was playing with a short deck. Bryant had suspended four players, and linebacker Eddie Lowe suffered a knee injury just before the game.

It was a strange game of *ifs,* with Alabama dominating three quarters and Texas whipping the Crimson Tide in the fourth.

Alabama led 7–0 at halftime, after split end Jesse Bendross caught a six-yard touchdown pass from Lewis and Peter Kim kicked the extra point at the 8:49 mark of the second quarter.

That score remained until the fourth quarter, when Kim kicked a 24-yard field goal with 12:27 remaining to raise it to 10–0.

Then the Longhorns took charge.

Quarterback Robert Brewer stunned the crowd—plus Alabama—by running 30 yards on a draw play for a touchdown on a third-down, twelve-yards-to-go play with 10:22 remaining. He was untouched. After Raul Allegre kicked the extra point, the Crimson Tide lead was only 10–7.

With 2:05 remaining, Texas halfback Terry Orr ran eight yards into the end zone, with Allegre kicking an extra point that gave the Longhorns a stunning 14–10 lead.

But the excitement was only starting.

Alabama split end Joey Jones took the ensuing kickoff and ran 61 yards; he was tripped from behind to save a touchdown. "I don't know if I had the right," he said, "but I offered a prayer asking God to let me run it all the way."

Jones only got a Cotton Bowl kickoff return record.

With 1:54 remaining and the football at the Texas 38-yard line, the Crimson Tide tried a surprise pass on first down. Lewis tried to throw to split end Timmy Clark in the end zone, but safety William Graham intercepted for the Longhorns at the one-foot line. Running all alone on the pass play at the 15-yard line was Alabama halfback Joe Carter, whom the quarterback could not see because of a heavy rush.

"I've seen the greatest of pro quarterbacks throw to the wrong man," said Bryant after the game. "Walter Lewis is only a college sophomore."

Lewis was back in the spotlight after Texas took an intentional safety and kicked to Alabama with 48 seconds remaining. The Crimson Tide had the football at its 41-yard line, needing about 30 yards to give Kim a chance to save the game with a field goal.

Lewis was sacked on first down. He scrambled on the final play, trying to run for a touchdown instead of getting out of bounds to stop the clock for one last desperation pass.

Alabama was defeated.

"Texas dominated us in the fourth quarter," Bryant said in reflection. "They got stronger as the game went on. If the game had gone ten more minutes, I think they would have won by two touchdowns. Even at halftime I was concerned about us holding out. And, we blew a few opportunities."

Fleet-footed Joey Jones.

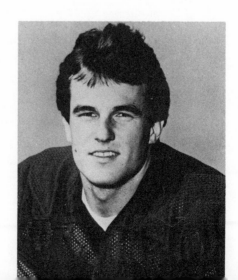

Powerful Ricky Moore.

One early opportunity came when Alabama quarterback Alan Gray fumbled on the first possession inside the Texas 10-yard line.

The Longhorns, on the other hand, converted six times on third down with at least ten yards to go for important first downs.

Even with the Texas offense producing when it had to, Alabama linebacker Robbie Jones was named defensive player of the game after making twelve tackles.

"That didn't make it an any less tough loss," Robbie Jones later reflected. "It was tough to swallow after all we'd gone through."

For Texas coach Fred Akers, it was a most memorable win. "I think it was the greatest win of my career," he said. "You couldn't have found a classier man than Bear Bryant or a classier program than Alabama. Coach Bryant had been my inspiration through the years."

Bryant was more than that to the members of the Cotton Bowl team selection committee. He was the reason, perhaps, Alabama, and not Southern Cal, was chosen to face Texas that year.

The Cotton Bowl took heat from critics because the Crimson Tide had played in Dallas the previous year.

"We were proud of our selection," said Field Scovell, the founding father of the Cotton Bowl. "We'll take our chances with Texas and Alabama any year. For class people, we could never improve on Alabama folks. And, of course, Texas and Alabama have great traditions. Any time you can get two teams with those type reputations, you'll have a good show many more times than not."

The Cotton Bowl did in 1982.

1982 Liberty Bowl Game

Alabama 21   Illinois 15

The famous tower on Thomas Field on the University of Alabama campus has been taken down, to the disgust of many Crimson Tide football fans. They viewed it as reverently as many graduates of The Capstone look upon Denny Chimes on The Quadrangle. It was from The Tower that Paul "Bear" Bryant coached Alabama football from 1958 through 1982.

Coach Ray Perkins had The Tower disassembled before spring practice started in 1983. He favored on-the-field observation.

That action, which did not endear Perkins to many Alabama supporters, makes December 21, 1982, an even more noteworthy date in the proud history of Crimson Tide football.

It was on that morning that Bryant climbed the steps leading to the top of The Tower for the last time. He went to the summit to watch his last Alabama team conclude on-campus preparations for the 1982 Liberty Bowl on December 29, his last game as leader of the Crimson Tide.

The victory over Illinois, 21–16, with the nation watching the end of an unparalleled coaching career, makes for happy remembrance.

The mood was less flamboyant as Bryant strolled from the practice field in Tuscaloosa for the last time, with a cool breeze blowing and his eyes glistening as he reflected on his days on campus.

"I couldn't help but think about it as I went up The Tower for the last time," Bryant said as he walked from the practice field. "It's been thirty-one years in one capacity or another on Alabama practice fields, either as a player or a coach. It's twenty-six bowl games in some capacity. That's a lot of time.

Quick and determined Jesse Bendross.

"Some of it has been good. Some of it has been bad. But I'll cherish every minute of it.

"I've been richly blessed."

Then, as was his practice during the holiday season, the sixty-nine-year-old man eight days away from his triumphant farewell game said, "Have a merry Christmas, gentlemen, and a nice next year."

Bryant took time that day to talk to his players.

"He told us at the last Tuscaloosa practice that he'd expected a lot of us prior to the season," said Russ Wood, a senior defensive end on a struggling team that took a 7–4 record into the Liberty Bowl. "He told us he'd let us down, that that was why he'd decided to retire, that it was up to us to play for ourselves in his last game.

"But we decided to play and win the Liberty Bowl for him. We had let him down, as well as ourselves, and it was our last chance to make up for it."

The countdown to glory had started. A standing ovation awaited Bryant after the victory in the Liberty Bowl.

The countdown to sadness also had started. Bryant, a man who had said, "I'll probably croak as soon as I quit coaching," and "If I had it my way, I'd die on the sideline during a game," died after

304

Defense Alabama style!

suffering a massive coronary on Jan. 26, 1983, less than a month after his last game. That prompted tributes to his greatness that were previously unheard of for a coach.

In many ways, the grief may never end for most Alabama fans.

In all ways, memories of the man will linger forever.

Most of the reflections are good, evidenced by his record as a coach: 323 wins in 38 seasons, 24 straight bowl games at Alabama.

At the Liberty Bowl coaches news conference.

It was an eventful final month for Paul William Bryant, no doubt about it, from a final win on the field to the ultimate victory in life.

The eve of the Liberty Bowl was reflective.

"I don't have any emotion whatsoever," Bryant said as the game against Illinois drew near. "I'll probably have a lot of emotion at this time next week when it's all over. But now it's just another game."

Illinois coach Mike White had a contrary view.

"I'm the other guy this week, right?" he said. "I think it's a great moment. This game, with the circumstances surrounding it, has turned into a national event. For me, it's an opportunity to be with Coach Bryant, an opportunity to shake his hand after the game, no matter what the outcome, and a chance to be close to history. In the locker room before practice yesterday, our players were peeking around the corner just to get a look at the great man. I didn't try to stop them. Coach Bryant is that special. He deserves such attention and respect."

The pregame talk in the Alabama dressing room was sobering.

"Coach Bryant started talking slowly, as he usually did, and much quieter than usual," said Jeremiah Castille, an Alabama defensive halfback who tied a Liberty Bowl record with three pass interceptions in that important game. "It didn't take long for us to realize he was emotional.

"Coach Bryant thanked us for our contributions to the season and to Alabama football. He told us to play the game for ourselves, particularly the seniors, that it was important that we gave our best at all times. He told us how much he'd remember the game in future years, how we'd all be special to him because we were the players on his last team. He told us to win for ourselves, not for him, that we'd be remembered more because of that game. He apologized because his last game had put so much pressure on us. He told us to play in a way that'd bring credit to ourselves and to Alabama. He said, win or lose, that was the only way we'd leave that night without having regrets.

"Coach Bryant broke down a few times while talking to us that night. He'd say a few words, then his voice would crack a little when tears came to his eyes. It was a time with him that none of us will forget. I'm proud to have been one of those players in that dressing room."

The pregame warmups were watched by a multitude of news media representatives.

"I'm freezing to death," Bryant said as he leaned on a goal post for a final time on a night when the chill factor was eight degrees. The coach was reminded that he had once said after a frigid practice in Tuscaloosa, "Coldness is in the mind."

He smiled and answered, "Well, that's a bunch of bull as far as I can tell right now."

Then came his infectious grin.

Lights flashed and cameras clicked as his steps were recorded for history. Alabama fans shouted such words as "We love you, Bear, go out as a winner," and Illinois fans, who admitted to having mixed emotions about victory and defeat on this night, kept their eyes on the rival coach.

The game was a hard-hitting affair as an Alabama defense played the Bryant way while protecting an end zone assaulted many times by the Illini.

Alabama surrendered 423 yards passing to Illinois, which had standout quarterback Tony Eason. But the Crimson Tide intercepted seven passes and knocked the rival quarterback out of action three times with crunching tackles.

"Alabama just likes to hit hard, that's all," said Eason. "That's obvious to me and everybody else. It was the hardest-hitting game I've ever been in."

Walter Lewis hands off to Ricky Moore.

In the closely contested game, Alabama kept making crucial plays to protect the honor of its departing coach.

The first "big play" came when defensive tackle Randy Edward blocked an Illinois field goal attempt.

The Alabama offense followed with a two-yard touchdown run by fullback Ricky Moore in the first quarter. Peter Kim kicked the extra point. Quarterback Walter Lewis had passed 50 yards to split end Joey Jones to set up the score.

Illinois, which drove inside the Alabama 25-yard line five times during the first half, got to within a point, 7–6, when halfback Joe Curtis ran two yards for a touchdown in the second quarter.

In the third quarter the Crimson Tide got an eight-yard touchdown run on a reverse play from split end Jesse Bendross. Kim kicked the extra point to push the score to 14–6 going into the fourth quarter.

The Illini bounced back early in the fourth quarter behind Eason, who led his team on a thirteen-play scoring drive that culminated with a two-yard pass to split end Oliver Williams. A pass for the two-point conversion was incomplete, with Castille breaking it up, leaving Alabama with a 14–12 lead.

The Crimson Tide took the ensuing kickoff and drove for a two-yard touchdown run by fullback Craig Turner. Kim kicked the extra point to extend the Alabama lead to 21–12.

Mike Bass kicked a 23-yard field goal for Illinois to fix the final margin of victory for the Crimson Tide. Illinois had two more serious scoring threats in the fourth quarter that went for naught.

"I'm sure our defensive effort in the last quarter pleased Coach Bryant until his death," said Jackie Cline, a Crimson Tide defensive tackle that memorable season. "He seemed pleased when we gave him the game ball. It was more like giving him a trophy than anything else. He cried."

Bryant worked hard until the end, almost constantly screaming encouragement to his frantic team, often chastising assistant coaches when plays failed. Then it was over, and he was hoisted to the shoulders of his players as a mob scene developed on the playing field. The scoreboard flashed a message: "Thanks For The Memories!"

"It was great listening to Coach Bryant talk to us as we rode

Craig Turner driving for hard-earned yardage.

him on our shoulders to the trophy presentation," said Wood. "It was a happy time. It was an exciting time. It was sort of a sad time. Probably the most vivid thing that stood out was when Coach Bryant shook my hand in the dressing room after the game. He had tears in his eyes."

The postgame press conference, which was conducted under a huge tent outside the stadium, was sentimental. Many of the 54,123 fans who watched the game, a Liberty Bowl record, stayed for a final look at the coach.

"I'm thankful to have won my final game," Bryant said at the start of his press conference. "I'm proud of the state of Alabama, the team, the media and those people who support our program.

"I've been fortunate to have been associated with top-notch people throughout my career. I've been fortunate in that those people have reached most of the goals we've set throughout the years.

"I'm tremendously proud of the team for winning. I told our players before the game that, whether they liked it or not or I liked it or not, people would always remember them for what they did in this game. I'm flattered they responded like they did. I think they wanted it for themselves and for me.

"I have looked at the last roundup forever, too, and this'll make my memories of it a lot more pleasant. I thought about that several times during the fourth quarter. A loss wouldn't have been so pleasant at this final stage in my coaching career.

"Again, I'm so appreciative of my players and assistant coaches."

Robbie Jones, an Alabama linebacker that year, knew Bryant was sincere when he said that. "We didn't want to win for The Gipper, as Notre Dame once did," he said while expressing the players' point of view, "but we sure wanted to win one for The Bear."

The final month of Bryant's life was hectic.

Bryant returned to Tuscaloosa after the Liberty Bowl and began making preparations for the arrival of Ray Perkins as his successor. Privately, he said he planned to remain as athletic director for "maybe six months, no more than a year" before "getting out of the way."

The retired coach continued recruiting prospects for Alabama. He mixed that grind with pleasure, which included taking a trip by automobile to visit longtime friends and relatives in Fordyce, Arkansas, his hometown.

His health, meanwhile, was deteriorating. "I'd like to be young again, like fifty instead of seventy, but that's not gonna happen,"

310

Bryant said privately. He made frequent visits to his doctor. Quietly, after experiencing discomfort in his chest, he checked into Druid City Hospital in Tuscaloosa.

At 12:24 p.m. on January 26, Bryant was struck with a massive coronary, after resting comfortably the previous evening. After sixty-six minutes of extraordinary medical procedures, he was dead.

Current Alabama players were told about his death as they worked out in a weight room at Memorial Coliseum. More than a few of them dropped to their knees upon hearing the sad news. There were a lot of tears.

An entire nation, former friends and former rivals alike, mourned the death of a coach who had become a legend in his time.

Associated Press began combing the country for reaction to the death of Bryant, who posted a 323–85–17 record, in the process leaving little doubt about his greatness.

The top on the story read:

"A hero who always seemed larger than life. Bigger than the game itself. A man's man. A monumental figure in intercollegiate athletics. The best that's ever been. A master coach.

"The tributes poured in Wednesday, each seemingly more glowing than the last one, as the stunned world of college football tried to find the proper words to pay tribute to Paul "Bear" Bryant, who died of a massive heart attack at the age of 69.

"But in the final analysis, Bryant was simply a football coach. And, one after another, his adulators kept coming back to the same phrase, the greatest football coach of all time."

Among the first people to react to the death was President Ronald Reagan. He telephoned Mary Harmon Bryant on the evening after her husband's death to offer condolences to the charming widow. Then he issued a statement: "Bryant made legends out of ordinary people. He was a hard but loved taskmaster. He was patriotic to the core. He was devoted to his players. He was inspired by a winning spirit that would not quit. Bear Bryant gave his country the gift of life unsurpassed. In making the impossible seem easy, he lived what we all strive to be."

But much more was said.

From former Ohio State coach Woody Hayes: "He was a winner. He was honorable. He won with clean clubs. His kids played great football. He was an enormously fine winner."

From Alabama President Dr. Joab Thomas: "He was a great teacher. He was a great man. He was more than a great football coach."

Graveside at Elmwood Cemetery.

From Mayor Tom Wynne III of Fordyce, Arkansas: "The notoriety Bryant brought to our city, we couldn't buy that with a city budget."

From former Alabama player and Miami Dolphins defensive halfback Don McNeal: "Coach Bryant was like a father to me."

From former Alabama player and Duke coach Steve Sloan: "He was like a godfather to everybody in coaching. The saddest thing about it is he was looking forward to spending some time playing golf, hunting and fishing. He never got to enjoy his retirement."

From Oklahoma coach Barry Switzer: "He was bigger than the game itself. I doubt anybody will ever approach his record in terms of total impact on the game."

From former Alabama player and New York Jets defensive tackle Marty Lyons: "I just hope and pray he will be rewarded properly for all the things he has done for people, not just for football."

From former Alabama assistant coach and Auburn coach Pat Dye: "His presence made the world a better place in which to live. His teaching will last forever in the lives of those he touched."

From Michigan coach Bo Schembechler: "College football has lost its greatest coach and friend."

From former Nebraska coach and Nebraska athletic director Bob Devaney: "In my opinion, college football has lost its greatest coach of all time."

From former Alabama player and Clemson coach Danny Ford: "He will be missed by so many people because he helped so many people. That was his main goal in life. He related football to life. He taught all of his former players so much about life. He reached so many of us. Everybody who was under his teachings came out a better person. When you think about the thousands of people who wore his colors, Alabama red, it is not hard to determine this world is a little bit better because of Coach Bryant."

From former United States President Gerald Ford: "I am terribly saddened by the passing of an old and dear friend. Bryant was a superstar in the history of American football."

From Penn State coach Joe Paterno: "His death is almost impossible to believe. Coach Bryant appeared to be indestructible."

The nation had lost a hero. The state of Alabama had lost its most famous adopted son. The University of Alabama had lost some of its magic.

That is why the masses turned out the day he was buried in Birmingham. About 30,000 mourners were in the immediate vicinity of First United Methodist Church in Tuscaloosa when his funeral was held. About 40,000 mourners were in the immediate vicinity of Elmwood Cemetery when he was buried. Alabama State Troopers estimated that including mourners who lined city streets and an interstate highway to pay homage to him as the funeral processional passed on that unseasonably warm day, about 650,000 people paid their respects to him.

More than that shed tears.

A winner was gone.

The first victory came on September 28 in 1945.

The 100th victory came on November 7 in 1959.

The 200th victory came on September 10 in 1971.

The 300th victory came on October 5 in 1980.

The historic 315th victory came on November 28 in 1981.

The last victory came on December 29 in 1982.

Vivid is the memory of what Paul "Bear" Bryant said to a throng of admiring Crimson Tide fans as he departed his final press conference.

One of the admirers said, "We love you, Bear. And thank you."

Bryant doffed his famous houndstooth hat, grinned at the fans and said, "Ya'll keep cheering for Alabama, you hear?"

1983 Sun Bowl Game

Alabama 28   SMU 7

Bobby Collins lit the fuse that ignited a University of Alabama explosion in the 1983 Sun Bowl. The Southern Methodist coach, who was miffed because his nationally fifth-ranked team did not receive an invitation to play in a major bowl game, was outspoken in early December.

"It'd be easy to say this is the way it is and go on about our business," Collins said, "but I'm not gonna do it that way."

Collins was mad because his 10–1 team was bypassed by major bowl games because of a fear that SMU fans would not attend such a game in large numbers. That situation developed after the Mustangs lost 15–12 to Texas in an October game that ultimately deprived them of a Southwest Conference championship and a berth in the Cotton Bowl.

"We're going to the Sun Bowl and have a great time, but some of the things I spoke out against I'll continue to pursue," Collins said about a week before the Sun Bowl game against Alabama. "We deserve to be in a New Year's Day bowl game. You can slice it any way you want.

"We've got a saying at SMU that we'll have to prove ourselves one more time. That's what we'll do in the Sun Bowl against Alabama."

Collins and most of the remainder of the world of college football got surprised when the Crimson Tide, completing an 8–4 season, defeated SMU, 28–7, on a frigid afternoon on which Alabama had a hot hand.

Interestingly, the people of El Paso turned their backs on a Texas-based team to enthusiastically support the Crimson Tide.

"The whole town became Alabama fans," said Crimson Tide

coach Ray Perkins, who was completing his first season after replac-
ing legendary Paul "Bear" Bryant. "It's safe to say the fan support
got us off to a fast start. The emotional aspects of SMU not really
wanting to be there to play us also seemed to help our players.

"I'm not so sure SMU didn't deserve a better bowl game invitation with all the talent they had at the time."

That would appear to be the case.

But the Mustangs were no match for highly motivated Alabama
in the fiftieth renewal of the Sun Bowl when the chill factor dropped
the temperature to six degrees. No sooner had the cheers that greeted
the arrival of the Crimson Tide on the playing field subsided than the
victors began an awesome display.

It was 28–0 by halftime.

It is doubtful Collins said anything critical about bowl game
team selection committees during the halftime break. He was working too hard on his defense after Alabama quarterback Walter Lewis
led the Crimson Tide to four touchdowns and four extra points on its
first six possessions.

Wes Neighbors congratulating Ricky Moore.

Walter Lewis calling signals.

The victory enabled Alabama to tie Southern Cal for the most bowl victories in history, with twenty. It also raised the overall post-season record for the Crimson Tide to 20–14–3.

"I thought our players were absolutely great against a fine SMU team," Perkins said. "The defense did a super job. Walter Lewis did a fantastic job directing the offense in the first half.

"Before the game, somebody asked me if Walter had to have a good game in order for us to have a chance to win. I told them he would have a good game. He was back in mid-season form."

Lewis, a senior who was wrapping up his career as the all-time total offense leader in the history of a tradition-rich program, was named winner of the C. M. Hendricks most valuable player award. Wes Neighbors, a freshman center, was named winner of the Chuck Hughes most valuable lineman award after manhandling heralded SMU middle guard Michael Carter.

"I'd read a story in El Paso in which Carter said he was gonna shotput me out of the end zone," Neighbors said.

317

Curt Jarvis, All-SEC nose guard.

"Wes told me he felt great before the game," said Billy Neighbors, a proud father and former All-American tackle on the 1961 national championship team from Alabama. "But he was worried before the game that Carter would win the award for a good performance Wes got."

Actually, there was good reason for everybody from Alabama to be more than a little concerned entering the game. SMU had the second best defense in the nation, having allowed only 9.9 points per game, as well as only four rushing touchdowns during the season.

Alabama got 28 points in a half. The Crimson Tide scored three of its touchdowns on the ground.

Alabama drove 59 yards in seven plays on its second possession. Fullback Ricky Moore, who had 113 yards rushing in the game, scored on a one-yard run.

The Crimson Tide defense helped Alabama to its second touchdown. Safety Sammy Hood recovered a fumble by SMU quarterback Lancy McIlhenny. Three plays later, after a 54-yard drive, Moore scored his second touchdown on an 11-yard run.

Alabama drove 91 yards in fifteen plays for its third touch-down, taking six minutes, with Lewis scoring on a one-yard run. The quarterback completed three passes for 33 yards on the march.

The Crimson Tide defense struck again as the Mustangs attempted to get back into the game. Safety Freddie Robinson intercepted a pass at the Alabama 38-yard line. Lewis moved the offense 62 yards in four plays, completing a 19-yard pass to split end Joey Jones for the touchdown, and freshman placekicker Van Tiffin added his four extra points for an astonishing 28–0 lead.

Alabama had 303 yards offense in the first half. SMU had two first downs the first 25 minutes.

"Once we got ahead like that, the crowd really got behind us, which only added to the enjoyment," said Perkins.

A somewhat helpless Collins watched in disbelief. "Give Alabama credit," he said after the game. "They played extremely well. I was particularly impressed with Lewis. What a tremendous talent he is."

Lewis preferred to compliment his teammates when looking back on an enjoyable afternoon. "It was just a great team effort," he said. "We decided to finish up the season on a high note so that the guys coming back would have something to look forward to. Everybody seemed to execute at a high efficiency level. It was our best game of the season."

That was understandable.

Alabama, laboring through a coaching transition, had an up-and-down season in 1983. It started impressively, with four consecutive victories, then took a dip with back-to-back heartbreaking defeats. A highly publicized and most questionable call by an official deprived the rallying Crimson Tide of a touchdown late in a 34–28 loss at Penn State. That was followed by an exciting loss to Tennessee, 41–34, in Birmingham. Following three consecutive victories came back-to-back losses at Boston College, 20–13, and to Auburn, 23–20, on national television.

"Nobody really beat us except ourselves," said Randy Edwards, a defensive tackle at Alabama in 1983. "It breaks my heart that we didn't play all season like we did against SMU. You could see in their eyes that we'd whipped them good."

The Sun Bowl victory, and the closeness of every defeat during the regular season, indicate it was an Alabama team that jelled too late. "I'm positive the victory over SMU in the Sun Bowl was good for us," said Perkins, "but I'm still disappointed in that 8–4 record."

The Sun Bowl match became a reality after Perkins campaigned hard to get Alabama a berth in the Fiesta Bowl. It prompted some laughter among national observers, although the Mustangs were only favored by four points.

SMU had two super running backs, Reggie Dupard and Jeff Atkins, who had combined for 2,186 yards and sixteen touchdowns after Eric Dickerson and Craig James had led the Mustangs similarly in previous years. They were expected to run through what had at times been a porous Crimson Tide defense. Neither player scored or was much of a factor in the game.

The matchup featuring two quarterbacks of little national note, Lewis against McIlhenny, drew a lot of attention.

Steve Johnson of *The Decatur Daily* looked at Lewis:

"As far as numbers go, Walter Lewis is a perfect 10. He has them all beat: Bart Starr, Joe Namath, Kenny Stabler, Steve Sloan, Scott Hunter, Jeff Rutledge, Richard Todd, the best of a long line of Alabama quarterbacks.

"Statistics make him second to none going into the Sun Bowl. He passed them all becoming Alabama's all-time offensive leader with 5,690 yards, more than three miles.

"'Stabler and Namath and some of those other quarterbacks have done something I wasn't able to do,' said Lewis. 'They won national championships. They were able to attain something I didn't. I'll have to live with that.'"

But Lewis's passing against SMU was strong, with nine completions in fourteen attempts for 148 yards.

"I wish we had Walter Lewis a couple more years," Perkins said after the most valuable player performance.

The middle guard on that Alabama team was freshman Curt Jarvis. He noticed the SMU players complaining and the El Paso fans cheering the Crimson Tide.

"We looked at it like they (SMU players) didn't respect us much," Jarvis said. "They did a lot of moaning and groaning, that much I know, as if they thought they should be matched against a better team in a bigger bowl. We took the game a lot more serious after they started all that talk. It motivated us in an important way.

"Then hearing the fans cheering us like that was definitely a key to our performance. We wanted to play well for them. We didn't want the Sun Bowl people and the fans out there to think they had a bad team on their hands. I think we proved that."

The Mustangs might not have wanted to be in El Paso on that day, but Richard "Daddy Wags" Wagner did.

Wagner was an outside linebacker at Alabama in 1983 who had

Making decisions on the sideline.

a unique problem. He had to tell his wife she could not go to the Sun
Bowl because their eight-year-old son could not stay with anybody.
"Neither my wife nor my son got to go," said Wagner, who in 1983
was still playing college football at thirty years of age.

Wagner entered college eight years after graduating from high
school in Fort Payne, Alabama, where he played as a 6-foot-2, 140-
pounder. "I wanted to play college football," said Wagner, who completed his career in the Sun Bowl. "But I didn't have the size."

"I thought I'd make the military a career," Wagner said.
"About two years before my six-year hitch was over, I was stationed

in Las Vegas, where I started going to the weight room. I weighed 165 pounds then. Four months later, I was up to 215."

Wagner started watching more football on television. He walked on at Alabama in 1979 but was cut from the squad. He was told his age and an eight-year layoff were the reasons. He walked on again in 1980 and made the team.

Wagner played in one varsity game in 1982. He played in four varsity games, plus the Sun Bowl, in 1983.

"Daddy Wags" was wrapping up his career at Alabama.

Perkins had just started his. It had been a season of triumph and disappointment. It ended on a high note after some low days.

"It wasn't that hard for us to put the losses to Boston College and Auburn out of our minds," said Jarvis. "You can't worry about this and that all the time. We put it behind and thought about things we could control. Those losses were there. We couldn't change that. But we sure could do something about ending the year on a positive note.

"That's another difference in our approach to the Sun Bowl and the one used by SMU. We went out there to take care of our business first, then to have a good time. Their players didn't even want to be there. We wanted to win. They didn't really care. That showed on the field."

What happened off the field is left to the imagination. Jarvis nor anybody else wanted to talk much about what happened at night in El Paso or over the Mexican border in Juarez. "I'm afraid my grandmother might read what I say," Jarvis said with a laugh.

So remembering the Sun Bowl was pleasant for Alabama players, even four years later, and the first season for Perkins was eventful.

"It's been an interesting year," Perkins said a few days after the Sun Bowl. "It's been an educational year. It's been a learning process.

"I'm disappointed with the record. But I think we made a lot of progress. I think we'll make a lot more progress in the near future with a group of young players to work with. I believe in setting high goals and going after them. I've always been that way. I don't intend to change."

That last statement by Perkins is the reason he was so disappointed with what happened to Alabama in 1984.

The record was 5–6. That was Alabama's first losing season since 1957. There was no bowl invitation awaiting the Crimson Tide, the first time that had happened since 1959.

1985 Aloha Bowl Game

Alabama 24   **Southern Cal 3**

There was almost a disaster at the start.

There was almost a disaster at the end.

In between, the University of Alabama claimed a 24–3 victory over Southern Cal in an Aloha Bowl played between two of the tradition-rich programs in the sport.

Middle guard Curt Jarvis, then a junior with all-star credentials, recalls the landing the Crimson Tide made in Honolulu. "We landed so hard part of the ceiling came out of the plane," Jarvis said. "It was bumpy as the devil. It scared me out of my mind.

"People were hollering. I was about in tears myself. Then the woman came on the public address system and said, 'Welcome to Hawaii.' Wow! We had bottomed out. I thought I was dead. I saw that water. I was looking for a way out, I just knew we would sink and never be heard from again. That plane was going all over the place. That was as scared as I have been in my life. I really did think we were dead."

The scene on the Alabama plane as the Crimson Tide left Hawaii was more amusing, at least to Jarvis, although there was an injured player on board. On the night after the victory, which was secured on December 29, two Alabama players, center Wes Neighbors and offensive tackle Gary Otten, decided to body surf in unforgiving waters.

They left the Waikiki Beach motel, went past Diamond Head, and stopped on the North Shore, where the waves are made for championship surfing with a board. In fact, a sign read, "Danger: No Surfing." But Neighbors and Otten went into the water.

It took only one wave to dampen their spirits. Neighbors was knocked upside down by the force, but Otten got the worst of it. He was picked up and driven into the sand. He suffered a bruised spine, a strained neck, a black eye, and numerous cuts.

Playing against Southern Cal had not been as tough as that.

"That's the best of the memories from the Aloha Bowl, 'Ooter' trying to body surf," Jarvis said. "He and Wes went into the water over where they have the national surfing championships. In fact, they'd cancelled all surfing there that day because the waves were too bad.

"So 'Big Wes' and 'Ooter' decided they're gonna body surf in thirty-foot waves. Wes gave it a try and got out of there. 'Ooter' said he'd give it a go.

"Those waves pulled all the water out from under him. That's how they do over there. Those waves formed hands and grabbed 'Ooter.' Then they just dumped him down into the sand. He hit hard, too, real hard. He just shot down into the ground like a bullet fired from a gun.

Another serious moment occurred at halftime, when the Crimson Tide and the Trojans went to the dressing room tied 3–3.

"Yeah, it was an interesting halftime chat, to say the least," said Jarvis. "Coach Perkins threatened us within an inch of our lives after the way we played the first half. He said, 'I don't know what's wrong with you. I don't know if you went out and partied too much or what. But if you don't play better in the second half, you won't live through offseason workouts.'

"We knew what he meant. He was mad. We'd played like dogs out there."

Linebacker Joe Godwin put it another way as he looked back on the game.

"I think we might have been wrapped up in the atmosphere of Hawaii," Godwin said. "The coaches realized that. They got our attitudes straightened out. Coach Perkins said we better get our act straight. He told us if we didn't, the underclassmen would go through the toughest offseason in history at Alabama. He told us we were too good to sit down just because the last game of the season had come."

Those reactions came from defensive players after they had shut down Southern Cal.

The offense was struggling even more, thanks to a lot of penalties that stopped potential drives.

"It wasn't pretty in that dressing room," said Neighbors. "We just sat there and waited for the explosion."

But it led to something beautiful in the eyes of Perkins, who

324

Gene Jelks with another slick move.

All-star Wes Neighbors celebrating victory.

denied he was that tough on his players during halftime. "We didn't tell our players much at halftime," he said. "The players just responded well and did the things they were told to do.

"Basically, we told them they would win the game if they did two things, play smart and play physical. It was the worst first half I'd seen for a team to play so great in the second half."

Van Tiffin had scored the first three points for Alabama with a 48-yard field goal in the first quarter. Southern Cal had tied it with a 24-yard field goal in the second quarter.

Alabama scored one touchdown in the third quarter, then two in the fourth quarter.

Fullback Craig Turner scored on a one-yard run in the third quarter. He did so at the end of a 42-yard drive. Tiffin kicked the extra point.

The Crimson Tide gained 115 yards to 20 for the Trojans during that 15-minute period.

The game became a blowout of sorts in the fourth quarter, when quarterback Mike Shula passed 24 yards to tight end Clay Whitehurst for a touchdown, split end Al Bell ran 14 yards for a touchdown on a reverse, and Tiffin kicked two more extra points. The pass to Whitehurst came on third down, with one yard to go for a first down. The Trojans were definitely caught off-balance.

Bell, a Los Angeles native playing against a team from that city, picked up a convoy of blockers on his touchdown run. Southern Cal had little chance to stop him.

The victory meant a lot to Alabama players for two reasons. First, Southern Cal has such a tradition of greatness. Second, the last time the two powers had met, in 1978, the Trojans won, 24–14, and split the national championship with the Crimson Tide.

That·Alabama had an encouraging 8–2–1 record and Southern Cal had a dismal 6–5 record did not take any luster away from the game.

"I remember Charles White showing up in Birmingham and running through us," Godwin said. "I was an Alabama fan then, but I remembered it when we learned we'd be playing them in Hawaii. It was sort of a revenge factor in the Aloha Bowl.

"USC is such a football powerhouse. Alabama is, too. I knew if we could beat them it'd mean a lot to our program. We knew USC would be a good opponent, even with a 6–5 record. That was a major consideration when the team voted to go to the Aloha Bowl. We knew it'd be hard to get into a good football atmosphere in Hawaii. We knew it'd be easier against a name team."

So Alabama had on a game face while in Hawaii, at least partly.

"It's a big island with a lot to do," said Jarvis, "good stuff and bad stuff. We worked hard during the morning and afternoon, starting early and working sort of late. Then, we'd watch the sky and wait for sundown. All the cats came out at night."

Godwin liked the daylight "because there's some good bikini watching to be had in Hawaii. We stayed on the beaches a lot, naturally. It was some kind of unbelievable experience for a country boy

Albert Bell on the loose.

from Alabama. I liked the beautiful environment. It was sort of like I was on a sightseeing trip."

Jarvis admits some of players saw sights different from the ones discussed by Godwin. For instance, the third time was a charm for a bouncer at one nightclub.

"I'd never tell you names, but some of us got out and about pretty good," Jarvis said. "The funniest thing, I guess, was one of my friends dancing on a stage in this out-of-the-way establishment with a couple of people we'd met. He was trying to take off his clothes, too, and the bouncer threw us out of there.

"They told us not to show up again, but we went back the next day for a wet T-shirt contest. My friend did the soaking, a face and all, and we got pitched out of there again.

"The bouncer told us to never, never show up there again.

"We went back the next night. This time he remembered us. We didn't get in, for sure.

"I forget the name of the place. It was something like The Paradise Club, a strip joint."

The eyes wandered, perhaps, but the heart stayed focused on Southern Cal. "That's obvious," said Jarvis. "Teams like Notre Dame and Southern Cal, they're big business."

Yes.

Southern Cal could be dubbed "Tailback U." The Heisman Trophy has gone to more than a few such Trojans.

But it was an Alabama tailback that stole the spotlight in the Aloha Bowl. Gene Jelks was named most outstanding offensive player after running for 79 yards on seventeen carries. Another Crimson Tide player, Bobby Humphrey, had 55 yards on fourteen carries.

Interestingly, Southern Cal tailbacks managed only 44 yards on 19 carries. That might explain why Alabama outside linebacker Cornelius Bennett won most outstanding defensive player honors.

Unbelievably, much of the crowd at the game liked that, even though Alabama had to fly across the nation to get to Hawaii, over Los Angeles in the process.

"Coach Perkins had told us we might face a pro-USC crowd in Hawaii, because that is about as far west as a person can go," Jarvis said. "When he said that, I looked at Wes Neighbors, winked, and said, 'All he has to do is give us an hour on the beach and we'll have all the fans we need.'"

1986 Sun Bowl Game

Alabama 28   Washington 6

On Christmas Day, 1986, the University of Alabama football team proved there is sunlight at the end of a dark tunnel. The Crimson Tide had lost three games along the way to the Sun Bowl, plus two teammates who died prior to the season; but it was not to be denied a happy conclusion when it played the University of Washington in El Paso.

Coach Ray Perkins called the 28–6 victory "another challenge accepted and met by an incredible group of young men."

"It was a great victory," he said. "Even though it wasn't for a national championship, it was for pride. Our guys just made up their minds they were going to win this one. I had changed my philosophy about the bowl game this year. In the past we always said our goal was to win the game first and to have fun second. This time I told them to have fun first, and then see about winning the game."

That attitude summed up the situation in grand fashion.

Alabama players capped their 10–3 season while wearing black decals on the back of their helmets in memory of George Scruggs and Willie Ryles, teammates who died earlier in the year. Scruggs, a freshman running back, was killed in an automobile accident in April; and Ryles, a sophomore defensive tackle, died after collapsing during preseason practice during August.

At the start of its longest season in history, the Crimson Tide defeated Ohio State 16–10 in the Kickoff Classic in late August, then flew to Ryles' funeral from East Rutherford, New Jersey, before returning to campus.

"It's been a tough season," explained Joe Godwin, a senior linebacker. "There's no way to express the sorrow we felt after losing two teammates like we did. This team has had a lot of pressure on it

329

Curt Jarvis and Ray Perkins.

throughout the season. That's why it's so nice to end on such a positive note."

Adding to the pressure was the expectation among Crimson Tide fans that the team would win a national championship. For a while it appeared Alabama was up to that challenge. Then came Penn State on a schedule that ranked as one of the toughest in the nation.

Alabama was 7–0 and was ranked second in the nation when it lost to the Nittany Lions, 23–3, in a game played in Tuscaloosa. There had been victories over such powerhouse teams as Ohio State, Florida, Notre Dame, and Tennessee.

The victory over Notre Dame was the first in the history of the Alabama program. The Crimson Tide had suffered four dramatic losses to the Fighting Irish previously, and the victory over Tennessee was the first since 1981, following four straight defeats on the treasured third Saturday in October.

"There never was a break in the emotion," said Curt Jarvis, a senior middle guard. "It was big game after big game for us. It became difficult to get up week after week. So Penn State just manhandled us. I have never felt so defeated after a game. It was thorough. They whipped us. There was no doubt about it.

"We had won, and won against quality teams. Maybe we just got tired. All I know is the Sun Bowl victory was the first since the win over Tennessee in October that we could really be proud of. I think we just lost our edge along the way."

That is understandable. It looked that way to Alabama fans as the season came down the stretch. The Crimson Tide lost to Louisiana State, 14–10, and to Auburn, 21–17, with the Sugar Bowl-bound Bengal Tigers taking advantage of numerous breaks and the intrastate Tigers scoring the decisive touchdown in the final minute.

"We beat ourselves in those games," Jarvis said. "Nobody will ever convince me otherwise."

So it was a drained and crestfallen Alabama team that went to El Paso to play Washington, which had an 8–2–1 record. Washington coach Don James said it was "perhaps the finest team" he had fielded in his twelve seasons at the Pacific-10 Conference runnerup.

But Alabama treated them with no respect on the field.

That is why a national television audience saw a multitude of smiling fans on the Alabama sideline during the final minutes of the game. One of them belonged to senior linebacker Cornelius Bennett, who was selected the Most Oustanding Player in the game. He looked into a camera and said, "Mom, I'll be home for Christmas in about five hours. I want a big plate of everything."

Bennett, who won the Lombardi Award as the top collegiate lineman in the country, had already feasted on Washington quarterback Chris Chandler. The Crimson Tide star disrupted the Huskies'

Cornelius Bennett in another dominating performance.

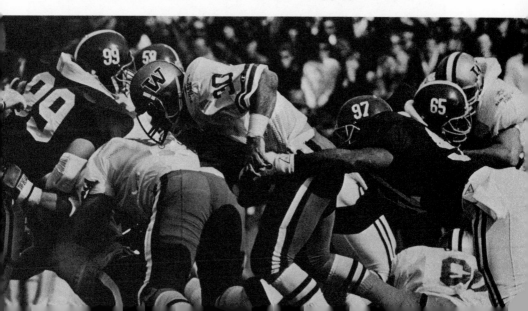

offense all afternoon, picking up twelve tackles and creating havoc on the other side of the line. Washington gained only 68 yards rushing. Chandler, who had passed for twenty touchdowns during the regular season, completed only 20 of 43 passes for 199 yards.

"That's the most pressure I've ever faced," said Chandler. "Bennett was in my face the whole day. When it wasn't him, it was one of the others. I'll be the first to admit that I didn't have a lot of pressure on me during the regular season. I didn't respond to it too well."

Chandler was frustrated.

Bennett was beaming.

"It's great to end my career as a most valuable player," said Bennett. "It's a great feeling. We wanted the Sun Bowl championship. We set our goals to win it. It's something all of us can look back on and feel extremely good."

The Crimson Tide got its offense rolling in the second half, after leading only 7–6 at halftime. The offensive stars of the game clearly were sophomore halfback Bobby Humphrey and Shula.

Humphrey scored three touchdowns against a defense that had allowed an average of two per game during the regular season. He rushed for 159 yards on 28 attempts against a defense that allowed 89 per game during the season. And he did all of this while fighting influenza.

Bobby Humphrey breaking free for a long touchdown.

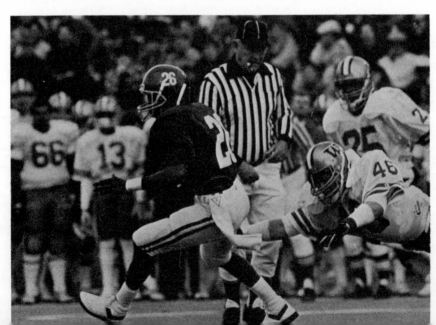

Humphrey scored his touchdowns on a 64-yard run with 13:45 remaining in the second quarter, breaking a scoreless duel, a 17-yard pass from Shula with :13 remaining in the third quarter, and a three-yard run with 7:16 remaining in the fourth quarter.

The other Alabama touchdown came on a 32-yard pass from Shula to senior split end Greg Richardson with 6:24 remaining in the third quarter, which is when the Crimson Tide started to dominate the game.

Van Tiffin kicked four extra points for Alabama, ending his career with 139 straight without a miss, a national record.

The scoring outburst came against a Washington team that ranked fifteenth nationally, allowing only 15.4 points per game.

Washington scored its points on field goals by Jeff Jaeger. He made one from 31 yards with 5:55 remaining in the second quarter, and he made the other from 34 yards with :38 remaining in the second quarter. That pushed his total for the season to 19 field goals in 23 attempts. He scored a national record 100 points for the Huskies.

"There were times when we couldn't do anything on offense because of their defense," Coach James said in reflection. "We didn't have time to do anything."

Washington's offensive line was larger than the line of some professional teams, averaging almost 270 pounds per man.

"Size is a myth," said James. "Speed and quickness is the name of the game."

Alabama defensive coordinator Joe Kines agreed. "Speed won't always beat size, but it's hard for them to hit you if they can't catch you."

And while Washington toppled, Humphrey rolled. He capped a brilliant sophomore season in the Sun Bowl. He had three games in which he rushed for 200 yards or more, and in eight games he rushed for 100 yards or more. He had 1,471 yards rushing during the regular season, a school record, and he scored 17 touchdowns during the regular season, also a school record. Coach Perkins dubbed him, "The best running back I've been around, including those I saw in the National Football League."

Will there be a Heisman Trophy push on behalf of the running back in 1987?

"We might do that," Perkins asnwered.

"I wouldn't complain," Humphrey said.

Neither did Don Shula, father of Mike Shula and coach of the Miami Dolphins, complain. It was the first time he had been at a game in which his son played since high school. "It's emotional," he

333

said from the stands. "I'm thinking about things I'd do if I was coaching in this game. But there's nothing I can do, except sit and watch. I'm proud of what Mike has accomplished at Alabama."

Don Shula spoke those words during the first half when son Mike and the Alabama offense was struggling. In the second half Mike was sharp enough to earn the Most Outstanding Back award, finishing with 15 completions in 26 attempts for 188 yards.

"Shula displayed tremendous poise," said Parseghian.

"If I was a NFL team looking to draft a backup quarterback, I'd take a close look at Mike Shula," said Brent Musburger, who handled play-by-play announcing duties for CBS-TV. "He has the pedigree, if nothing else. He didn't become rattled against a fine Washington defense."

The same can be said about the Alabama offense in general, especially after it was limited to 141 yards during the first half. The second half was a different story, with the Crimson Tide driving 47, 83, and 92 yards for its touchdowns. This made it the second consecutive bowl game in which the Crimson Tide looked impressive in the second half.

Mike Shula directing the assault.

Van Tiffin, a perfect 139 for 139 points after touchdown.

Perkins termed the display in El Paso "the best Christmas present anybody could receive." It pushed his bowl record in four seasons at Alabama to 3–0, and it was the tenth bowl game victory for Alabama in its most recent eleven postseason appearances.

The victory came amid strong speculation that Perkins was leaving the Crimson Tide to become coach of the Tampa Bay Buccaneers of the NFL. For almost a month before the game, the rumor mill said Tampa owner Hugh Culverhouse, an Alabama graduate, would offer the job to Perkins. Two days before the Sun Bowl Perkins said, "I'm going to be at Alabama a long time. As far as I know there's not an opening in Tampa. . . . I haven't talked with anybody with the Bucs.

"I'm happy with my job at Alabama. It'd take a godfather-like deal for me to make a move anywhere."

Less than a week later, Perkins announced that the rigors of coaching at the collegiate level were too time-consuming, and he was taking the position of head coach at Tampa Bay. President Joab Thomas wasted little time in hiring Steve Sloan as athletic director and Bill Curry as head coach. Curry wasted little time in reinstalling The Tower on Thomas Field.

Their appointments soothed some of the disenchantment among Alabama fans. They had carried high hopes of a national championship into the season, and a Southeastern Conference championship at the very least. For the first time in Crimson Tide history, the school did not have to charter a train or a plane to transport supporters to a bowl game. Only about 250 Alabama fans purchased Sun Bowl tickets.

Those who stayed home missed a good game and a couple of national records. Alabama made its 39th bowl game appearance, extending its record, won its 22nd bowl victory, giving the Crimson Tide a one-game edge over Southern Cal, which was preparing for its Citrus Bowl loss January 1 against Auburn.

The victory by Alabama in the 53rd Sun Bowl enabled the Crimson Tide to come full circle in the bowl game business. Alabama made its first postseason appearance in the 1926 Rose Bowl, defeating favored Washington, 20–19, to shed the cloak of inferiority that had covered football in Dixie.

Alabama players wore leather helmets and high-topped shoes in 1926.

The Crimson Tide dressed better in 1986, of course. But it carried something to El Paso that long ago had become commonplace at Alabama: pride. And it was Alabama pride that was evident on a pleasant day in the sun as the bowlingest football program in the nation kept rolling along.

1988 Hall of Fame Bowl

Michigan 28   Alabama 24

In retrospect, the arrival of Bill Curry as coach at Alabama created what could be compared to a marriage doomed from the start—with fault resting with both partners.

The new leader of the Crimson Tide talked a good game, and for a while it appeared he could coach one. His first team got off to a nice start, 4–1 with the loss to upstart Florida. However, a loss to Memphis State and a profound tailspin at the end of the season left Alabama with a 7–5 record and at the mercy of howling wolves.

Such disappointment was magnified by a small faction of Crimson Tide supporters who wrote hate mail. Also, if you choose to believe everything alleged by Curry, there were life-threatening telephone calls. Making matters worse for the coach was his background: Georgia Tech educated and previously employed. To veteran Alabama fans, that was akin to a Russian occupying the White House.

Meanwhile, devoted Alabama followers, including members of the athletic department, began noticing a lack of discipline in a program that had thrived on military-like organization. They also did not like the somewhat soft way in which practices were conducted and, at times, games were played. Nor did they take to excuses after losses, which has never been the Crimson Tide way.

In summary, Alabama was fast becoming a ship divided by the time the Crimson Tide arrived in Tampa, Florida for a historic battle against Michigan in the 1988 Hall of Fame Bowl. That in itself was sad, because the game matched two of the more tradition-rich programs in history.

"Players didn't pay any attention to all of that talk," said Roger Shultz, then an aspiring Crimson Tide freshman center. "We

337

just played football and did what the coaching staff told us. Personally, I wasn't affected by the controversy. I figured anybody making life-threatening telephone calls was sick and needed to be in a hospital. I wasn't going to worry about that."

For Curry, the Hall of Fame Bowl mirrored his up-and-down debut season at Alabama. The Crimson Tide looked bad during the first half, rallied to take matters in hand at sunset in the fourth quarter, and allowed victory to slip away in the last minute of the game. The Wolverines, with their pride still in tow, scored late to claim a 28–24 victory in what was an outstanding game to watch.

"They got us with some last-minute heroics," said Shultz. "It was a hard pill to swallow."

On a wonderfully sun-splashed January 2, 1988, a crowd of 60,156 watched a superb offensive display by a pair of proud teams with uncharacteristic 7–4 records at Tampa Stadium. Alabama produced 460 yards; Michigan produced 414, with 346 coming by way of the run. The Wolverines led 14–3 at halftime and 21–3 during the third quarter. After seeing a dreadful touchdown drought reach eleven quarters, the Crimson Tide scored three in four possessions to take a 24–21 lead with 3:45 remaining in the game.

Michigan of the Big Ten Conference became the victor, as the title of its fight song would favor, when quarterback Demetrius Brown passed twenty yards to Jon Kolesar for a touchdown with 48 seconds remaining. It was a desperation effort by the Wolverines, on fourth down with three yards to go for a first down, and the receiver caught the lofted football in the back corner of the end zone with Alabama defensive back John Mangum providing excellent coverage.

"I thought we had the game won," said Shultz. "We were on the sideline thinking about a great comeback win. John Mangum had the guy covered just right. It was a perfect pass and a perfect catch—just one of those things that can happen in football."

Obviously, emotion is also a large part of football. The Wolverines played in the Hall of Fame Bowl while their legendary coach Bo Schembechler recovered from heart surgery in Ann Arbor. Highly motivated Michigan was led by assistant head coach Gary Moeller, who made a gutsy decision at the end of the game.

"I was sitting at home thinking, 'That Moeller, he better go for the win or I'll kill him,'" said Schembechler, who admits he had second thoughts related to the grandness of what would have been a game-tying field goal. "I was proud of him and the players."

Shultz saw evidence of that kind of feeling during the game,

Center Roger Shultz and Jeff Dunn, quarterback

after feeling some loftiness himself just before the opening kickoff.

"Just before the game started, I found myself thinking, 'Gosh, this is Alabama and Michigan, two of the all-time great programs playing for the first time,'" said Shultz. "We were enormously thankful for the chance to take part in something like that. If nothing else, I got to get close to those striped helmets they wear. I always wondered if they were stickers or spray-painted.

"But what I noticed most was how motivated the Michigan players were to win the game for Bo Schembechler. Man, they had his name written on their arms in ink—even on their shoes and pants. You could see the emotion carrying them for a long time, especially during the first half."

Among the more motivated Michigan players that afternoon was halfback Jamie Morris. He ran for 234 yards and three touchdowns that covered 25, 14, and 77 yards. He was named most valuable player.

"Bo is like a father to me," said Morris. "This was my best game, and it was for him."

Alabama was not without stars. Quarterback Jeff Dunn completed twenty-three passes to set a school record for a bowl game, unseating Steve Sloan who completed twenty in the 1966 Orange Bowl. Halfback Bobby Humphrey ran for 149 yards, and placekicker Phillip Doyle had a 51-yard field goal to open the scoring, a school record for the longest in history in a bowl game.

When it was over and Alabama returned home to face a controversial future, Tampa sports columnist Tom McEwen wrote about a memorable football game:

"Good show.

"No, make that great show.

"Great weather. Great setting. Great pre-game and halftime show. Great crowd. And, great game."

Those few words definitely were appropriate.

Jeff Dunn

1988 Sun Bowl

Alabama 29   Army 28

To borrow from a weary thought, a person had to get up early in the morning to find something that would take his mind off the controversy that plagued the Alabama football program during the 1988 season.

So, it happened in Texas . . .

"It was still dark when we got to the stadium in El Paso," said Roger Shultz, a center on the team that defeated Army, 29–28, in the 1988 Sun Bowl. "It was a morning football game. It was weird getting dressed that early, sort of like the days when I played in a pee-wee league."

There was nothing small-fry about the unsettling winds of distrust that continued to blow through Tuscaloosa that year. They rumbled in hurricane-like fashion in other places, as it worked out, and the coach Bill Curry era appeared to be destined to fail.

By the time Alabama arrived in El Paso, the coaching situation had become so unpredictable that press conferences were called to offer votes of confidence in the leadership in place. It is proper to think the Crimson Tide avoided a complete disaster because of its dignified name in college football. As it was, the record was a respectable 9–3, with talented players credited for making it that way more so than their leader.

"Coach Curry has had a tough year, but I think things are going pretty well considering the injuries we've had," said Roger Sayers, then the acting University of Alabama president. Interestingly, he was speaking during October, when the Crimson Tide had a 5–1 overall record and a 3–1 Southeastern Conference record.

Perhaps the remarks were made to quiet a storm that had become national in scope. After the loss to Ole Miss in Tuscaloosa, Curry reported that a brick had been thrown through his office

341

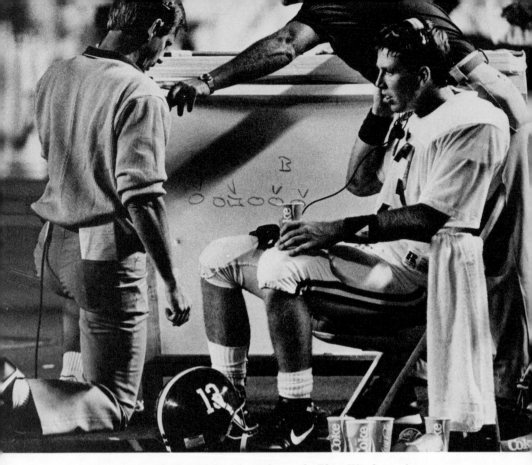

Quarterback David Smith and coach Chip Wisdom plot strategy as they receive instructions from the press box.

window, causing the program to receive more negative exposure in the news media. Meanwhile, some ranking members in the athletic department contended that the story about the broken window was a ploy used by the coaching staff to defuse a more alarming revelation, that an assistant coach had gone into the stands after the loss to fight booing Crimson Tide fans. Incredibly, they claimed that the enormous amount of glass on the ground outside the office indicated the brick had been thrown from inside.

Also, there was widespread talk about players getting into trouble off the field, with paperwork to that effect produced by athletic department members. Curry denied each allegation, but he remained in the spotlight. The wildness reached a peak when he refused to take his team to College Station, Texas, for a game against Texas A&M because weather forecasters predicted a hurricane in the area. It was a noble gesture of sorts, but the wisdom behind it became questionable when the scheduled game day came and went with the weather nice.

So Alabama completed a 9–3 season with a rescheduled victory over Texas A&M in the Hurricane Bowl and a victory over Army in the Sun Bowl. Just before the latter, the University of Alabama Board of Trustees issued a statement in El Paso that affirmed that the contract of the coach was "not for sale." This happened as Curry announced quarterback Jeff Dunn and linebacker John Sullins were suspended from the game because they had violated team guidelines.

That the Crimson Tide was able to accomplish so much under duress was due to the ingenious contributions of offensive coordinator Homer Smith. Perhaps the bowl game meant more to him because he was head coach at Army from 1974 through 1978.

"I'd call Homer Smith a genius," said Shultz. "I'm talking about when it comes to football and otherwise. It takes a while to learn his complicated offensive system, but it's amazing how well it works. Also, he made sure everybody knew what everybody was doing, meaning I had to know what the running backs were doing and why, and they had to understand what the center was doing and why. He was such a smart man that I sat stunned during my first meeting with him and thought, 'Uh oh, I'll need a dictionary to understand this guy.' He definitely had interesting ways to get across his points during practices, meetings, and everyday conversations.

"For instance, he arrived for a meeting with the offense one afternoon with his shirt buttoned out of line. Finally, (quarterback) Gary Hollingsworth said, 'Coach Smith, I believe you've got your buttons messed up.' Just like that, Coach Smith said, 'That's right, Gary. It's the same with football. If the basics aren't there, then nothing about the offense is going to look right or work right.' Once, he was preaching about gripping the football tightly to avoid fumbles. He told a player to toss him a football, and he gripped it and the air went out of it. He had it staged. He knew the football was about out of air anyway, and he made his point in a dramatic way.

"I'll always be indebted to Coach Smith for what he did for us. In a way, I love the man."

After the victory over Army in the Sun Bowl, quarterback David Smith felt the same way, only magnified. He had a record-shattering morning and early afternoon in El Paso, completing thirty-three of fifty-two passes for 412 yards and two touchdowns as Alabama came from behind to win. Afterward, he handed the game football to Homer Smith.

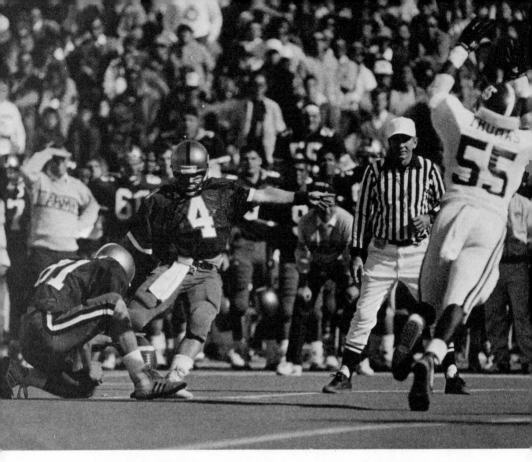

Derrick Thomas moves in to block his second Keith Walker field goal
[PHOTO: NESBITT].

"Everything felt perfect," David Smith said about the Sun Bowl. "The receivers were always where I thought they'd be. The pass protection was super. I just sat back there and had a picnic."

For a while, however, it appeared the Crimson Tide was going to be in for a disappointing Christmas Eve, as 48,719 fans who attended the game will attest.

Army led 14–3, then 14–13 at halftime. The Cadets scored a touchdown in the first three minutes, with Mike Mayweather running one yard after Ben Barnett ran 51 to set it up. The men from West Point missed other scoring opportunities late in the first half when Alabama linebacker Derrick Thomas blocked two field goal attempts, from 22 and 44 yards.

Alabama went ahead 20–14 when Smith passed 23 yards for a touchdown to Greg Payne, only to see the Cadets regain the lead 21–20, then stretch it to 28–20 at the end of the third quarter.

The Crimson Tide rallied in the fourth quarter with a 32-yard field goal by Phillip Doyle, which cut the lead to five points. A touchdown dive by David Casteal with 4:01 remaining provided the slim final margin.

"They had a small defensive line that slanted a lot," said Shultz. "That's why it was easy to block them for pass attempts. We changed our game plan that way to take advantage."

Army was a 14-point underdog with a 9–2 record. The Cadets used the wishbone offense to perfection, utilizing the basic variety like Alabama once employed, and they piled up 350 yards rushing and none passing. The Crimson Tide went the other route, through the air, with Payne and Marco Battle establishing a school record for a bowl game by catching nine passes each.

"We didn't go to El Paso for a moral victory," said Jim Young, then the Army coach. "We didn't play to keep from getting blown out by Alabama. We thought we could win. I think we could've won."

Alabama players were impressed by the Cadets, on the field and off. "They displayed unusual discipline," said Shultz. "They were good guys. As soon as the game ended, I swapped my shoes for a pair worn by one of the Cadets."

Obviously, the Crimson Tide walked in larger shoes because it won with superior talent. *Football News* selected Smith, Thomas, and Doyle for its all-bowl-games team after their performances. Payne and Battle could have been included on that unit without anybody protesting.

1990 Sugar Bowl

Miami 33   **Alabama 25**

Sugar Bowl Executive Director Mickey Holmes remembers it as "one of the better games in our history." He adds, "Remember, Alabama was playing the eventual national champion, and the Crimson Tide had a lot of off-the-field distractions to deal with that year. Also, Alabama might have come to New Orleans a little down after its historic loss at Auburn."

Ole Mickey said a mouthful, most of it on the money.

While the victory by Miami, 33–25, might not have been full of drama in the fourth quarter when the Hurricanes' defense seemed to have the whip hand, Alabama did show pride as it made its first Sugar Bowl appearance in a decade.

Miami was a nine-point favorite, having achieved a 10–1 record and number two national ranking. Alabama was also 10–1, ranked seventh, but the Crimson Tide was smarting from a 30–20 loss to Auburn at the end of the regular season, the result of the first meeting with its intrastate rival on Auburn's home field.

"Personally, I think we had ourselves back together and were motivated to play in the Sugar Bowl," said Roger Shultz, an Alabama center that season. "There was a lot of excitement involved with our game at Auburn—honestly, I sort of liked the atmosphere down there—and that loss did hurt a lot. We thought we'd beat them and go to New Orleans unbeaten and untied with a shot at the national championship. Still, I think we gave Miami our best effort. It just wasn't enough."

Overmatched Alabama gave the Hurricanes all the fight they wanted, particularly after a week of jawing back and forth among some players. The pre-game taunting became so enthusiastic that a gathering of the two squads at Pat O'Brien's bar in the French

Philip Doyle kicks another one.

Quarter became comical, with Miami linebacker Bernard Clark leading the way when it came to hurling insults. People who were not within earshot were treated to a heavy dose of the cutting remarks in the New Orleans newspapers.

After the game, a couple of Miami representatives offered remarks that indicate how competitive Alabama was.

From Coach Dennis Erickson: "This was our best offensive game of the year."

From Clark: "They have a good team. The difference was we started playing Miami defense in the second half."

Alabama managed only 89 yards in the second half, after getting 163 in the first half. The halftime score was 20–17. Phillip Doyle missed a field goal attempt from 40 yards in the final seconds that would have deadlocked the game, and an entertained crowd of 77,452 had reason to believe an upset might be in the making. After all, the Crimson Tide had put a large dent in a defense that had allowed only 9.3 points per game during the regular season.

On the flipside, and more telling, Miami never trailed.

Stephen McGuire scored a touchdown on a three-yard run and Carlos Huerta kicked the extra point for a 7–0 lead with 4:55 remaining in the first quarter.

Alabama tied the game, 7–7, on a four-yard touchdown pass

347

from Gary Hollingsworth to Marco Battle and a Phillip Doyle extra point.

Miami went ahead, 13–7, on an 18-yard touchdown pass from Craig Erickson to Wesley Carroll.

Doyle kicked a 45-yard field goal to cut the lead to 13–10.

Alex Johnson scored a touchdown on a three-yard run, and Huerta kicked the extra point to give Miami a 20–10 lead.

Alabama rallied when Hollingsworth passed seven yards for a touchdown to Lamonde Russell with 40 seconds remaining in the first half. Doyle kicked the extra point to set the score at 20–17, then missed the field goal that would have tied the game at halftime.

In the second half, Erickson had two touchdown passes: 11 yards to Rod Chudzinski and 12 yards to Randy Bethen, with Huerta adding one extra point, and Miami led 33–17.

A nine-yard touchdown pass from Hollingsworth to Prince Wimbley and a two-point conversion pass to Russell fixed the final margin.

It was the final game for Bill Curry as coach at Alabama. He saw his team lose to a powerhouse that amassed 227 yards running and 250 yards passing.

"They simply ran the offense and defense and beat us," Curry said. "We didn't find a weakness."

All of that considered, Alabama found its way back to a familiar setting that season—New Orleans—and the season left Crimson Tide supporters excited about the future.

Bill Curry was gone, making his way to Kentucky. He offered a somewhat forced resignation after much deliberation.

Gene Stallings was summoned, making his way from Phoenix. He offered a needed fresh breath for the program. After a false start of sorts, he got Alabama rolling again.

1991 Fiesta Bowl

Louisville 34   Alabama 7

Rarely is Alabama embarrassed on the football field.

But that was the case in every way on January 1, 1991, when the Crimson Tide was defeated by Louisville, 34–7, in the Fiesta Bowl.

The score was 25–0 after one quarter.

Need there be anything else said?

Perhaps.

"Man!" said Roger Shultz, an Alabama senior center in that game. "Their quarterback, Browning Nagle, had a career day. They played inspired football from the start. We were a little flat. No, a whole lot flat. They beat us bad in every way. They got us early and never gave us a chance to catch our breath. At halftime we were thinking, 'Man, do we really have to go back out there and play some more?' It was thorough. We took a beating all the way around."

The score was 25–7 at halftime. It was 32–7 after three quarters. A safety put the caps on a misadventure for Alabama at the end of a 7–5 season that started slowly, picked up pace, and ended dismally.

In retrospect, a few contributing factors should be explained since an Alabama team coached in a bowl for the first time by Gene Stallings got whipped by a Louisville team coached by Howard Schnellenberger.

First of all, Alabama players partied too much in Tempe, Arizona, at the end of a rollercoaster-like season, while Louisville players concentrated hard on a game that elevated the national status of that program. In some ways, that is understandable because the Crimson Tide did have reason to breathe a sigh of relief.

Alabama started the Gene Stallings era with three consecutive losses, 27–24 to Mississippi, 17–13 to Florida, and 17–16 to Georgia. Obviously, the Crimson Tide had a chance to win all of those games but tossed them away by making foolish mistakes, particularly in the kicking game. The debacle had many observers wondering if another coach was on his way out less than a year after he had settled in.

But once the rough spots were leveled, Alabama lost only one more regular season game, 9–0 to Penn State, and capped the merriment with a 16–7 victory over intrastate rival Auburn. At that moment, Stallings was being labeled a savior for the program.

Then the euphoria of survival lingered too long.

"I'm sure we viewed the trip to the Fiesta Bowl as a reward," said Shultz. "Maybe we didn't take Louisville as seriously as we should have."

There was another distraction, one magnified because of the history the State of Alabama has when it comes to civil rights and race relations. Because the state of Arizona does not celebrate a holiday in honor of the late Dr. Martin Luther King, Jr., several college football programs made an issue of the controversy and said they would not take part in the Fiesta Bowl. Then eyebrows across the nation were raised when the Crimson Tide was invited to the game, with observers wondering if they would accept the invitation.

"Coach Stallings put it straight to us," said Shultz. "We had a team meeting, and he asked if we wanted to go to the Fiesta Bowl. We all voted to go. Then he asked if there were any objections from anybody because of the Dr. Martin Luther King issue. There weren't any—not one thing said—so it was agreed that we'd go out there and play Louisville.

"Of course, we wore black armbands as a tribute to Dr. King."

As it worked out, there was not much of a pall hanging over the festivities in Tempe, except from an Alabama standpoint on the scoreboard. The fun nature of the Fiesta Bowl was apparent, especially when the controversy made the hosts more determined to show their guests a good time.

Schnellenberger, an assistant coach at Alabama from 1961 through 1965 as well as the architect who started the dynasty at Miami, had his team at a feverish pitch for the game. The Cardinals had ended their regular season in early November, which gave them much more time to prepare. He had them ready and motivated, confident they could win over a highly touted program.

Roger Shultz, Alabama's senior center

All of this showed in a hurry.

Nagle passed 75 yards for a touchdown to Lattrell Ware with 7:35 remaining in the first quarter.

Ralph Dawkins scored on a five-yard run with 3:40 remaining in the first quarter.

Nagle passed 37 yards for a touchdown to Anthony Cummings.

Louisville blocked a punt and recovered it in the end zone for another touchdown.

The Louisville quarterback had a career during the first quarter, leading the Cardinals to a 25–0 lead. Dismantling a vaunted Alabama defense, he finished the game with 20 pass completions in 33 attempts for an astounding 451 yards. "He was hot, and there wasn't anything we could do," said Shultz.

The Alabama offense failed, too. The Crimson Tide managed only 189 yards and got its only touchdown on a 49-yard pass interception return by Charles Gardner.

Pure and simple, *embarrassing* was the operative word when summing up what the Fiesta Bowl was to proud Alabama.

"That's what happens when one team makes plays and the other team only comes close to making plays," Stallings said while reflecting on the loss to Louisville. "It's hard to get things turned around during a game when one team gets off to a 25–0 lead.

"Also, we didn't prepare for the game the way I had intended. I let the players take off after the victory over Auburn with the thought we'd do a lot of heavy work in Arizona. Then the weather was bad when we got there, so we didn't get much accomplished.

"Then there was Louisville. The other side had a lot to do with what happened in that Fiesta Bowl. They had a good team. Remember, they had several players who went high in the pro draft that year.

"But I'm a firm believer that something good can come from something bad. In fact, I'm certain getting beat like we did by Louisville helped us get ready for the nice things that happened to us in 1991."

1991 Blockbuster Bowl

Alabama 30   **Colorado 25**

Coach Gene Stallings found himself in an interesting position just before Alabama went to Miami to play Colorado in the 1991 Blockbuster Bowl. He was being asked to come up with excuses for the alleged poor performance of a team that had won ten of eleven games during the regular season, including the last nine in a row.

"I'll bet there are a lot of programs who'd like to trade places with us," Stallings said when slapped in the face with the idea the Crimson Tide was the worst 10–1 team in history. "I couldn't care less about the margins of victory we've had. I'm not going to distract a bit from what these players have accomplished."

The reason for such criticism was the fact Alabama had won its last five games by a touchdown or less each, with the first over Tennessee and the last over Auburn. The offense had struggled in spots, although there were blistering paces in stretches, and the defense had pretty much saved the season, although it had shown many signs of weakness until its back was against the goal line.

"I've always believed you play forty-five to fifty-five plays a game for the chance to make four or five that make the difference," Stallings said. "We made the ones that counted most of the year. We had the number one rushing team in the Southeastern Conference, which isn't weak. We gave up less than eleven points per game. How can you be an average team and do that?

"We struggled most of the year, yes, but that's because we had an inexperienced team in a lot of areas.

"I'm proud of what our players did."

Regardless of how a person feels about the 1991 regular season, Alabama had momentum when it went to the Blockbuster Bowl. Fans were again dreaming of a national championship at some point in the near future. After all, only a 35–0 loss to Florida in

Siran Stacy was a standout in his last game at Alabama.

early September had kept the Crimson Tide from being in the chase for top honors when the holiday season arrived.

Colorado had played a similar regular season. The Buffaloes defense allowed 13.6 points per game while their offense had good moments and bad moments. The record was 8–2–1.

So what did odds-makers do? They called it a "pick it" game.

So what did most analysts say? They vowed points would be scarce in Miami.

Well, Alabama won, 30–25, in one of the more entertaining bowl games of the holiday season. The contest featured explosive offense, clutch defense, and about anything else a fan would want— including a punt return for a touchdown, a safety, and a rally at the end by Colorado after it appeared the Crimson Tide was home free.

The crowd was slack after a rainy afternoon, with 46,123 watching, but it was the only bowl game that December 28 and a national television audience was entertained by it. Fans saw an Alabama team determined to shake off the lingering effects of the Fiesta Bowl from the previous season and hoping to keep rolling along toward what was starting to look like a most promising 1992.

"The Fiesta Bowl loss to Louisville was a disgrace, an embarrassment," said Jay Barker, a redshirt freshman quarterback who led the Crimson Tide down the triumphant stretch leading to the Blockbuster Bowl. "We returned from Arizona with a bitter taste in our mouths. We went to Miami determined to redeem ourselves in front of a national audience. We wanted a sweet taste to carry into spring practice in 1992."

Such determination showed on the first touchdown of the Blockbuster Bowl, a sparkling 52-yard punt return by Alabama freshman David Palmer. It was a major league effort, a show-stopper, as "The Deuce" got loose with a high-step move, faked out a couple of other would-be tacklers, and followed a convoy into the end zone.

The extra point by Matt Wettington gave Alabama a 7–0 lead with 6:11 remaining in the first quarter.

Meanwhile, the touchdown made Colorado Coach Bill Mc-Cartney appear prophetic. A few days before the game, he had said, "If he (Palmer) breaks one, I hope he breaks one early." He knew the "Pocket Rocket" had returned three punts for touchdowns during the regular season while piling up 1,113 all-purpose yards.

Colorado tied the game with 1:34 remaining in the first quarter when Scott Phillips ran one yard for a touchdown and Jim Harper kicked the extra point.

About three minutes later, the Buffaloes took the lead, 9–7, when Ted Johnson tackled Alabama fullback Martin Houston in the end zone for a safety. That started a wave of six lead changes.

Another one came with 2:00 remaining in the second quarter, when Wettington kicked a 25-yard field goal.

Four seconds before intermission, Harper kicked a field goal to give Colorado a 12–10 lead and bring what had become a strange first half to an end. The Buffaloes had been stuffed by an inspired Alabama defense, but they were ahead on the scoreboard because the Crimson Tide offense had been fairly productive from a yardage standpoint, yet erratic while in scoring position.

The complexion changed in the second half. Maybe this happened because Alabama running back Siran Stacy had a few choice words for his teammates in the dressing room during the break.

"Yes, I got up and spoke to the other guys," said Stacy, who was miffed by a poor offensive performance in the first half and was concerned about his last game for the Crimson Tide being a failure. "I was disgusted. I was embarrassed. Basically, I just said, 'Hey, we can do better than this, so let's do it.'"

Barker remembers something else happening at halftime. "We decided to gamble more on offense," he said, "to mix in the pass with the run." He responded with a dandy evening, 12 completions in 16 attempts for 154 yards. Alabama got 153 yards rushing in the game. The defense held Colorado to minus 11 yards rushing and 210 passing.

Barker passed 13 yards to an inspired Stacy for the first touchdown of the second half for a 16–12 lead with 10:54 remaining in the third quarter.

Colorado regained the lead with a touchdown 18 seconds later, when Darian Hagen passed 62 yards to Michael Westbrooks. An extra point kick by Harper set the score at 19–16.

With 6:55 remaining in the third quarter, Barker passed 12 yards to Kevin Lee for a touchdown. An extra point kick by Wettington gave Alabama a 23–19 lead.

Then came a dramatic play that pretty much iced the victory for the Crimson Tide. From five yards out Barker lofted the football toward the back left corner of the end zone, where Palmer stretched his arms and made a fingertip catch while falling to the ground. The extra point kick by Wettington gave Alabama a 30–19 lead with 8:10 remaining in the game.

"Jay made a perfect throw, and I made a perfect catch," said Palmer in describing the play. His performance convinced voters to make him the most outstanding player in the game.

Colorado rallied for another touchdown with 3:30 remaining in the game to fix the final margin. Also the Buffaloes drove the ball on their next possession but were stopped on a fourth down, short-yardage run by a suddenly inspired Alabama defense.

Kevin Turner, Mal Moore, and Gene Stallings (left to right)

Surely, Alabama fans remember what happened a few minutes after that. A smiling Stallings was interviewed by CBS-TV Sports at the end of "a mighty long game." The coach said, "It's fun being at Alabama."

It was indeed enjoyable again for Alabama and its fans—at long last, after some agony.

Appendix

(Information supplied by University of Alabama)

Alabama's Great Bowl Tradition

Total Bowl Appearances—44
Record Consecutive Bowl Apearances—25 (1959–1983)
Won 24, Lost 17, Tied 3

THE ORANGE BOWL—
MIAMI, FLORIDA
Record: Won 4, Lost 3

1943—Alabama 37, Boston College 21
1953—Alabama 61, Syracuse 6
1963—Alabama 17, Oklahoma 0
1965—Texas 21, Alabama 17
1966—Alabama 39, Nebraska 28
1972—Nebraska 38, Alabama 6
1975—Notre Dame 13, Alabama 11

THE COTTON BOWL—
DALLAS, TEXAS
Record: Won 2, Lost 4

1942—Alabama 29, Texas A&M 21
1954—Rice 28, Alabama 6
1968—Texas A&M 20, Alabama 16
1973—Texas 17, Alabama 13
1981—Alabama 30, Baylor 2
1982—Texas 14, Alabama 12

THE SUGAR BOWL—
NEW ORLEANS, LOUISIANA
Record: Won 7, Lost 4

1945—Duke 29, Alabama 26
1948—Texas 27, Alabama 7
1962—Alabama 10, Arkansas 3
1964—Alabama 12, Mississippi 7
1967—Alabama 34, Nebraska 7
1973—Notre Dame 24, Alabama 23
1975—Alabama 13, Penn State 6
1978—Alabama 35, Ohio State 6
1979—Alabama 14, Penn State 7
1980—Alabama 24, Arkansas 9
1990—Miami 33, Alabama 25

THE GATOR BOWL—
JACKSONVILLE, FLORIDA
Record: Won 0, Lost 1

1968—Missouri 35, Alabama 10

THE HALL OF FAME BOWL—
TAMPA, FLORIDA
Record: Won 0, Lost 1

1988—Michigan 28, Alabama 24

THE FIESTA BOWL—
TEMPE, ARIZONA
Record: Won 0, Lost 1

1991—Louisville 34, Alabama 7

THE ROSE BOWL—
PASADENA, CALIFORNIA
Record: Won 4, Lost 1, Tied 1

1926—Alabama 20, Washington 19
1927—Alabama 7, Stanford 7
1931—Alabama 24, Washington State 0
1935—Alabama 29, Stanford 13
1938—California 13, Alabama 0
1946—Alabama 34, Southern Cal 14

THE ASTRO-BLUEBONNET BOWL—
HOUSTON, TEXAS
Record: Won 0, Lost 0, Tied 2

1960—Alabama 3, Texas 3
1970—Alabama 24, Oklahoma 24

THE LIBERTY BOWL—
PHILADELPHIA & MEMPHIS
Record: Won 2, Lost 2

1959—Penn State 7, Alabama 0
1969—Colorado 47, Alabama 33
1976—Alabama 36, UCLA 6
1982—Alabama 21, Illinois 15

THE SUN BOWL—
EL PASO, TEXAS
Record: Won 3, Lost 0

1983—Alabama 28, SMU 7
1986—Alabama 28, Washington 6
1988—Alabama 29, Army 28

THE ALOHA BOWL—
HONOLULU, HAWAII
Record: Won 1, Lost 0

1985—Alabama 24, Southern Cal 3

THE BLOCKBUSTER BOWL—
MIAMI, FLORIDA
Record, Won 1, Lost 0

1991—Alabama 30, Colorado 25

359

Alabama's Outstanding Bowl Performers

ALOHA BOWL OUTSTANDING PLAYER AWARDS:

1985—Linebacker Cornelius Bennett
(Defense)
1985—Halfback Gene Jelks (Offense)

ASTRO-BLUEBONNET BOWL OUTSTANDING PLAYER AWARD:

1960—Linebacker Lee Roy Jordan
(Outstanding Defense Player)
1970—Linebacker Jeff Rouzie
(Outstanding Defensive Player)

BLOCKBUSTER BOWL BRIAN PICCOLO AWARD:

1991—David Palmer
(Most Valuable Player)

COTTON BOWL OUTSTANDING PLAYER AWARD:

1942—End Holt Rast,
Tackle Don Whitmire and
Halfback Jimmy Nelson
1981—Halfback Major Ogilvie and
Middle Guard Warren Lyles
1982—Linebacker Robbie Jones

LIBERTY BOWL OUTSTANDING PLAYER AWARD:

1976—Linebacker Barry Krauss
1982—Defensive Back Jeremiah Castille

ORANGE BOWL OUTSTANDING PLAYER AWARDS:

1963—Linebacker Lee Roy Jordan
1965—Quarterback Joe Namath
1966—Quarterback Steve Sloan

SUGAR BOWL OUTSTANDING PLAYER AWARDS:

1962—Fullback Mike Fracchia
1964—Field Goal Kicker Tim Davis

1967—Quarterback Ken Stabler
1975—Quarterback Richard Todd
1978—Quarterback Jeff Rutledge
1979—Linebacker Barry Krauss
1980—Halfback Major Ogilvie

SUN BOWL OUTSTANDING PLAYER AWARDS:

1983—Quarterback Walter Lewis
(Most Valuable Player)
1983—Center Wes Neighbors
(Most Outstanding Lineman)
1986—Linebacker Cornelius Bennett
(Most Valuable Player)
1988—Quarterback David Smith
(Most Valuable Player)
Linebacker Derrick Thomas
(Most Outstanding Lineman)

ALABAMA PLAYERS ON ALL-TIME BOWL TEAMS:

Rose Bowl
Halfback Johnny Mack Brown, 1926
Halfback Millard "Dixie" Howell, 1935

Sugar Bowl
Center Vaughn Mancha, 1945
Tackle Tom Whitley, 1948
Halfback Harry Gilmer, 1945
Guard Ray Richeson, 1948

Cotton Bowl
End Holt Rast, 1942
Tackle Don Whitmire, 1942
Halfback Jimmy Nelson, 1942

Orange Bowl
Center Joe Domnanovich, 1943
Tackle Don Whitmire, 1943
Linebacker Lee Roy Jordan, 1963
Quarterback Joe Namath, 1965
End Ray Perkins, 1966
Quarterback Steve Sloan, 1966
Guard John Hannah, 1972
End Leroy Cook, 1975
Cornerback Mike Washington, 1975

Alabama Record Against All Opponents

Opponent	W	L	T	Pts.	Op.	Opponent	W	L	T	Pts.	Op.
Arkansas	2	0	0	34	12	Mississippi State	62	11	3	1679	608
Arkansas State	1	0	0	34	7	Missouri	1	2	0	55	75
Army	1	0	0	29	28	Montgomery AC	1	0	0	16	0
Auburn	32	23	1	1057	859	Nashville	1	0	0	17	0
Baylor	2	0	0	75	2	Nebraska	3	2	0	123	107
Birmingham	2	3	0	56	19	New Orleans AC	0	1	0	0	21
Birmingham HS	2	0	0	113	0	North Carolina State	3	0	0	61	7
Birmingham-						Notre Dame	1	5	0	86	112
Southern	11	0	0	551	12	Oglethorpe	2	0	0	75	0
Boston College	1	3	0	88	92	Ohio Am Corp.	1	0	0	7	0
Bryson College	1	0	0	95	0	Ohio State	2	0	0	51	16
California	1	1	0	66	13	Oklahoma	1	0	1	41	24
Camp Gordon	0	1	0	6	19	Pennsylvania	1	0	0	9	7
Carlisle	0	1	0	3	20	Penn State	8	5	0	203	181
Case College	1	0	0	40	0	Pensacola AC	1	0	0	10	5
Centre	2	1	0	33	17	Pensacola N.A.B.	2	0	0	82	6
Chattanooga	9	0	0	337	55	Richmond	1	0	0	66	0
Cincinnati	5	0	0	156	27	Rice	0	3	0	19	68
Clemson	11	3	0	356	122	Rutgers	2	0	0	48	20
Cumberland	0	1	0	0	44	St. Mary's	1	0	0	6	0
Colorado	1	1	0	60	72	Sewanee	17	10	3	495	288
Davidson	1	0	0	16	6	South Carolina	7	0	0	194	20
Delta State	1	0	0	89	0	Southern Cal	5	2	0	150	120
Duke	1	1	0	61	41	Southern Methodist	2	0	0	84	10
Duquesne	3	0	0	122	14	Southern Military					
Florida	17	8	0	582	276	Inst.	1	0	0	59	0
Florida State	3	0	1	66	44	Southern Mississippi	22	4	2	869	306
Fordham	1	1	0	7	8	Southwestern	2	0	0	76	6
Furman	5	0	0	160	19	S. W. Louisiana	8	0	0	296	53
George Washington	3	0	0	86	6	Spring Hill	3	0	0	112	7
Georgia	33	22	4	885	623	Stanford	1	0	1	36	20
Georgia Pre-Flight	0	1	0	19	35	Syracuse	1	1	0	61	29
Georgia Tech	28	21	3	692	556	Tampa	1	0	0	34	6
Haskell	1	0	0	9	8	Taylor School	1	0	0	35	0
Houston	7	0	0	133	57	Temple	3	0	0	102	17
Howard	20	0	1	669	34	Tennessee	40	27	7	1186	888
Illinois	1	0	0	21	15	Texas	0	7	1	62	131
Keesler Field	1	0	0	21	0	Texas A&M	3	1	0	98	61
Kentucky	30	1	1	761	161	Texas Christian	2	3	0	93	75
LSU	36	14	5	1031	543	Tulane	24	10	3	594	297
Louisiana Tech	1	0	0	34	0	Tulsa	3	0	0	116	19
Louisville	2	1	0	86	43	Tuscaloosa AC	2	0	0	22	5
Loyola (N.O.)	1	0	0	13	6	UCLA	1	0	0	36	6
Marion Institute	9	0	0	482	0	Union	4	0	0	136	0
Maryland	2	1	0	48	44	Vanderbilt	47	18	4	1618	869
Maryville	3	0	0	40	0	Villanova	0	1	0	18	41
Memphis State	7	1	0	192	56	Virginia Tech	10	0	0	346	70
Mercer	2	0	0	40	0	Washington	4	0	0	120	42
Miami	13	3	0	416	168	Washington & Lee	1	0	0	9	0
Michigan	0	1	0	24	28	Washington State	1	0	0	24	0
Millsaps	3	0	0	155	0	Wetumpka	1	0	0	24	0
Mississippi	31	6	2	1157	357	Wichita State	1	0	0	38	0
Mississippi College	7	0	0	283	10	Wisconsin	0	1	0	0	15

Alabama's Football Records Year-by-Year

Year	Coach	Captain	Record	Pts.	Opp.
1892	E. N. Beaumont (Penn)	W. G. Little	2-2-0	96	37
1893	Eli Abbott (Penn)	G. H. Kyzer	0-4-0	24	74
1894	Eli Abbott	S. B. Slone	3-1-0	60	16
1895	Eli Abbott	H. M. Bankhead	0-4-0	12	112
1896	Otto Wagonhurst (Penn)	S. B. Slone	2-1-0	56	10
1897	Allen McCants (Alabama)	Frank S. White, Jr.	1-0-0	6	0
1898	No Team	T. G. Burk—Elected	No Team		
1899	W. A. Hartin (Virginia)	T. W. Wert	3-1-0	39	31
1900	M. Griffin	W. E. Drennen	2-3-0	52	99
1901	M. H. Harvey (Auburn)	W. E. Drennen	2-1-2	92	23
1902	Eli Abbott, J. O. Heyworth	J. R. Forman	4-4-0	191	49
1903	W. B. Blount (Yale)	W. S. Wyatt	3-4-0	60	114
1904	W. B. Blount	W. S. Wyatt	7-3-0	100	62
1905	Jack Leavenworth (Yale)	B. A. Burks	6-4-0	178	113
1906	J. W. H. Pollard (Dartmouth)	Washington Moody	5-1-0	97	82
1907	J. W. H. Pollard	Emile Hannon	5-1-2	70	64
1908	J. W. H. Pollard	Henry Burks	6-1-1	107	31
1909	J. W. H. Pollard	Derrill Pratt	5-1-2	68	17
1910	Guy S. Lowman (Springfield)	O. G. Gresham	4-4-0	65	107
1911	D. V. Graves (Missouri)	R. H. Bumgardner	5-2-2	153	31
1912	D. V. Graves	Farley W. Moody	5-3-1	156	55
1913	D. V. Graves	C. H. Van de Graaff	6-3-0	188	40
1914	D. V. Graves	C. A. "Tubby" Long	5-4-0	211	64
1915	Thomas Kelly (Chicago)	William L. Harsh	6-2-0	250	51
1916	Thomas Kelly	Lowndes Morton	6-3-0	156	62
1917	Thomas Kelly	Jack Hovater	5-2-1	168	29
1918	No Team	Dan Boone—Elected	No Team		
1919	Xen C. Scott (Western Reserve)	Isaac J. Rogers	8-1-0	280	22
1920	Xen C. Scott	Sid Johnston	10-1-0	377	35
1921	Xen C. Scott	Al Clemens	5-4-2	241	104
1922	Xen C. Scott	Ernest C. Cooper	6-3-1	300	81
1923	Wallace Wade (Brown)	Al Clemens	7-2-1	222	50
1924	Wallace Wade	A. T. S. Hubert	8-1-0	290	24
1925	Wallace Wade	Bruce Jones	10-0-0	297	26
1926	Wallace Wade	Emile "Red" Barnes	9-0-1	249	27
1927	Wallace Wade	Freddie Pickhard	5-4-1	154	73
1928	Wallace Wade	Earle Smith	6-3-0	187	75
1929	Wallace Wade	Billy Hicks	6-3-0	196	58
1930	Wallace Wade	Charles B. Clement	10-0-0	271	13
1931	Frank W. Thomas (Notre Dame)	Joe Sharpe	9-1-0	370	57
1932	Frank W. Thomas	Joe Cain	8-2-0	200	51
1933	Frank W. Thomas	Foy Leach	7-1-1	130	17
1934	Frank W. Thomas	Bill Lee	10-0-0	316	45
1935	Frank W. Thomas	James Walker	6-2-1	185	55
1936	Frank W. Thomas	Jas. "Bubber" Nisbet	8-0-1	168	35
1937	Frank W. Thomas	Leroy Monsky	9-1-0	225	33
1938	Frank W. Thomas	Lew Bostick	7-1-1	149	40
1939	Frank W. Thomas	Carey Cox	5-3-1	101	53
1940	Frank W. Thomas	Harold Newman	7-2-0	166	80
1941	Frank W. Thomas	John Wyhonic	9-2-0	263	85
1942	Frank W. Thomas	Joe Domnanovich	8-3-0	246	97
1943	No Team	No Team	No Team		
1944	Frank W. Thomas	Game Captains	5-2-2	272	83
1945	Frank W. Thomas	Game Captains	10-0-0	430	80

Year	Coach	Captain	Record	Pts.	Opp.
1946	Frank W. Thomas	Game Captains	7-4-0	186	110
1947	H. D. Drew (Bates)	John Wozniak	8-3-0	210	101
1948	H. D. Drew	Ray Richeson	6-4-1	228	170
1949	H. D. Drew	Doug Lockridge	6-3-1	227	130
1950	H. D. Drew	Mike Mizerany	9-2-0	328	107
1951	H. D. Drew	Jack Brown	5-6-0	263	188
1952	H. D. Drew	Bobby Wilson	10-2-0	325	139
1953	H. D. Drew	Bud Willis	6-3-3	178	152
1954	H. D. Drew	Sid Youngleman	4-5-2	123	104
1955	J. B. Whitworth (Alabama)	Nick Germanos	0-10-0	48	256
1956	J. B. Whitworth	Jim Cunningham-Wes Thompson	2-7-1	85	208
1957	J. B. Whitworth	Jim Loftis-Clay Walls	2-7-1	69	173
1958	Paul W. Bryant (Alabama)	Dave Sington-Bobby Smith	5-4-1	106	75
1959	Paul W. Bryant	Marlin Dyess-Jim Blevins	7-2-2	95	59
1960	Paul W. Bryant	Leon Fuller-Bobby Boylston	8-1-2	183	56
1961	Paul W. Bryant	Pat Trammell-Billy Neighbors	11-0-0	297	25
1962	Paul W. Bryant	Lee Roy Jordan-Jimmy Sharpe	10-1-0	289	39
1963	Paul W. Bryant	Benny Nelson-Steve Allen	9-2-0	227	95
1964	Paul W. Bryant	Joe Namath-Ray Odgen	10-1-0	250	88
1965	Paul W. Bryant	Steven Sloan-Paul Crane	9-1-1	256	107
1966	Paul W. Bryant	Ray Perkins-Richard Cole	11-0-0	301	44
1967	Paul W. Bryant	Ken Stabler-Bobby Johns	8-2-1	204	131
1968	Paul W. Bryant	Mike Hall-Donnie Sutton	8-3-0	184	139
1969	Paul W. Bryant	Danny Ford-Alvin Samples	6-5-0	314	268
1970	Paul W. Bryant	Danny Gilbert-Dave Brungard	6-5-1	334	264
1971	Paul W. Bryant	Johnny Musso-Robin Parkhouse	11-1-0	368	122
1972	Paul W. Bryant	Terry Davis-John Mitchell	10-2-0	406	150
1973	Paul W. Bryant	Wilbur Jackson-Chuck Strickland	11-1-0	477	113
1974	Paul W. Bryant	Sylvester Croom-Ricky Davis	11-1-0	329	96
1975	Paul W. Bryant	Richard Todd-Leroy Cook	11-1-0	374	72
1976	Paul W. Bryant	Thad Flanagan-Charles Hannah	9-3-0	327	140
1977	Paul W. Bryant	Mike Tucker-Ozzie Newsome	11-1-0	380	139
1978	Paul W. Bryant	Marty Lyons-Jeff Rutledge-Tony Nathan	11-1-0	335	168
1979	Paul W. Bryant	Don McNeal-Steve Whitman	12-0-0	383	67
1980	Paul W. Bryant	Major Ogilvie-Randy Scott	10-2-0	362	88
1981	Paul W. Bryant	Warren Lyles-Alan Gray	9-2-1	296	151
1982	Paul W. Bryant	Eddie Lowe-Steve Mott	8-4-0	317	201
1983	Ray Perkins (Alabama)	Walter Lewis-Randy Edwards	8-4-0	366	229
1984	Ray Perkins	Paul Ott Carruth-Emanuel King	5-6-0	226	208
1985	Ray Perkins	Jon Hand-Thornton Chandler	9-2-1	318	181
1986	Ray Perkins	Mike Shula-Cornelius Bennett	10-3-0	351	163
1987	Bill Curry (Georgia Tech)	Kerry Goode-Randy Rockwell	7-5-0	268	213
1988	Bill Curry	David Smith-Derrick Thomas	9-3-0	317	188
1989	Bill Curry	Marco Battle-Willie Wyatt	10-2-0	357	217
1990	Gene Stallings (Texas A&M)	Gary Hollingsworth-Efrum Thomas-Philip Doyle	7-5-0	260	161
1991	Gene Stallings	Robert Stewart-John Sullins-Kevin Turner	11-1-0	324	143

University of Alabama All-Time Football Record

WON 669, LOST 234, TIED 43, 73%
(1892-PRESENT)

1892—WON 2, LOST 2

56	B'him H. Sch.	0	Birmingham	Nov. 11
4	B'ham A. C.	5	Birmingham	Nov. 12
14	B'ham A. C.	10	Birmingham	Nov. 4
22	Auburn	32	B'ham	Feb. 22, 1893
96		37		

1893—WON 0, LOST 4

0	B'ham A. C.	4	Tuscaloosa	Oct. 14
8	B'ham A. C.	10	Birmingham	Nov. 4
0	Sewanee	20	Birmingham	Nov. 11
16	Auburn	40	Montgomery	Nov. 30
24		74		

1894—WON 3, LOST 1

0	Mississippi	6	Jackson, Miss.	Oct. 27
18	Tulane	6	New Orleans	Nov. 3
24	Sewanee	4	Birmingham	Nov. 15
18	Auburn	0	Montgomery	Nov. 29
60		16		

1895—WON 0, LOST 4

6	Georgia	30	Columbus, Ga.	Nov. 9
0	Tulane	22	New Orleans	Nov. 6
6	L.S.U.	12	B. Rouge, La.	Nov. 18
0	Auburn	48	Tuscaloosa	Nov. 23
12		112		

1896—WON 2, LOST 1

30	B'ham A. C.	0
6	Sewanee	10
20	Miss. State	0
56		10

1897—WON 1, LOST 0

6	Tuscaloosa A. C.	0	Tuscaloosa

1898—(NO TEAM)

1899—WON 3, LOST 1

16	Tuscaloosa A.C.	5	Tuscaloosa	Oct. 21
16	Montgomery A.C.	0	Tuscaloosa	Nov. 11
7	Mississippi	5	Jackson, Miss.	Nov. 24
0	N. Orleans A.C.	21	New Orleans	Nov. 25
39		31		

1900—WON 2, LOST 3

35	Taylor Sch.	0	Tuscaloosa	Oct. 21
12	Mississippi	5	Tuscaloosa	Oct. 26
0	Tulane	6	Tuscaloosa	Nov. 3
5	Auburn	53	Montgomery	Nov. 17
0	Clemson	35	Birmingham	Nov. 29
52		99		

1901—WON 2, LOST 1, TIED 2

41	Mississippi	6	Tuscaloosa	Oct. 19
0	Georgia	0	Montgomery	Nov. 9
0	Auburn	17	Tuscaloosa	Nov. 15
45	Miss. State	0	Tuscaloosa	Nov. 28
6	Tennessee	6	Birmingham	Nov. 28
92		23		

1902—WON 4, LOST 4

57	B'ham H. S.	0	Tuscaloosa	Oct. 10
81	Marion Inst.	0	Tuscaloosa	Oct. 13
0	Auburn	23	Birmingham	Oct. 18
0	Georgia	5	Birmingham	Nov. 1
27	Miss. State	0	Tuscaloosa	Nov. 8
0	Texas	10	Tuscaloosa	Nov. 11
26	Ga. Tech	0	Birmingham	Nov. 27
0	L.S.U.	11	Tuscaloosa	Nov. 29
191		49		

1903—WON 4, LOST 4

0	Vanderbilt	30	Nashville	Oct. 10
0	Miss. State	11	Columbus, Miss.	Oct. 16
18	Auburn	6	Montgomery	Oct. 23
0	Sewanee	23	Birmingham	Nov. 2
18	L.S.U.	0	Tuscaloosa	Nov. 9
0	Cumberland U.	44	Tuscaloosa	Nov. 14
24	Tennessee	0	Birmingham	Nov. 26
60		114		

1904—WON 7, LOST 3

29	Florida	0	Tuscaloosa	Oct. 3
0	Clemson	18	Birmingham	Oct. 8
6	Miss. State	0	Columbus, Miss.	Oct. 15
17	Nashville U.	0	Tuscaloosa	Oct. 24
16	Georgia	5	Tuscaloosa	Nov. 5
5	Auburn	29	Birmingham	Nov. 12
0	Tennessee	0	Birmingham	Nov. 24
11	L.S.U.	0	B. Rouge	Dec. 2
6	Tulane	0	N. Orleans	Dec. 4
10	Pensacola A.C.	5	Pensacola, Fla.	Dec. 4
100		62		

1905—WON 6, LOST 4

17	Maryville	0	Tuscaloosa	Oct. 3
0	Vanderbilt	34	Nashville	Oct. 7
34	Miss. State	0	Tuscaloosa	Oct. 14
5	Georgia Tech	12	Atlanta	Oct. 21
0	Clemson	25	Columbia, S.C.	Oct. 25
36	Georgia	0	Birmingham	Nov. 4
21	Centre	0	Tuscaloosa	Nov. 9
30	Auburn	0	Birmingham	Nov. 18
6	Sewanee	42	Birmingham	Nov. 23
29	Tennessee	0	Birmingham	Nov. 30
178		113		

1906—WON 5, LOST 1

6	Maryville	0	Tuscaloosa	Oct. 6
14	Howard Co.	0	Tuscaloosa	Oct. 13
0	Vanderbilt	78	Nashville	Oct. 20
16	Miss. State	4	Starkville, Miss	Nov. 3
10	Auburn	0	Birmingham	Nov. 17
51	Tennessee	0	Birmingham	Nov. 29
97		82		

1907—WON 5, LOST 1, TIED 2

17	Maryville	0	Tuscaloosa	Oct. 5
20	Mississippi	0	Columbus, Miss.	Oct. 12
4	Sewanee	54	Tuscaloosa	Oct. 21
0	Georgia	0	Montgomery	Oct. 25
12	Centre	0	Birmingham	Nov. 2
6	Auburn	6	Birmingham	Nov. 16
6	L.S.U.	4	Mobile	Nov. 23
5	Tennessee	0	Birmingham	Nov. 28
70		82		

1908—WON 6, LOST 1, TIED 1

27	Wetumpka	0	Tuscaloosa	Oct. 3
17	Howard	0	Birmingham	Oct. 10
16	Cincinnati	0	Birmingham	Oct. 17
6	Ga. Tech	11	Atlanta	Oct. 24
23	Chattanooga U.	6	Tuscaloosa	Oct. 31
6	Georgia	6	Birmingham	Nov. 14
9	Haskell Inst.	8	Tuscaloosa	Nov. 20
4	Tennessee	0	Birmingham	Nov. 26
108		31		

1909—WON 5, LOST, 1, TIED 2

16	Union	0	Tuscaloosa	Oct. 2
14	Howard	0	Tuscaloosa	Oct. 9
3	Clemson	0	Birmingham	Oct. 16
0	Mississippi	0	Jackson, Miss.	Oct. 23
14	Georgia	0	Atlanta	Oct. 30
10	Tennessee	0	Knoxville	Nov. 13
5	Tulane	5	N. Orleans	Nov. 20
6	L.S.U.	12	Birmingham	Nov. 25
68		17		

1910—WON 4, LOST 4

25	B'ham Sou.	0	Tuscaloosa	Oct. 1
26	Marion Inst.	0	Tuscaloosa	Oct. 8
0	Georgia	22	Birmingham	Oct. 15
0	Ga. Tech	36	Tuscaloosa	Oct. 22
0	Mississippi	16	Greenville, Miss.	Nov. 5
0	Sewanee	30	Birmingham	Nov. 12
5	Tulane	3	N. Orleans	Nov. 19
9	Wash. & Lee	0	Birmingham	Nov. 24
65		107		

1911—WON 5, LOST 2, TIED 2

24	Howard	0	Tuscaloosa	Sept. 30
47	B'ham Sou.	5	Birmingham	Oct. 14
3	Georgia	11	Tuscaloosa	Oct. 7
6	Miss. State	6	Columbus, Miss.	Oct. 21
0	Ga. Tech	0	Atlanta	Oct. 29
35	Marion Inst.	0	Marion, Ala.	Nov. 4
0	Sewanee	3	Tuscaloosa	Nov. 11
22	Tulane	0	Birmingham	Nov. 18
16	Davidson Col.	6	Birmingham	Nov. 30
153		31		

1912—WON 5, LOST 3, TIED 1

52	Marion Inst.	0	Tuscaloosa	Sept. 28
62	B'ham Sou.	0	Tuscaloosa	Oct. 5
3	Ga. Tech	20	Atlanta	Oct. 12
0	Miss. State	7	Aberdeen, Miss.	Oct. 18
9	Georgia	13	Columbus, Ga.	Oct. 26
7	Tulane	0	N. Orleans	Nov. 2
10	Mississippi	9	Tuscaloosa	Nov. 9
6	Sewanee	6	Birmingham	Nov. 16
7	Tennessee	0	Birmingham	Nov. 28
156		55		

1913—WON 6, LOST 3

27	Howard	0	Tuscaloosa	Sept. 27
81	B'ham Sou.	0	Tuscaloosa	Oct. 4
20	Clemson	0	Tuscaloosa	Oct. 11
0	Georgia	20	Tuscaloosa	Oct. 18
26	Tulane	0	N. Orleans	Oct. 25
21	Miss. Col.	3	Jackson, Miss.	Nov. 1
7	Sewanee	10	Birmingham	Nov. 9
6	Tennessee	0	Tuscaloosa	Nov. 14
0	Miss. State	7	Birmingham	Nov. 27
188		40		

1914—WON 5, LOST 4

13	Howard	0	Tuscaloosa	Oct. 3
54	B'ham Sou.	0	Tuscaloosa	Oct. 10
13	Ga. Tech	0	Birmingham	Oct. 17
7	Tennessee	17	Knoxville	Oct. 24
58	Tulane	0	Tuscaloosa	Oct. 31
0	Sewanee	18	Birmingham	Nov. 7
63	Chattanooga	0	Tuscaloosa	Nov. 13
0	Miss. State	9	Birmingham	Nov. 26
3	Carlisle	20	Birmingham	Dec. 5
211		64		

*1915—WON 6, LOST 2

44	Howard	0	Tuscaloosa	Oct. 2
67	B'ham Sou.	0	Tuscaloosa	Oct. 9
40	Miss. Col.	0	Tuscaloosa	Oct. 16
16	Tulane	0	Tuscaloosa	Oct. 23
23	Sewanee	10	Birmingham	Oct. 30
7	Ga. Tech	21	Atlanta	Nov. 6
0	Texas	20	Austin, Tex.	Nov. 13
53	Mississippi	0	Birmingham	Nov. 25
250		51		

1916—WON 6, LOST 3

13	B'ham Sou.	0	Tuscaloosa	Sept. 30
80	Sou. Univ.	0	Tuscaloosa	Oct. 7
13	Miss. Col.	7	Tuscaloosa	Oct. 14
16	Florida	0	Jacksonville, Fla.	Oct. 21
27	Mississippi	0	Tuscaloosa	Oct. 28
7	Sewanee	6	Birmingham	Nov. 4
0	Ga. Tech	13	Atlanta	Nov. 11
0	Tulane	33	N. Orleans	Nov. 18
0	Georgia	3	Birmingham	Nov. 30
156		62		

1917—WON 5, LOST 2, TIED 1

7	Ohio Am. Corp.	0	Montgomery	Oct. 3
13	Marion Inst.	0	Tuscaloosa	Oct. 12
46	Miss. Col.	0	Tuscaloosa	Oct. 20
64	Mississippi	0	Tuscaloosa	Oct. 26
3	Sewanee	3	Birmingham	Nov. 3
2	Vanderbilt	7	Birmingham	Nov. 10
27	Kentucky	0	Lexington	Nov. 17
6	Cp. Gordon	19	Birmingham	Nov. 29
168		29		

1918—(NO TEAM)

1919—WON 8, LOST 1

27	B'ham Sou.	0	Tuscaloosa	Oct. 4
49	Mississippi	0	Tuscaloosa	Oct. 11
48	Howard	0	Tuscaloosa	Oct. 18
61	Marion Inst.	0	Tuscaloosa	Oct. 24
40	Sewanee	0	Birmingham	Nov. 1
12	Vanderbilt	16	Nashville	Nov. 8
23	L.S.U.	0	B. Rouge	Nov. 15
6	Georgia	0	Atlanta	Nov. 22
14	Miss. State	6	Birmingham	Nov. 27
280		22		

1920—WON 10, LOST 1

59	Sou. Mil. Inst.	0	Tuscaloosa	Sept. 25
49	Marion Inst.	0	Tuscaloosa	Oct. 2
45	B'ham Sou.	0	Tuscaloosa	Oct. 9
57	Miss. Col.	0	Tuscaloosa	Oct. 16
33	Howard	0	Tuscaloosa	Oct. 23
21	Sewanee	0	Birmingham	Oct. 30
14	Vanderbilt	7	Birmingham	Nov. 6
21	L.S.U.	0	Tuscaloosa	Nov. 11
14	Georgia	21	Atlanta	Nov. 20
24	Miss. State	7	Birmingham	Nov. 25
40	Case College	0	Cleveland O.	Nov. 27
377		35		

1921—WON 5, LOST 4, TIED 2

34	Howard	14	Tuscaloosa	Sept. 24
27	Spring Hill	7	Tuscaloosa	Oct. 1
55	Marion Inst.	0	Tuscaloosa	Oct. 8
95	Bryson (N.C.)	0	Tuscaloosa	Oct. 15
0	Sewanee	17	Birmingham	Oct. 22
7	L.S.U.	7	N. Orleans	Oct. 29
0	Vanderbilt	14	Birmingham	Nov. 5
2	Florida	9	Tuscaloosa	Nov. 11
0	Georgia	22	Atlanta	Nov. 19
7	Miss. State	7	Birmingham	Nov. 24
14	Tulane	7	N. Orleans	Dec. 3
241		104		

1922—WON 6, LOST 3, TIED 1

110	Marion Inst.	0	Tuscaloosa	Sept. 30
41	Oglethorpe	0	Tuscaloosa	Oct. 7
7	Ga. Tech	33	Atlanta	Oct. 14
7	Sewanee	7	Birmingham	Oct. 21
10	Texas	19	Austin, Tex.	Oct. 28
9	Pennsylvania	7	Philadelphia	Nov. 4
47	L.S.U.	3	Tuscaloosa	Nov. 10
0	Kentucky	6	Lexington	Nov. 18
10	Georgia	6	Montgomery	Nov. 25
59	Miss. State	0	Birmingham	Nov. 30
300		81		

1923—WON 7, LOST 2, TIED 1

12	Union	0	Tuscaloosa	Sept. 29
56	Mississippi	0	Tuscaloosa	Oct. 6
0	Syracuse	23	Syracuse, N.Y.	Oct. 13
7	Sewanee	0	Birmingham	Oct. 20
59	Spring Hill	0	Mobile	Oct. 27
0	Ga. Tech	0	Atlanta	Nov. 3
16	Kentucky	8	Tuscaloosa	Nov. 10
30	L.S.U.	3	Montgomery	Nov. 16
36	Georgia	0	Montgomery	Nov. 24
6	Florida	16	Birmingham	Nov. 29
222		**50**		

1924—WON 8, LOST 1

55	Union	0	Tuscaloosa	Sept. 27
20	Furman Univ.	0	Greenville, S.C.	Oct. 4
51	Miss. Col.	0	Tuscaloosa	Oct. 11
14	Sewanee	0	Birmingham	Oct. 18
14	Ga. Tech	0	Atlanta	Oct. 25
61	Mississippi	0	Montgomery	Nov. 1
42	Kentucky	7	Tuscaloosa	Nov. 8
0	Centre Col.	17	Birmingham	Nov. 15
33	Georgia	0	Birmingham	Nov. 27
290		**24**		

1925—WON 10, LOST 0

53	Union Col.	0	Tuscaloosa	Sept. 26
50	B'ham Sou.	7	Tuscaloosa	Oct. 2
42	L.S.U.	0	Birmingham	Oct. 17
27	Sewanee	0	B. Rouge	Oct. 10
7	Ga. Tech	0	Atlanta	Oct. 24
6	Miss. State	0	Tuscaloosa	Oct. 31
31	Kentucky	0	Birmingham	Nov. 7
34	Florida	0	Montgomery	Nov. 14
27	Georgia	0	Birmingham	Nov. 26
*20	U. of Wash.	19	Rose Bowl	Jan. 1, '26
297		**26**		

1926—WON 9, LOST 0, TIED 1

54	Milsaps	0	Tuscaloosa	Sept. 24
19	Vanderbilt	7	Nashville	Oct. 2
26	Miss. State	7	Meridian, Miss.	Oct. 9
21	Ga. Tech	0	Atlanta	Oct. 16
2	Sewanee	0	Birmingham	Oct. 23
24	L.S.U.	0	Tuscaloosa	Oct. 30
14	Kentucky	0	Birmingham	Nov. 6
49	Florida	0	Montgomery	Nov. 13
33	Georgia	6	Birmingham	Nov. 25
* 7	Stanford	7	Rose Bowl	Jan. 1, 27
249		**27**		

1927—WON 5, LOST 4, TIED 1

46	Milsaps	0	Tuscaloosa	Sept. 24
31	So. Pres. U.	0	Tuscaloosa	Sept. 30
0	L.S.U.	0	Birmingham	Oct. 8
0	Ga. Tech	13	Atlanta	Oct. 15
24	Sewanee	0	Birmingham	Oct. 22
13	Miss. State	7	Tuscaloosa	Oct. 29
21	Kentucky	6	Birmingham	Nov. 5
6	Florida	13	Montgomery	Nov. 12
+ 6	Georgia	20	Birmingham	Nov. 24
7	Vanderbilt	14	Birmingham	Dec. 3
154		**73**		

1928—WON 6, LOST 3

27	Mississippi	0	Tuscaloosa	Oct. 6
46	Miss. State	15	St'kville, Miss.	Oct. 13
13	Tennessee	15	Tuscaloosa	Oct. 20
42	Sewanee	12	Montgomery	Oct. 27
0	Wisconsin	15	Madison, Wis.	Nov. 3
14	Kentucky	0	Montgomery	Nov. 10
13	Ga. Tech	33	Atlanta	Nov. 17
19	Georgia	0	Birmingham	Nov. 29
13	L.S.U.	0	Birmingham	Dec. 8
187		**75**		

1929—WON 6, LOST 3

55	Miss. Col.	0	Tuscaloosa	Sept. 28
22	Mississippi	7	Tuscaloosa	Oct. 5
46	Chattanooga	0	Tuscaloosa	Oct. 12
0	Tennessee	6	Knoxville	Oct. 19
35	Sewanee	7	Birmingham	Oct. 26
0	Vanderbilt	13	Nashville	Nov. 2
24	Kentucky	13	Montgomery	Nov. 9
14	Ga. Tech	0	Atlanta	Nov. 16
0	Georgia	12	Birmingham	Nov. 28
196		**58**		

1930—WON 10, LOST 0

43	Howard	0	Tuscaloosa	Sept. 27
64	Mississippi	0	Tuscaloosa	Oct. 4
25	Sewanee	0	Birmingham	Oct. 11
18	Tennessee	6	Tuscaloosa	Oct. 18
12	Vanderbilt	7	Birmingham	Oct. 25
19	Kentucky	0	Lexington	Nov. 1
20	Florida	0	Gainesville	Nov. 8
33	L.S.U.	0	Montgomery	Nov. 15
13	Georgia	0	Birmingham	Nov. 27
*24	Wash. State	0	Rose Bowl, Jan. 1, '31	
271		**13**		

1931—WON 9, LOST 1

42	Howard	0	Tuscaloosa	Sept. 28
55	Mississippi	6	Tuscaloosa	Oct. 3
53	Miss. State	0	Meridian, Miss.	Oct. 10
0	Tennessee	25	Knoxville	Oct. 17
33	Sewanee	0	Birmingham	Oct. 24
9	Kentucky	7	Tuscaloosa	Oct. 31
41	Florida	0	Birmingham	Nov. 7
74	Clemson	7	Montgomery	Nov. 14
14	Vanderbilt	6	Nashville	Nov. 26
49	Chattanooga	0	Chattanooga	Dec. 2
370		**57**		

1932—WON 8, LOST 2

45	Southwestern	6	Tuscaloosa	Sept. 24
53	Miss. State	0	Montgomery	Oct. 1
28	George Wash.	6	Wash., D. C.	Oct. 8
3	Tennessee	7	Birmingham	Oct. 15
24	Mississippi	13	Tuscaloosa	Oct. 22
12	Kentucky	7	Lexington	Oct. 29
9	V. P. I.	6	Tuscaloosa	Nov. 5
0	Ga. Tech	6	Atlanta	Nov. 12
20	Vanderbilt	0	Birmingham	Nov. 24
6	St. Mary's	0	San Francisco	Dec. 5
200		**51**		

1933—WON 7, LOST 1, TIED 1
SEC CHAMPIONS

34	Oglethorpe	0	Tuscaloosa	Sept. 30
0	Mississippi	0	Birmingham	Oct. 7
18	Miss. State	0	Tuscaloosa	Oct. 14
12	Tennessee	6	Knoxville	Oct. 21
0	Fordham	2	New York	Oct. 28
20	Kentucky	0	Birmingham	Nov. 4
27	V. P. I.	0	Tuscaloosa	Nov. 11
12	Ga. Tech	9	Atlanta	Nov. 18
7	Vanderbilt	0	Nashville	Nov. 30
130		**17**		

1934—WON 10, LOST 0
SEC CHAMPIONS

24	Howard	0	Tuscaloosa	Sept. 29
35	Sewanee	6	Montgomery	Oct. 5
41	Miss. State	0	Tuscaloosa	Oct. 13
13	Tennessee	6	Birmingham	Oct. 20
26	Georgia	6	Birmingham	Oct. 27
34	Kentucky	14	Lexington	Nov. 3
40	Clemson	0	Tuscaloosa	Nov. 10
40	Ga. Tech	0	Atlanta	Nov. 17
34	Vanderbilt	0	Birmingham	Nov. 29
*29	Stanford	13	Rose Bowl, Jan. 1, '35	
316		**45**		

1935—WON 6, LOST 2, TIED 1

7	Howard	7	Tuscaloosa	Sept. 28
39	Geo. Wash.	0	Wash., D. C.	Oct. 5
7	Miss. State	20	Tuscaloosa	Oct. 12
25	Tennessee	0	Knoxville	Oct. 19
17	Georgia	7	Athens, Ga.	Oct. 26
13	Kentucky	0	Birmingham	Nov. 2
33	Clemson	0	Tuscaloosa	Nov. 9
38	Ga. Tech	7	Birmingham	Nov. 16
6	Vanderbilt	14	Nashville	Nov. 28
185		**55**		

1936—WON 8, LOST 0, TIED 1

34	Howard	0	Tuscaloosa	Sept. 26
32	Clemson	0	Tuscaloosa	Oct. 3
7	Miss. State	0	Tuscaloosa	Oct. 10
0	Tennessee	0	Birmingham	Oct. 17
13	Loyola, N. O.	6	N. Orleans	Oct. 24
14	Kentucky	0	Lexington	Oct. 31
34	Tulane	7	Birmingham	Nov. 7
20	Ga. Tech	16	Atlanta	Nov. 14
14	Vanderbilt	6	Birmingham	Nov. 25
168		**35**		

1937—WON 9, LOST 1*
SEC CHAMPIONS

41	Howard	0	Tuscaloosa	Sept. 25
65	Sewanee	0	Birmingham	Oct. 2
20	S. Carolina	0	Tuscaloosa	Oct. 9
14	Tennessee	7	Knoxville	Oct. 16
19	Geo. Wash.	0	Wash., D. C.	Oct. 23
41	Kentucky	0	Tuscaloosa	Oct. 30
9	Tulane	6	N. Orleans	Nov. 6
7	Ga. Tech	0	Birmingham	Nov. 13
9	Vanderbilt	7	Nashville	Nov. 25
* 0	California	13	Rose Bowl, Jan. 1, '38	
225		**33**		

1938—WON 7, LOST 1, TIED 1

19	So. Calif	7	Los Angeles	Sept. 24
34	Howard	0	Tuscaloosa	Oct. 1
14	N. Car. State	0	Tuscaloosa	Oct. 8
0	Tennessee	13	Birmingham	Oct. 15
32	Sewanee	0	Tuscaloosa	Oct. 22
26	Kentucky	6	Lexington	Oct. 29
3	Tulane	0	Birmingham	Nov. 5
14	Ga. Tech	14	Atlanta	Nov. 12
7	Vanderbilt	0	Birmingham	Nov. 24
149		**40**		

1939—WON 5, LOST 3, TIED 1

21	Howard	0	Tuscaloosa	Sept. 30
7	Fordham	6	New York	Oct. 7
20	Mercer	0	Tuscaloosa	Oct. 14
0	Tennessee	21	Knoxville	Oct. 21
7	Miss. State	0	Tuscaloosa	Oct. 28
7	Kentucky	0	Birmingham	Nov. 4
0	Tulane	13	N. Orleans	Nov. 11
0	Ga. Tech	0	Birmingham	Nov. 18
39	Vanderbilt	0	Nashville	Nov. 30
101		**53**		

1940—WON 7, LOST 2

+26	Spring Hill	0	Mobile (N)	Sept. 27
20	Mercer	0	Tuscaloosa	Oct. 5
31	Howard	0	Tuscaloosa	Oct. 12
12	Tennessee	27	Birmingham	Oct. 19
25	Kentucky	0	Lexington	Nov. 2
13	Tulane	6	Birmingham	Nov. 9
14	Ga. Tech	13	Atlanta	Nov. 16
25	Vanderbilt	21	Birmingham	Nov. 23
0	Miss. State	13	Tuscaloosa	Nov. 30
166		**80**		

1941—WON 9, LOST 2

47	S'wes. La. Inst.	6	Tuscaloosa	Sept. 27
0	Miss. State	14	Tuscaloosa	Oct. 4
61	Howard	0	Birmingham	Oct. 11
9	Tennessee	2	Knoxville	Oct. 18
27	Georgia	14	Birmingham	Oct. 25
30	Kentucky	0	Tuscaloosa	Nov. 1
19	Tulane	14	N. Orleans	Nov. 8
20	Ga. Tech	0	Birmingham	Nov. 15
0	Vanderbilt	7	Nashville	Nov. 22
21	Miami (Fla.)	7	Miami (N)	Nov. 28
*29	Texas A&M	21	Cotton Bowl, Jan. 1, '42	
263		**85**		

1942—WON 8, LOST 3

54	S'wes. La. Inst.	0	Montgomery (N)	Sept. 25
21	Miss. State	6	Tuscaloosa	Oct. 3
27	Pen'cola N.A.S.	0	Mobile	Oct. 10
8	Tennessee	0	Birmingham	Oct. 17
14	Kentucky	0	Lexington	Oct. 24
10	Georgia	21	Atlanta	Oct. 31
29	S. Carolina	0	Tuscaloosa	Nov. 7
0	Ga. Tech	7	Atlanta	Nov. 14
27	Vanderbilt	7	Birmingham	Nov. 21
19	Ga. N. Pre-Flt	35	Birmingham	Nov. 28
*37	Boston Col.	21	Orange Bowl, Jan. 1, '43	
246		**97**		

1943—(NO TEAM)

1944—WON 5, LOST 2, TIED 2

27	L. S. U.	27	B. Rouge (N)	Sept. 30
63	Howard	7	Birmingham	Oct. 7
55	Millsaps	0	Tuscaloosa	Oct. 14
0	Tennessee	0	Knoxville	Oct. 21
41	Kentucky	0	Montgomery (N)	Oct. 27
7	Georgia	14	Birmingham	Nov. 4
34	Mississippi	6	Mobile	Nov. 11
19	Miss. State	0	Tuscaloosa	Nov. 18
*26	Duke	29	Sugar Bowl, Jan. 1, '45	
272		**83**		

1945—WON 10, LOST 0
SEC CHAMPIONS

21	Keesler A.A.F.	0	Biloxi, Miss.	Sept. 29
26	L. S. U.	7	B. Rouge (N)	Oct. 6
55	S. Carolina	0	Montgomery	Oct. 13
25	Tennessee	7	Birmingham	Oct. 20
28	Georgia	14	Birmingham	Oct. 27
60	Kentucky	19	Louisville	Nov. 3
71	Vanderbilt	0	Nashville	Nov. 17
55	Pen'cola N.A.S.	6	Tuscaloosa	Nov. 24
55	Miss. State	13	Tuscaloosa	Dec. 1
*34	Sou. Calif.	14	Rose Bowl, Jan. 1, '46	
430		**80**		

1946—WON 7, LOST 4

26	Furman	7	Birmingham	Sept. 20
7	Tulane	6	N. Orleans	Sept. 28
14	S. Carolina	6	Columbia, S.C.	Oct. 5
54	S'wes. La. Inst.	0	Tuscaloosa	Oct. 12
0	Tennessee	12	Knoxville	Oct. 19
21	Kentucky	7	Montgomery	Oct. 26
0	Georgia	14	Athens, Ga.	Nov. 2
21	L. S. U.	31	Baton Rouge	Nov. 9
12	Vanderbilt	7	Birmingham	Nov. 16
7	Boston Col.	13	Boston	Nov. 23
24	Miss. State	7	Tuscaloosa	Nov. 30
186		**110**		

1947—WON 8, LOST 3

34	Miss. Southern	7	Birmingham (N)	Sept. 20
20	Tulane	21	New Orleans	Sept. 27
7	Vanderbilt	14	Nashville	Oct. 4
26	Duquesne	0	Tuscaloosa	Oct. 11
10	Tennessee	0	Birmingham	Oct. 18
17	Georgia	7	Athens, Ga.	Oct. 25
13	Kentucky	0	Lexington	Nov. 1
14	Ga. Tech	7	Birmingham	Nov. 15
41	L. S. U.	12	Tuscaloosa	Nov. 22
21	Miami (Fla.)	6	Miami	Nov. 29
* 7	Texas	27	Sugar Bowl, Jan. 1, '48	
210		**101**		

1948—WON 6, LOST 4, TIED 1

14	Tulane	21	New Orleans	Sept. 25
14	Vanderbilt	14	Mobile	Oct. 2
48	Duquesne	6	Tuscaloosa (N)	Oct. 8
6	Tennessee	21	Knoxville	Oct. 16
10	Miss. State	7	Starkville	Oct. 23
0	Georgia	35	Birmingham	Oct. 30
27	Miss. Southern	0	Tuscaloosa	Nov. 6
14	Georgia Tech	12	Atlanta	Nov. 13
6	L. S. U.	26	Baton Rouge	Nov. 20
34	Florida	28	Tuscaloosa	Nov. 27
55	Auburn	0	Birmingham	Dec. 4
228		170		

1949—WON 6, LOST 3, TIED 1

14	Tulane	28	Mobile	Sept. 24
7	Vanderbilt	14	Nashville	Oct. 1
48	Duquesne	8	Tuscaloosa (N)	Oct. 7
7	Tennessee	7	Birmingham	Oct. 15
35	Miss. State	6	Tuscaloosa	Oct. 22
14	Georgia	7	Athens	Oct. 29
20	Ga. Tech	7	Birmingham	Nov. 12
34	Miss. Southern	26	Tuscaloosa	Nov. 19
35	Florida	13	Gainesville	Nov. 26
13	Auburn	14	Birmingham	Dec. 3
227		130		

1950—WON 9, LOST 2

27	Chattanooga	0	Birmingham	Sept. 23
26	Tulane	14	New Orleans	Sept. 30
22	Vanderbilt	27	Mobile	Oct. 1
34	Furman	6	Tuscaloosa (N)	Oct. 13
9	Tennessee	14	Knoxville	Oct. 21
14	Miss. State	7	Tuscaloosa	Oct. 28
14	Georgia	7	Birmingham	Nov. 4
53	Miss. Southern	0	Tuscaloosa	Nov. 11
54	Ga. Tech	19	Atlanta	Nov. 18
41	Florida	13	Jacksonville	Nov. 25
34	Auburn	0	Birmingham	Dec. 2
328		107		

1951—WON 5, LOST 6

89	Delta State	0	Montgomery (N)	Sept. 21
7	L. S. U.	13	Mobile (N)	Sept. 29
20	Vanderbilt	22	Nashville (N)	Oct. 6
18	Villanova	41	Tuscaloosa	Oct. 12
13	Tennessee	27	Birmingham	Oct. 20
7	Miss. State	0	Starkville	Oct. 27
16	Georgia	14	Athens	Nov. 3
40	Miss. Southern	7	Tuscaloosa	Nov. 10
7	Georgia Tech	27	Birmingham	Nov. 17
21	Florida	30	Tuscaloosa	Nov. 24
25	Auburn	7	Birmingham	Dec. 1
263		188		

1952—WON 10, LOST 2

20	Miss. Southern	6	Montgomery (N)	Sept. 19
21	L. S. U.	20	Baton Rouge (N)	Sept. 27
21	Miami	7	Miami (N)	Oct. 3
33	Virginia Tech	0	Tuscaloosa	Oct. 11
0	Tennessee	20	Knoxville	Oct. 18
42	Miss. State	19	Tuscaloosa	Oct. 25
34	Georgia	19	Birmingham	Nov. 1
42	Chattanooga	28	Tuscaloosa	Nov. 8
3	Georgia Tech	7	Atlanta	Nov. 15
27	Maryland	7	Mobile	Nov. 22
21	Auburn	0	Birmingham	Nov. 29
*61	Syracuse	6	Orange Bowl, Jan. 1, '53	
325		139		

1953—WON 6, LOST 3, TIED 3
SEC CHAMPIONS

19	Miss. Southern	25	Montgomery (N)	Sept. 18
7	L. S. U.	7	Mobile (N)	Sept. 26
21	Vanderbilt	12	Nashville (N)	Oct. 3
41	Tulsa	13	Tuscaloosa	Oct. 10
0	Tennessee	0	Birmingham	Oct. 17
7	Miss. State	7	Tuscaloosa	Oct. 24
33	Georgia	12	Athens	Oct. 31
21	Chattanooga	14	Tuscaloosa	Nov. 7
13	Georgia Tech	6	Birmingham	Nov. 14
0	Maryland	21	College Park	Nov. 21
10	Auburn	7	Birmingham	Nov. 28
* 6	Rice	28	Cotton Bowl, Jan. 1, '54	
178		152		

1954—WON 4, LOST 5, TIED 2

2	Miss. Southern	7	Montgomery (N)	Sept. 17
12	L. S. U.	0	Baton Rouge (N)	Sept. 25
28	Vanderbilt	14	Mobile (N)	Oct. 2
40	Tulsa	0	Tuscaloosa	Oct. 9
27	Tennessee	0	Knoxville	Oct. 16
7	Miss. State	12	Tuscaloosa	Oct. 23
0	Georgia	0	Birmingham	Oct. 30
0	Tulane	0	New Orleans	Nov. 6
0	Georgia Tech	20	Atlanta	Nov. 13
7	Miami	23	Miami (N)	Nov. 19
0	Auburn	28	Birmingham	Nov. 27
123		104		

1955—WON 0, LOST 10, TIED 0

0	Rice	20	Houston (N)	Sept. 24
6	Vanderbilt	21	Nashville (N)	Oct. 1
0	T. C. U.	21	Tuscaloosa	Oct. 8
0	Tennessee	20	Birmingham	Oct. 15
7	Miss. State	26	Tuscaloosa	Oct. 22
14	Georgia	35	Athens	Oct. 29
7	Tulane	27	Mobile	Nov. 5
2	Georgia Tech	26	Birmingham	Nov. 12
12	Miami	34	Miami (N)	Nov. 18
0	Auburn	26	Birmingham	Nov. 26
48		256		

1956—WON 2, LOST 7, TIED 1

13	Rice	20	Houston (N)	Sept. 22
7	Vanderbilt	32	Mobile (N)	Oct. 6
6	T. C. U.	23	Tuscaloosa	Oct. 13
0	Tennessee	24	Knoxville	Oct. 20
13	Miss. State	12	Tuscaloosa	Oct. 27
13	Georgia	16	Birmingham	Nov. 3
13	Tulane	7	New Orleans	Nov. 10
0	Georgia Tech	27	Atlanta	Nov. 17
13	Miss. Southern	13	Tuscaloosa	Nov. 24
7	Auburn	34	Birmingham	Dec. 1
85		208		

1957—WON 2, LOST 7, TIED 1

0	L. S. U.	28	Baton Rouge (N)	Sept. 28
6	Vanderbilt	6	Nashville (N)	Oct. 5
0	T. C. U.	28	Ft. Worth (N)	Oct. 12
0	Tennessee	14	Birmingham	Oct. 19
13	Miss. State	25	Tuscaloosa	Oct. 26
14	Georgia	13	Athens	Nov. 2
0	Tulane	7	Mobile	Nov. 9
7	Georgia Tech	10	Birmingham	Nov. 16
29	Miss. Southern	2	Tuscaloosa	Nov. 23
0	Auburn	40	Birmingham	Nov. 30
69		173		

1958—WON 5, LOST 4, TIED 1

3	L. S. U.	13	Mobile (N)	Sept. 27
0	Vanderbilt	0	Birmingham (N)	Oct. 4
29	Furman	6	Tuscaloosa (N)	Oct. 11
7	Tennessee	14	Knoxville	Oct. 18
9	Miss. State	7	Starkville	Oct. 25
12	Georgia	0	Tuscaloosa	Nov. 1
7	Tulane	13	New Orleans (N)	Nov. 8
17	Georgia Tech	8	Atlanta	Nov. 15
14	Memphis State	0	Tuscaloosa	Nov. 22
8	Auburn	14	Birmingham	Nov. 29
106		75		

1959—WON 7, LOST 2, TIED 2

3	Georgia	17	Athens	Sept. 19
3	Houston	0	Houston (N)	Sept. 26
7	Vanderbilt	7	Nashville (N)	Oct. 3
13	Chattanooga	0	Tuscaloosa	Oct. 10
7	Tennessee	7	Birmingham	Oct. 17
10	Miss. State	0	Tuscaloosa	Oct. 24
19	Tulane	7	Mobile (N)	Nov. 7
9	Ga. Tech	7	Birmingham	Nov. 14
14	Memphis State	7	Tuscaloosa	Nov. 21
10	Auburn	0	Birmingham	Nov. 28
* 0	Penn State	7	Liberty Bowl	Dec. 19
95		59		

1960—WON 8, LOST 1, TIED 2

21	Georgia	6	Birmingham	Sept. 17
6	Tulane	6	New Orleans (N)	Sept. 24
21	Vanderbilt	0	Birmingham (N)	Oct. 1
7	Tennessee	20	Knoxville	Oct. 15
14	Houston	0	Tuscaloosa	Oct. 22
7	Miss. State	0	Starkville	Oct. 29
51	Furman	0	Tuscaloosa	Nov. 5
16	Ga. Tech	15	Atlanta	Nov. 12
34	Tampa	6	Tuscaloosa	Nov. 19
3	Auburn	0	Birmingham	Nov. 26
* 3	Texas	3	Bluebonnet Bowl	Dec. 17
183		56		

1961—WON 11, LOST 0
NATIONAL CHAMPIONS
SEC CHAMPIONS

32	Georgia	6	Athens	Sept. 23
9	Tulane	0	Mobile (N)	Sept. 30
35	Vanderbilt	6	Nashville (N)	Oct. 7
26	N. C. State	7	Tuscaloosa	Oct. 14
34	Tennessee	3	Birmingham	Oct. 21
17	Houston	0	Houston (N)	Oct. 28
24	Miss. State	0	Tuscaloosa	Nov. 4
66	Richmond	0	Tuscaloosa	Nov. 11
10	Ga. Tech	0	Birmingham	Nov. 18
34	Auburn	0	Birmingham	Dec. 2
*10	Arkansas	3	Sugar Bowl, Jan. 1, '62	
297		25		

1962—WON 10, LOST 1

35	Georgia	0	Birmingham (N)	Sept. 22
44	Tulane	6	New Orleans (N)	Sept. 28
17	Vanderbilt	7	Birmingham (N)	Oct. 6
14	Houston	3	Tuscaloosa	Oct. 13
27	Tennessee	7	Knoxville	Oct. 20
35	Tulsa	6	Tuscaloosa	Oct. 27
20	Miss. State	0	Starkville	Nov. 3
36	Miami	3	Tuscaloosa	Nov. 10
6	Georgia Tech	7	Atlanta	Nov. 17
38	Auburn	0	Birmingham	Dec. 1
*17	Oklahoma	0	Orange Bowl, Jan. 1, '63	
289		39		

1963—WON 9, LOST 2

32	Georgia	7	Athens	Sept. 21
28	Tulane	0	Mobile (N)	Sept. 28
21	Vanderbilt	6	Nashville (N)	Oct. 5
6	Florida	10	Tuscaloosa	Oct. 12
35	Tennessee	0	Birmingham	Oct. 19
21	Houston	13	Tuscaloosa	Oct. 26
20	Miss. State	19	Tuscaloosa	Nov. 2
27	Georgia Tech	11	Birmingham	Nov. 16
8	Auburn	10	Birmingham	Nov. 30
17	Miami	12	Miami	Dec. 14
*12	Mississippi	7	Sugar Bowl, Jan. 1, '64	
227		95		

1964—WON 10, LOST 1
NATIONAL CHAMPIONS
SEC CHAMPIONS

31	Georgia	3	Tuscaloosa (N)	Sept. 19
36	Tulane	6	Mobile (N)	Sept. 26
24	Vanderbilt	0	Birmingham (N)	Oct. 3
21	N. C. State	0	Tuscaloosa	Oct. 10
19	Tennessee	8	Knoxville	Oct. 17
17	Florida	14	Tuscaloosa	Oct. 24
23	Miss. State	6	Jackson (N)	Oct. 31
17	L. S. U.	9	Birmingham	Nov. 7
24	Georgia Tech	7	Atlanta	Nov. 14
21	Auburn	14	Birmingham	Nov. 26
*17	Texas	21	Orange Bowl (N), Jan. 1, '65	
250		88		

1965—WON 9, LOST 1, TIED 1
AP NATIONAL CHAMPIONS
SEC CHAMPIONS

17	Georgia	18	Athens	Sept. 18
27	Tulane	0	Mobile (N)	Sept. 25
17	Mississippi	16	Birmingham (N)	Oct. 2
22	Vanderbilt	7	Nashville (N)	Oct. 9
7	Tennessee	7	Birmingham	Oct. 16
21	Florida State	0	Tuscaloosa	Oct. 23
10	Miss. State	7	Jackson (N)	Oct. 30
31	L. S. U.	7	Baton Rouge	Nov. 6
35	So. Carolina	14	Tuscaloosa	Nov. 13
30	Auburn	3	Birmingham	Nov. 27
*39	Nebraska	28	Orange Bowl (N), Jan. 1, '66	
256		107		

1966—WON 11, LOST 0, TIED 0
SEC CHAMPIONS

34	La. Tech	0	Birmingham (N)	Sept. 24
17	Mississippi	7	Jackson (N)	Oct. 1
26	Clemson	0	Tuscaloosa	Oct. 8
11	Tennessee	10	Knoxville	Oct. 15
42	Vanderbilt	6	Birmingham	Oct. 22
27	Miss. State	14	Tuscaloosa	Oct. 29
21	L. S. U.	0	Birmingham	Nov. 5
24	South Carolina	0	Tuscaloosa	Nov. 12
34	Sou. Miss.	0	Mobile	Nov. 26
31	Auburn	0	Birmingham	Dec. 3
*34	Nebraska	7	Sugar Bowl, Jan. 2, '67	
301		44		

1967—WON 8, LOST 2, TIED 1

37	Florida State	37	Birmingham (N)	Sept. 23
25	Sou. Miss.	3	Mobile (N)	Sept. 30
21	Mississippi	7	Birmingham	Oct. 7
35	Vanderbilt	21	Nashville (N)	Oct. 14
13	Tennessee	24	Birmingham	Oct. 21
13	Clemson	10	Clemson	Oct. 28
13	Miss. State	0	Tuscaloosa	Nov. 4
7	L. S. U.	6	Baton Rouge (N)	Nov. 11
17	So. Carolina	0	Tuscaloosa	Nov. 18
7	Auburn	3	Birmingham	Dec. 2
*16	Texas A&M	20	Cotton Bowl, Jan. 1, '68	
204		131		

1968—WON 8, LOST 3

14	Va. Tech	7	Birmingham (N)	Sept. 21
17	Sou. Miss.	14	Mobile	Sept. 28
8	Mississippi	10	Jackson	Oct. 5
31	Vanderbilt	7	Tuscaloosa	Oct. 12
9	Tennessee	10	Knoxville	Oct. 19
21	Clemson	14	Tuscaloosa	Oct. 26
20	Miss. State	13	Tuscaloosa	Nov. 2
16	L. S. U.	7	Birmingham	Nov. 9
14	Miami	6	Miami (N)	Nov. 16
24	Auburn	16	Birmingham	Nov. 30
*10	Missouri	35	Gator Bowl	Dec. 28
184		139		

1969—WON 6, LOST 5

17	Va. Tech	13	Blacksburg	Sept. 20
63	So. Miss.	14	Tuscaloosa (N)	Sept. 27
33	Mississippi	32	Birmingham (N)	Oct. 4
10	Vanderbilt	14	Nashville (N)	Oct. 11
14	Tennessee	41	Birmingham	Oct. 18
38	Clemson	13	Clemson	Oct. 25
23	Miss. State	19	Jackson (N)	Nov. 1
15	L. S. U.	20	Baton Rouge (N)	Nov. 6
42	Miami	6	Tuscaloosa	Nov. 15
26	Auburn	49	Birmingham	Nov. 29
*33	Colorado	47	Liberty Bowl	Dec. 13
314		268		

369

1970—WON 6, LOST 5, TIED 1

21	Southern Cal.	42	Birmingham (N) Sept. 12
51	Virginia Tech	18	Birmingham (N) Sept. 19
46	Florida	15	Tuscaloosa ....Sept. 26
23	Mississippi	48	Jackson (N) ....Oct. 3
35	Vanderbilt	11	Tuscaloosa ....Oct. 10
0	Tennessee	24	Knoxville ....Oct. 17
30	Houston	21	Houston ....Oct. 24
35	Miss. State	6	Tuscaloosa ....Oct. 31
9	L. S. U.	14	Birmingham ....Nov. 7
32	Miami	8	Miami (N) ....Nov. 14
28	Auburn	33	Birmingham ....Nov. 28
*24	Oklahoma	24	Astro-Bluebonnet Bowl (N) ....Dec. 31

334   264

1971—WON 11, LOST 1
SEC CHAMPIONS

17	Southern Cal	10	Los Angeles (N) Sept. 10
42	Southern Miss.	6	Tuscaloosa ....Sept. 18
38	Florida	0	Gainesville .....Sept. 25
40	Mississippi	6	Birmingham ....Oct. 2
42	Vanderbilt	0	Nashville (N) ....Oct. 9
32	Tennessee	15	Birmingham ....Oct. 16
34	Houston	20	Tuscaloosa ....Oct. 23
41	Miss. State	10	Jackson (N) ....Oct. 30
14	L. S. U.	7	Baton Rouge (N) Nov. 6
31	Miami	3	Tuscaloosa ....Nov. 13
7	Auburn	7	Birmingham ....Nov. 27
* 6	Nebraska	38	Orange Bowl (N), Jan. 1, '72

368   122

1972—WON 10, LOST 2
SEC CHAMPIONS

35	Duke	12	Birmingham (N) Sept. 9
35	Kentucky	0	Birmingham (N) Sept. 23
48	Vanderbilt	21	Tuscaloosa (N) ...Sept. 30
25	Georgia	7	Athens ....Oct. 7
24	Florida	7	Tuscaloosa ....Oct. 14
17	Tennessee	10	Knoxville ....Oct. 21
48	Southern Miss.	11	Birmingham (N) ..Oct. 28
58	Miss. State	14	Tuscaloosa ....Nov. 4
35	L. S. U.	21	Birmingham ....Nov. 11
52	Virginia Tech	13	Tuscaloosa ....Nov. 18
16	Auburn	17	Birmingham ....Dec. 2
*13	Texas	17	Cotton Bowl ..Jan. 1, '73

406   150

1973—WON 11, LOST 1
UPI NATIONAL CHAMPIONS
SEC CHAMPIONS

66	California	0	Birmingham (N) Sept. 15
28	Kentucky	14	Lexington ....Sept. 22
44	Vanderbilt	0	Nashville (N) ...Sept. 29
28	Georgia	14	Tuscaloosa ....Oct. 6
35	Florida	14	Gainesville ....Oct. 13
42	Tennessee	21	Birmingham ....Oct. 20
77	Virginia Tech	6	Tuscaloosa (N) ...Oct. 27
35	Miss. State	0	Jackson (N) ....Nov. 3
43	Miami	13	Tuscaloosa ....Nov. 17
21	L. S. U.	7	Baton Rouge (N) Nov. 22
35	Auburn	0	Birmingham ....Dec. 1
*23	Notre Dame	24	Sugar Bowl (N) ...Dec. 31

477   113

1974—WON 11, LOST 1
SEC CHAMPIONS

21	Maryland	14	College Park ...Sept. 14
52	Southern Miss.	0	Birmingham (N) Sept. 21
23	Vanderbilt	10	Tuscaloosa ....Sept. 28
35	Ole Miss	21	Jackson ....Oct. 5
8	Florida State	7	Tuscaloosa ....Oct. 12
28	Tennessee	6	Knoxville ....Oct. 19
41	T. C. U.	3	Birmingham ....Oct. 26
35	Miss. State	0	Tuscaloosa ....Nov. 2
30	L. S. U.	0	Birmingham ....Nov. 9
28	Miami	7	Miami (N) ....Nov. 16
17	Auburn	13	Birmingham ....Nov. 29
*11	Notre Dame	13	Miami (N) ....Jan. 1, '75

1975—WON 11, LOST 1
SEC CHAMPIONS

7	Missouri	20	Birmingham (N) Sept. 8
56	Clemson	0	Tuscaloosa (N) .....Sept. 20
40	Vanderbilt	7	Nashville ....Sept. 27
32	Ole Miss	6	Birmingham ....Oct. 4
52	Washington	0	Tuscaloosa ....Oct. 11
30	Tennessee	7	Birmingham ....Oct. 18
45	T. C. U.	0	Birmingham ....Oct. 25
21	Miss. State	10	Jackson (N) ....Nov. 1
23	L. S. U.	10	Baton Rouge (N) Nov. 8
27	Southern Miss.	6	Tuscaloosa ....Nov. 15
28	Auburn	0	Birmingham ....Nov. 29
*13	Penn State	6	Sugar Bowl (N) ..Dec. 31

1976—WON 9, LOST 3

7	Ole Miss	10	Jackson (N) ....Sept. 11
56	SMU	3	Birmingham ....Sept. 18
42	Vanderbilt	14	Tuscaloosa ....Sept. 25
0	Georgia	21	Athens ....Oct. 2
24	Southern Miss.	8	Birmingham ....Oct. 9
20	Tennessee	13	Knoxville ....Oct. 16
24	Louisville	3	Tuscaloosa ....Oct. 23
34	Miss. State	17	Tuscaloosa ....Oct. 30
28	LSU	17	Birmingham ....Nov. 6
18	Notre Dame	21	South Bend ....Nov. 13
38	Auburn	7	Birmingham ....Nov. 27
*36	UCLA	6	Liberty Bowl (N) ...Dec. 20

327   140

1977—WON 11, LOST 1
SEC CHAMPIONS

34	Ole Miss	13	Birmingham (N) Sept. 10
24	Nebraska	31	Lincoln ....Sept. 17
24	Vanderbilt	12	Nashville ....Sept. 24
18	Georgia	10	Tuscaloosa ....Oct. 1
21	Southern Cal	20	Los Angeles ....Oct. 8
24	Tennessee	10	Birmingham ....Oct. 15
55	Louisville	6	Tuscaloosa ....Oct. 22
37	Miss. State	7	Jackson (N) ....Oct. 29
24	LSU	3	Baton Rouge ....Nov. 5
36	Miami	0	Tuscaloosa ....Nov. 12
48	Auburn	21	Birmingham ....Nov. 26
*35	Ohio State	6	Sugar Bowl ....Jan. 2, '78

380   139

1978—WON 11, LOST 1
AP NATIONAL CHAMPIONS
SEC CHAMPIONS

20	Nebraska	3	Birmingham (N) Sept. 2
38	Missouri	20	Columbia ....Sept. 16
14	Southern Cal	24	Birmingham ....Sept. 23
51	Vanderbilt	28	Tuscaloosa ....Sept. 30
20	Washington	17	Seattle ....Oct. 7
23	Florida	12	Tuscaloosa ....Oct. 14
30	Tennessee	17	Knoxville ....Oct. 21
35	Virginia Tech	0	Tuscaloosa ....Oct. 28
35	Miss. State	14	Birmingham ....Nov. 4
31	L. S. U.	10	Birmingham ....Nov. 11
34	Auburn	16	Birmingham ....Dec. 2
*14	Penn State	7	Sugar Bowl ....Jan. 1, '79

335   169

1979—WON 12, LOST 0
AP & UPI NATIONAL CHAMPIONS
SEC CHAMPIONS

30	Georgia Tech	6	Atlanta (TV) ....Sept. 8
45	Baylor	0	Birmingham (N) Sept. 22
66	Vanderbilt	3	Nashville ....Sept. 29
38	Wichita State	0	Tuscaloosa ....Oct. 6
40	Florida	0	Gainesville ....Oct. 13
27	Tennessee	17	Birmingham ....Oct. 20
31	Virginia Tech	7	Tuscaloosa ....Oct. 27
24	Miss. State	7	Tuscaloosa ....Nov. 3
3	LSU	0	Baton Rouge ....Nov. 10
30	Miami (Fla.)	0	Tuscaloosa (TV) Nov. 17
25	Auburn	18	Birmingham ....Dec. 1
*24	Arkansas	9	Sugar Bowl, Jan. 1, 1980

1980—WON 10, LOST 2

26	Georgia Tech	3	Birmingham ....Sept. 6
59	Mississippi	35	Jackson ....Sept. 20
41	Vanderbilt	0	Tuscaloosa ....Sept. 27
45	Kentucky	0	Birmingham ....Oct. 4
17	Rutgers	13	East Rutherford, N.J. ...Oct. 11
27	Tennessee	0	Knoxville ....Oct. 18
42	Southern Miss.	7	Tuscaloosa ....Oct. 25
3	Mississippi State	6	Jackson ....Nov. 1
28	Louisiana State	7	Tuscaloosa ....Nov. 8
0	Notre Dame	7	Birmingham ....Nov. 15
34	Auburn	18	Birmingham ....Nov. 28
30	Baylor	2	Cotton Bowl ....Jan. 1, 1981
352		98	

1981—WON 9, LOST 2, TIED 1
SEC CHAMPIONS

24	L.S.U.	7	Baton Rouge (TV) ....Sept. 5
21	Georgia Tech.	24	Birmingham ....Sept. 12
19	Kentucky	10	Lexington ....Sept. 19
28	Vanderbilt	7	Nashville ....Sept. 26
38	Mississippi	7	Tuscaloosa ....Oct. 3
13	S. Mississippi	13	Birmingham ....Oct. 10
38	Tennessee	19	Birmingham ....Oct. 17
31	Rutgers	7	Tuscaloosa ....Oct. 24
13	Miss. State	10	Tuscaloosa ....Oct. 31
31	Penn. State	16	University Pk. (TV) ....Nov. 14
28	Auburn	17	Birmingham (TV) ....Nov. 28
*12	Texas	14	Cotton Bowl ....Jan. 1, 1982
296		151	

1982—WON 8, LOST 4

45	Georgia Tech	7	Atlanta ....Sept. 11
42	Mississippi	14	Jackson ....Sept. 18
24	Vanderbilt	21	Tuscaloosa ....Sept. 25
34	Arkansas State	7	Birmingham (N) ....Oct. 2
42	Penn. State	21	Birmingham (TV) ....Oct. 9
28	Tennessee	35	Knoxville ....Oct. 16
21	Cincinnati	3	Tuscaloosa ....Oct. 23
20	Miss. State	12	Jackson ....Oct. 30
10	L.S.U.	20	Birmingham ....Nov. 6
29	S. Mississippi	38	Tuscaloosa ....Nov. 13
22	Auburn	23	Birmingham (TV) ....Nov. 27
*21	Illinois	15	Liberty Bowl (N) ....Dec. 29
338		216	

1983—WON 8, LOST 4

20	Georgia Tech	7	Birmingham ....Sept. 10
40	Mississippi	0	Tuscaloosa ....Sept. 17
44	Vanderbilt	24	Nashville (N) ....Sept. 24
44	Memphis State	13	Tuscaloosa ....Oct. 1
28	Penn. State	34	State College (TV) ....Oct. 8
34	Tennessee	41	Birmingham ....Oct. 15
35	Mississippi State	18	Tuscaloosa ....Oct. 29
32	L.S.U.	26	Baton Rouge (TV) ....Nov. 5
28	S. Mississippi	16	Birmingham ....Nov. 12
13	Boston College	20	Foxboro (TV) ....Nov. 25
20	Auburn	23	Birmingham (TV) ....Dec. 3
*28	SMU	7	Sun Bowl (TV) ....Dec. 24
366		229	

1984—WON 5, LOST 6

31	Boston College	38	Birmingham (TV) ....Sept. 8
6	Georgia Tech	16	Atlanta (TV) ....Sept. 15
37	SW Louisiana	14	Tuscaloosa ....Sept. 22
21	Vanderbilt	30	Tuscaloosa ....Sept. 29
14	Georgia	24	Birmingham (TV) ....Oct. 6
6	Penn. State	0	Tuscaloosa ....Oct. 13
27	Tennessee	28	Knoxville ....Oct. 20
24	Mississippi State	20	Jackson ....Nov. 3
14	L.S.U.	16	Birmingham ....Nov. 10
29	Cincinnati	7	Cincinnati ....Nov. 7
17	Auburn	15	Birmingham (TV) ....Dec. 1
226		208	

1985—WON 9, LOST 2, TIED 1

20	Georgia	16	Athens (TV) ....Sept. 2
23	Texas A&M	10	Birmingham (TV) ....Sept. 14
45	Cincinnati	10	Tuscaloosa ....Sept. 21
40	Vanderbilt	20	Nashville (TV) ....Sept. 28
17	Penn. State	19	State College (TV) ....Oct. 12
14	Tennessee	16	Birmingham (TV) ....Oct. 19
28	Memphis State	9	Memphis ....Oct. 26
44	Mississippi State	28	Tuscaloosa ....Nov. 2
14	L.S.U.	14	Baton Rouge (TV) ....Nov. 9
24	So. Mississippi	13	Tuscaloosa ....Nov. 16
25	Auburn	23	Birmingham (TV) ....Nov. 30
*24	So. California	3	Aloha Bowl (TV) ....Dec. 28
318		181	

1986—WON 10, LOST 3

16	Ohio State	10	E. Rutherford, N.J. (TV) ....Aug. 27
42	Vanderbilt	10	Tuscaloosa (TV) ....Sept. 6
31	S. Mississippi	17	Birmingham ....Sept. 13
21	Florida	0	Gainesville ....Sept. 20
28	Notre Dame	10	Birmingham (TV) ....Oct. 4
37	Memphis State	0	Tuscaloosa ....Oct. 11
56	Tennessee	28	Knoxville (TV) ....Oct. 18
3	Penn. State	23	Tuscaloosa ....Oct. 25
38	Mississippi State	3	Starkville (TV) ....Nov. 1
10	L.S.U.	14	Birmingham (TV) ....Nov. 8
24	Temple	14	Tuscaloosa ....Nov. 15
17	Auburn	21	Birmingham (TV) ....Nov. 22
*28	Washington	6	Sun Bowl (TV) ....Dec. 25
351		163	

1987—WON 7, LOST 5

38	Southern Miss	6	Birmingham ....Sept. 5
24	Penn State	13	State College (N) (TV) .Sept. 12
14	Florida	23	Birmingham (N) ....Sept. 19
30	Vanderbilt	23	Nashville (N) ....Sept. 26
38	SW Louisiana	10	Birmingham ....Oct. 3
10	Memphis State	13	Memphis ....Oct. 10
41	Tennessee	22	Birmingham (N) (TV) ....Oct. 17
21	Miss. State	18	Birmingham (N) ....Oct. 31
22	L.S.U.	10	Baton Rouge (N) (TV) ...Nov. 7
6	Notre Dame	37	South Bend (N) ....Nov. 14
0	Auburn	10	Birmingham (TV) ....Nov. 27
*24	Michigan	28	Hall of Fame (TV) ....Jan. 2
268		213	

1988—WON 9, LOST 3

37	Temple	0	Philadelphia (N) ....Sept. 10
44	Vanderbilt	10	Tuscaloosa ....Sept. 24
31	Kentucky	27	Lexington (TV) ....Oct. 1
12	Mississippi	22	Tuscaloosa (TV) ....Oct. 8
28	Tennessee	20	Knoxville ....Oct. 15
8	Penn State	3	Birmingham (TV) ....Oct. 22
53	Miss. State	34	Starkville ....Oct. 29
18	LSU	19	Tuscaloosa (TV) ....Nov. 5
17	SW Louisiana	0	Birmingham ....Nov. 12
10	Auburn	15	Birmingham (TV) ....Nov. 25
30	Texas A&M	10	College Station (N) (TV) ....Dec. 1
*29	Army	28	Sun Bowl (TV) ....Dec. 24
297		188	

1989—WON 10, LOST 2
SEC CHAMPIONS

35	Memphis State	7	Birmingham ....Sept. 16
15	Kentucky	3	Tuscaloosa (TV) ....Sept. 23
20	Vanderbilt	14	Nashville (TV) ....Sept. 30
62	Mississippi	27	Jackson ....Oct. 7
24	SW Louisiana	17	Tuscaloosa ....Oct. 14
47	Tennessee	30	Birmingham (TV) ....Oct. 21
17	Penn State	10	State College (TV) ....Oct. 28
23	Miss. State	10	Birmingham (TV) ....Nov. 4
32	L.S.U.	16	Baton Rouge (N) (TV) ...Nov. 11
37	Southern Miss	14	Tuscaloosa ....Nov. 18
20	Auburn	30	Auburn (TV) ....Dec. 2
*25	Miami	33	Sugar Bowl (N) (TV) .....Jan. 1
357		217	

1990—WON 7, LOST 5

24	Southern Miss	27	Birmingham ....Sept. 8
13	Florida	17	Tuscaloosa (TV) ....Sept. 15
16	Georgia	17	Athens (TV) ....Sept. 22
59	Vanderbilt	28	Tuscaloosa ....Sept. 29
25	SW Louisiana	6	Lafayette ....Oct. 6
9	Tennessee	6	Knoxville (TV) ....Oct. 20
0	Penn State	9	Tuscaloosa (TV) ....Oct. 27
22	Miss. State	0	Starkville (TV) ....Nov. 3
24	L.S.U.	3	Tuscaloosa ....Nov. 10
45	Cincinnati	7	Birmingham ....Nov. 17
16	Auburn	7	Birmingham (TV) ....Dec. 1
* 7	Louisville	34	Fiesta Bowl (TV) ....Jan. 1
260		161	

1991 WON 11, LOST 1

41	Temple	3	Birmingham ....Sept. 7
0	Florida	35	Gainesville (TV) ....Sept. 14
10	Georgia	0	Tuscaloosa (TV) ....Sept. 21
48	Vanderbilt	17	Nashville ....Sept. 28
53	UT-Chattanooga	7	Birmingham ....Oct. 5
62	Tulane	0	Tuscaloosa ....Oct. 12
24	Tennessee	19	Birmingham (TV) ....Oct. 19
13	Mississippi State	7	Tuscaloosa (TV) ....Nov. 2
20	L.S.U.	17	Baton Rouge (TV) ....Nov. 9
10	Memphis State	7	Memphis ....Nov. 16
13	Auburn	6	Birmingham (TV) ....Nov. 30
*30	Colorado	25	Blockbuster Bowl (TV) ..Dec. 28
324		143	

*Denotes bowl game

University of Alabama Bowl Records

TEAM RECORDS

Most Plays: 89 vs. Michigan, 1988 Hall of Fame

Most Yards: 586 vs. Syracuse, 1953 Orange

Highest Average Gain Per Play: 7.4 vs. Syracuse, 1953 Orange

Fewest Plays: 47 vs. Penn State, 1959 Liberty

Least Yards: 32 vs. Missouri, 1968 Gator

Rushing

Most Attempts: 68 vs. Ohio State, 1978 Sugar

Most Yards: 292 vs. Southern Cal., 1946 Rose

Most TDs: 4 vs. Syracuse, 1953 Orange

Fewest Rushes: 26 vs. Texas, 1964 Orange

Least Yards: −45 vs. Missouri, 1968 Gator

Passing

Most Attempts: 52 vs. Army, 1988 Sun

Most Yards: 412 vs. Army, 1988 Sun

Most Completions: 33 vs. Army, 1988 Sun

Most TDs: 3, last vs. Miami, 1990 Sugar

Fewest Attempts: 7 vs. Arkansas, 1980 Sugar

Fewest Completions: 2 vs. Penn State, 1959 Liberty

Least Yards: 16 vs. Texas A&M, 1992 Cotton

Most Interceptions: 3, last vs. Louisville, 1991 Fiesta

TOP TEN BOWL PERFORMANCES

TOTAL OFFENSE

Most Plays
89 vs. Michigan, 1988 Hall of Fame
88 vs. Army, 1988 Sun
86 vs. Nebraska, 1966 Orange
81 vs. Colorado, 1991 Blockbuster
80 vs. Colorado, 1969 Liberty
79 vs. Syracuse, 1953 Orange
79 vs. Ohio State, 1977 Sugar
79 vs. Baylor, 1981 Cotton
77 vs. Miami, 1990 Sugar
76 vs. SMU, 1983 Sun
75 vs. Penn State, 1979 Sugar

Fewest Plays
47 vs. Penn State, 1959 Liberty
51 vs. Rice, 1954 Cotton
56 vs. Missouri, 1968 Gator
57 vs. Texas, 1982 Cotton
60 vs. Arkansas, 1980 Sugar
60 vs. Texas, 1973 Cotton
61 vs. Penn State, 1975 Sugar
63 vs. UCLA, 1976 Liberty
67 vs. Washington, 1986 Sun
68 vs. Louisville, 1991 Fiesta

Most Yards
586 vs. Syracuse, 1953 Orange
518 vs. Nebraska, 1966 Orange
507 vs. Army, 1988 Sun
460 vs. Michigan, 1988 Hall of Fame
436 vs. Nebraska, 1967 Sugar
428 vs. Oklahoma, 1977 Bluebonnet
399 vs. SMU, 1983 Sun
389 vs. Washington, 1986 Sun
389 vs. Ohio State, 1978 Sugar
372 vs. UCLA, 1976 Liberty

Fewest Yards
23 vs. Missouri, 1968 Gator
75 vs. Texas A&M, 1942 Cotton
103 vs. Texas, 1948 Sugar
131 vs. Penn State, 1959
183 vs. California, 1937 Rose
189 vs. Louisville, 1991 Fiesta
194 vs. Ole Miss, 1964 Sugar
252 vs. Miami, 1990 Sugar
255 vs. Rice, 1954 Cotton
288 vs. Nebraska, 1972 Orange
299 vs. Penn State, 1979 Sugar

RUSHING

Most Rushes
68 vs. Ohio State, 1978 Sugar
67 vs. Baylor, 1980 Cotton
64 vs. Colorado, 1991 Blockbuster
62 vs. SMU, 1983 Sun
60 vs. Penn State, 1979 Sugar
58 vs. Mississippi, 1964 Sugar
58 vs. Nebraska, 1966 Sugar
58 vs. Nebraska, 1972 Orange
57 vs. Illinois, 1982 Liberty
55 vs. Southern Cal., 1985 Aloha

Fewest Rushes
26 vs. Texas, 1964 Orange
28 vs. Texas, 1948 Sugar
29 vs. Missouri, 1968 Gator
29 vs. Miami, 1990 Sugar
33 vs. Louisville, 1991 Fiesta
35 vs. Rice, 1954 Cotton
36 vs. Army, 1988 Sun
39 vs. Penn State, 1959 Liberty
41 vs. Washington, 1986 Sun
42 vs. Texas, 1973 Cotton
42 vs. Texas A&M, 1968 Cotton

Most Yards Rushing
292 vs. Southern Cal, 1946 Rose
286 vs. Syracuse, 1953 Orange
284 vs. Arkansas, 1980 Sugar
280 vs. Ohio State, 1978 Sugar
268 vs. Illinois, 1982 Liberty
268 vs. UCLA, 1976 Liberty
251 vs. SMU, 1983 Sun
244 vs. Boston College, 1942
    Orange
241 vs. Nebraska, 1972 Orange
241 vs. Baylor, 1981 Cotton
229 vs. Oklahoma, 1970
    Bluebonnet

Fewest Yards Rushing
− 45 vs. Missouri, 1968 Gator
38 vs. Miami, 1990 Sugar
41 vs. Texas, 1948 Sugar
49 vs. Texas, 1965 Orange
59 vs. Texas A&M, 1941
    Cotton
95 vs. Army, 1988 Sun
95 vs. Louisville, 1991 Fiesta
104 vs. Penn State, 1959 Liberty
106 vs. Penn State, 1975 Sugar
135 vs. Texas A&M, 1967
    Cotton
138 vs. Texas, 1973 Cotton

Most TDs Rushing
4 vs. Syracuse, 1953 Orange
3 vs. Nebraska, 1966 Sugar
3 vs. Nebraska, 1967 Cotton
3 vs. Colorado, 1969 Liberty
3 vs. Ohio State, 1978 Sugar
3 vs. Arkansas, 1980 Sugar
3 vs. Baylor, 1981 Cotton
3 vs. SMU, 1983 Sun

Fewest TDs Rushing
0, last vs. Colorado, 1991 Blockbuster

PASSING

Most Attempts
52 vs. Army, 1988 Sun
44 vs. Texas, 1965 Orange
43 vs. Miami, 1990 Sugar
40 vs. Michigan, 1988 Hall of
    Fame
35 vs. Louisville, 1991 Fiesta
34 vs. Colorado, 1969 Liberty
34 vs. Syracuse, 1953 Orange
29 vs. Nebraska, 1966 Sugar
29 vs. Notre Dame, 1975 Orange

Fewest Attempts
7 vs. Arkansas, 1980 Sugar
8 vs. Penn State, 1959 Liberty
11 vs. Ohio State, 1978 Sugar
11 vs. UCLA, 1976 Liberty
11 vs. Ole Miss, 1964 Sugar
12 vs. Penn State, 1975 Sugar
12 vs. Baylor, 1981 Cotton
13 vs. Illinois, 1982 Liberty
13 vs. Texas, 1982 Cotton
13 vs. Nebraska, 1972 Orange

Most Completions
33 vs. Army, 1988 Sun
27 vs. Miami, 1990 Sugar
23 vs. Michigan, 1988 Hall of
    Fame
22 vs. Syracuse, 1953 Orange
20 vs. Nebraska, 1966 Orange
20 vs. Texas, 1965 Orange
15 vs. Nebraska, 1967 Sugar
15 vs. Washington, 1986 Sun
15 vs. Notre Dame, 1975 Orange

Fewest Completions
2 vs. Penn State, 1959 Liberty
3 vs. Ole Miss, 1964 Sugar
3 vs. Nebraska, 1972 Orange

373

4 vs. Arkansas, 1980 Sugar
4 vs. Texas, 1948 Sugar
5 vs. Baylor, 1981 Cotton
7 vs. Missouri, 1968 Gator
7 vs. Rice, 1954 Cotton
7 vs. Illinois, 1982 Liberty

Most Yards
412 vs. Army, 1988 Sun
300 vs. Syracuse, 1953 Orange
298 vs. Texas, 1965 Orange
296 vs. Nebraska, 1966 Sugar
279 vs. Nebraska, 1967 Sugar
269 vs. Michigan, 1988 Hall of
Fame
223 vs. Notre Dame, 1975 Orange
214 vs. Miami, 1990 Sugar
212 vs. Colorado, 1969 Liberty
210 vs. Penn State, 1975 Sugar

Fewest Yards
16 vs. Texas A&M, 1942 Cotton
27 vs. Penn State, 1959 Liberty
29 vs. Ole Miss, 1964 Sugar
47 vs. Nebraska, 1972 Orange
62 vs. Texas, 1948 Sugar
67 vs. Rice, 1954 Cotton
68 vs. Missouri, 1968 Gator
70 vs. Arkansas, 1980 Sugar
86 vs. Oklahoma, 1963 Orange
91 vs. Penn State, 1979 Sugar

Most TDs Passing
3 vs. Colorado, 1991 Blockbuster
3 vs. Miami, 1990 Sugar
3 vs. Oklahoma, 1970, Bluebonnet
3 vs. Syracuse, 1953 Orange

Fewest TDs Passing
0, last vs. Louisville, 1991

Most Had Intercepted
3 vs. Louisville, 1991 Fiesta
3 vs. Texas A&M, 1968 Cotton
2 vs. Texas, 1965 Orange
2 vs. Nebraska, 1966 Sugar
2 vs. Missouri, 1968 Gator
2 vs. Texas, 1973 Cotton
2 vs. Syracuse, 1953 Orange
2 vs. Penn State, 1979 Sugar
2 vs. Notre Dame, 1975 Orange
2 vs. Illinois, 1982 Liberty

Fewest Had Intercepted
0, last vs. Washington, 1986 Sun

Most Yards Returned
123 vs. Colorado, 1991 Blockbuster
82 vs. Syracuse, 1953 Orange
78 vs. Illinois, 1982 Liberty
64 vs. Penn State, 1979 Sugar
52 vs. Arkansas, 1980 Sugar
51 vs. Ole Miss, 1964 Sugar

Fewest Yards Returned
0, last vs. Michigan, 1988 Hall of
Fame

PUNTING

Most Punts
16 vs. Texas A&M, 1942 Cotton
10 vs. Penn State, 1979 Sugar
10 vs. Missouri, 1968 Gator
9 vs. Washington, 1986 Sun
8 several, last vs. Miami, 1990 Sugar

Fewest Punts
1 vs. Ohio State, 1978 Sugar
2 vs. UCLA, 1976 Liberty
3 vs. Syracuse, 1953 Orange
4 vs. Army, 1988 Sun
4 vs. Michigan, 1988 Hall of Fame
4 vs. Oklahoma, 1970 Bluebonnet
4 vs. Nebraska, 1967 Sugar

Most Yards
581 vs. Texas A&M, 1942 Cotton
419 vs. Missouri, 1968 Gator
412 vs. Washington, 1986 Sun
388 vs. Penn State, 1979 Sugar
324 vs. Oklahoma, 1963 Orange
322 vs. Louisville, 1991 Fiesta
306 vs. Miami, 1990 Sugar
303 vs. Nebraska, 1972 Orange

Fewest Yards
33 vs. Ohio State, 1978 Sugar
53 vs. UCLA, 1976 Liberty
90 vs. Syracuse, 1953 Orange
141 vs. Nebraska, 1967 Orange
170 vs. Michigan, 1988 Hall of Fame

Best Average
45.7 vs. Washington, 1986 Sun
45.5 vs. Army, 1988 Sun
45.2 vs. Texas, 1980 Cotton
43.4 vs. Texas, 1965 Orange
43.3 vs. Nebraska, 1972 Orange
42.7 vs. Rice, 1954 Cotton
42.5 vs. Michigan, 1988 Hall of Fame

Worst Average
29.4 vs. Texas, 1973 Cotton

31.2 vs. Nebraska, 1966 Orange
33.0 vs. Texas A&M, 1968 Cotton
34.3 vs. Penn State, 1959 Liberty
35.2 vs. Nebraska, 1967 Sugar
36.2 vs. Arkansas, 1980 Sugar
36.3 vs. Texas A&M, 1942 Cotton

PUNT RETURNS

Most Returns
6 vs. Colorado, 1991 Blockbuster
6 vs. Nebraska, 1966 Orange
6 vs. Texas, 1965 Orange
5 vs. Notre Dame, 1975 Orange
5 vs. Texas A&M, 1968 Cotton
5 vs. Syracuse, 1953 Orange

Fewest Returns
0, last vs. Louisville, 1991 Fiesta

Most Return Yards
168 vs. Syracuse, 1953 Orange
136 vs. Nebraska, 1972 Orange
74 vs. Colorado, 1991 Blockbuster
64 vs. Penn State, 1979 Sugar
50 vs. Arkansas, 1980 Sugar

Fewest Return Yards
0 vs. Louisville, 1991 Fiesta
0 vs. Missouri, 1968 Gator
2 vs. Baylor, 1981 Cotton
3 vs. Texas, 1982 Cotton

KICKOFF RETURNS

Most Kickoff Returns
8 vs. Colorado, 1969 Liberty
6 vs. Louisville, 1991 Fiesta
6 vs. Miami, 1990 Sugar
5 vs. Army, 1988 Sun
5 vs. Michigan, 1988 Hall of Fame
5 vs. Missouri, 1968 Gator

Fewest Kickoff Returns
0 vs. Nebraska, 1972 Orange
0 vs. Penn State, 1959 Liberty
1, last vs. Washington, 1989 Sun

Most Kickoff Return Yards
127 vs. Colorado, 1969 Liberty
119 vs. Army, 1988 Sun
113 vs. Oklahoma, 1970 Bluebonnet
101 vs. Miami, 1990 Sugar
89 vs. Missouri, 1968 Gator

Fewest Kickoff Return Yards
0 vs. Nebraska, 1972 Orange
0 vs. Penn State, 1959 Liberty
16 vs. Baylor, 1981 Cotton

18 vs. Penn State, 1979 Sugar
19 vs. UCLA, 1976 Liberty

MOST FIRST DOWNS

Most Total First Downs
29 vs. Army, 1988 Sun
28 vs. Nebraska, 1966 Orange
28 vs. Michigan, 1988 Hall of Fame
25 vs. Syracuse, 1953 Orange
25 vs. Ohio State, 1978 Sugar
24 vs. Colorado, 1969 Liberty
23 vs. SMU, 1983 Sun
23 vs. UCLA, 1976 Liberty

Fewest Total First Downs
1 vs. Texas A&M, 1942 Cotton
6 vs. Missouri, 1968 Gator
7 vs. Texas, 1948 Sugar
8 vs. Penn State, 1959 Liberty
10 vs. Louisville, 1991 Fiesta
10 vs. Cal., 1937 Rose
11 vs. Rice, 1954 Cotton
12 vs. Penn State, 1979 Sugar
13 vs. Washington, 1986 Sun

Most First Downs by Rush
17 vs. UCLA, 1976 Liberty
17 vs. Ohio State, 1978 Sugar
16 vs. Syracuse, 1953 Orange
14 vs. Nebraska, 1966 Orange
14 vs. USC, 1985 Aloha
14 vs. Arkansas, 1980 Sugar
13 vs. Nebraska, 1972 Orange
13 vs. SMU, 1983 Sun
13 vs. Illinois, 1983 Liberty
13 vs. Colorado, 1991 Blockbuster

Fewest First Downs by Rush
0 vs. Texas A&M, 1942 Cotton
3 vs. Miami, 1990 Sugar
3 vs. Notre Dame, 1975 Orange
3 vs. Missouri, 1968 Gator
4 vs. Texas, 1965 Orange
5 vs. Louisville, 1991 Fiesta
5 vs. Army, 1988 Sun
5 vs. Texas A&M, 1968 Cotton

Most First Downs by Passing
23 vs. Army, 1988 Sun
18 vs. Michigan, 1988 Hall of Fame
14 vs. Texas, 1965 Orange
12 vs. Nebraska, 1966 Orange
11 vs. Notre Dame, 1975 Orange
10 vs. Miami, 1990 Sugar
10 vs. Oklahoma, 1970 Bluebonnet

Fewest First Downs by Passing
1 vs. Ole Miss, 1964 Sugar
1 vs. Texas A&M, 1942 Cotton
2 vs. Missouri, 1968 Gator
3 vs. Arkansas, 1980 Sugar
3 vs. Penn State, 1979 Sugar
3 vs. USC, 1985 Aloha
3 vs. Nebraska, 1972 Orange

Most First Downs by Penalty
4 vs. Miami, 1990 Sugar
4 vs. Colorado, 1969 Liberty
3 vs. SMU, 1983 Sun
3 vs. Texas A&M, 1968 Cotton
3 vs. Nebraska, 1966 Orange

Fewest First Downs by Penalty
0, last vs. Colorado, 1991
    Blockbuster

FUMBLES

Most Fumbles
10 vs. Ohio State, 1978 Sugar
7 vs. Penn State, 1959 Liberty
6 vs. Ole Miss, 1964 Sugar
5 vs. Texas A&M, 1968 Cotton
5 vs. Nebraska, 1972 Orange
5 vs. Baylor, 1981 Cotton
5 vs. Notre Dame, 1975 Orange

Fewest Fumbles
0, last vs. Miami, 1990 Sugar

Most Fumbles Lost
4 vs. Rice, 1954 Cotton
4 vs. Penn State, 1959 Liberty
3 vs. Illinois, 1982 Liberty

Fewest Fumbles Lost
0, last vs. Miami, 1990 Sugar

PENALTIES

Most Penalties
10 vs. USC, 1985 Aloha
8 vs. Nebraska, 1966 Orange
8 vs. Texas A&M, 1942 Cotton
7 vs. Louisville, 1991 Fiesta
7 vs. Army, 1988 Sun
7 vs. Arkansas, 1980 Sugar
7 vs. Oklahoma, 1970 Bluebonnet

Fewest Penalties
1 vs. Washington, 1986 Sun
1 vs. Texas, 1982 Cotton
1 vs. Ohio State, 1978 Sugar
1 vs. Notre Dame, 1975 Orange
1 vs. Oklahoma, 1963 Orange

Most Penalty Yards
93 vs. USC, 1985 Aloha
89 vs. Baylor, 1981 Cotton
81 vs. Texas A&M, 1942 Cotton
75 vs. Penn State, 1979 Sugar
65 vs. Rice, 1954 Cotton
62 vs. Nebraska, 1966 Orange

INDIVIDUAL RECORDS

Longest Punt Return
80 by Hootie Ingram vs. Syracuse,
    1953 Orange
72 by Jimmy Nelson vs. Texas
    A&M, 1942 Cotton
62 by Lou Ikners vs. Penn State,
    1979 Sugar
52 by David Palmer vs. Colorado,
    1991 Blockbuster
50 by Major Ogilvie vs. Arkansas,
    1980 Sugar

Longest Interception Return
75 by Hugh Morrow vs. Duke,
    1945 Sugar
60 by Buster Hill vs. Syracuse,
    1953 Orange
49 by Charles Gardner vs. Louis-

ville, 1991 Fiesta
49 by Mark McMillen vs.
    Colorado, 1991 Blockbuster
44 by Barry Krauss vs. UCLA,
    1976 Liberty
42 by Mike Clements vs. Penn
    State, 1979 Sugar
38 by Donnie Sutton vs. Missouri,
    1968 Gator

Most Points Scored in a Game
19 by Bobby Luna vs. Syracuse,
    1953 Orange (2 TDs, 7 PATs)
18 by Bobby Humphrey vs.
    Washington 1986 Sun (3 TDs)
12 by several, last by David Palmer
    vs. Colorado, 1991 Blockbuster

RUSHING

Most Attempts
28 by Bobby Humphrey vs.
Washington, 1986 Sun
28 by Ricky Moore vs. SMU, 1983
Sun
27 by Bobby Humphrey vs.
Michigan, 1988 Hall of Fame
27 by Johnny Musso vs. Oklahoma,
1970 Bluebonnet
26 by Siran Stacy vs. Colorado,
1991 Blockbuster
24 by Johnny Davis vs. Ohio State,
1978 Sugar

Most Yards Rushing
159 by Bobby Humphrey vs.
Washington, 1986 Sun
149 by Bobby Humphrey vs.
Michigan, 1988 Hall of Fame
138 by Johnny Musso vs.
Oklahoma, 1979 Bluebonnet
127 by Tony Nathan vs. Penn State,
1979 Sugar
120 by Wilbur Jackson vs.
Arkansas, 1980 Sugar
116 by Harry Gilmer vs. USC,
1946 Rose
113 by Ricky Moore vs. SMU,
1983 Sun

Most Touchdowns Rushing
2 by several, last by Bobby
Humphrey vs. Michigan, 1988
Hall of Fame

Longest Rushing Touchdown
67 by Dixie Howell vs. Stanford,
1935 Rose
64 by Bobby Humphrey vs.
Washington, 1986 Sun
43 by Monk Campbell vs.
Washington State, 1931 Rose
40 by Bobby Jenkins vs. Boston
College, 1943 Orange
38 by Bobby Luna vs. Syracuse,
1953 Orange

PASSING

Most Passes Attempted
52 by David Smith vs. Army, 1988
Sun
43 by Gary Hollingsworth vs.
Miami, 1990 Sugar
40 by Jeff Dunn vs. Michigan,
1988 Hall of Fame

37 by Scott Hunter vs. Missouri,
1968 Gator
37 by Joe Namath vs. Texas, 1965
Orange

Most Passes Completed
33 by David Smith vs. Army, 1988
Sun
27 by Gary Hollingsworth vs.
Miami, 1990 Sugar
23 by Jeff Dunn vs. Michigan,
1988 Hall of Fame
20 by Steve Sloan vs. Nebraska,
1966 Orange
15 by Mike Shula vs. Washington,
1986 Sun

Most Yards Passing
296 by Steve Sloan vs. Nebraska,
1966 Orange
207 by Clell Hobson vs. Syracuse,
1953 Orange

Best Completion Percentage
1,000 by Harry Gilmer vs. Duke
(8-8), 1945 Sugar
.833 by Richard Todd vs. Penn
State (10-12), 1975 Sugar

Longest Pass Completion
61, Johnny Cain to John Suther vs.
Washington, 1931 Rose
59, Dixie Howell to Don Hutson
vs. Stanford, 1935 Rose
59, Grant Gillis to J. M. Brown vs.
Washington, 1926 Rose
55, Neb Hayden, to Griff Langston
vs. Colorado, 1969 Liberty
55, Richard Todd to Ozzie
Newsome vs. Penn State, 1975
Sugar
54, Joe Riley to Don Hutson vs.
Stanford, 1935 Rose
50, Clell Hobson to Corky Tharp
vs. Syracuse, 1953 Orange

RECEIVING

Most Receptions
9 by Marco Battle vs. SMU, 1988
Sun
9 by Greg Payne vs. SMU, 1988
Sun
8 by Joe Curtis (65 yards) vs. Syracuse, 1953 Orange
6 by Howard Cross vs. Michigan,
1988 Hall of Fame

6 by Clay Whitehurst vs. Michigan,
1988 Hall of Fame

6 by Ozzie Newsome vs. Notre
Dame, 1975 Orange

Most Yards Receiving
178 by Ray Perkins vs. Nebraska,
1967 Sugar

126 by Russ Schamun vs. Notre
Dame, 1975 Sugar

107 by Greg Payne vs. Army, 1988
Sun

KICKOFF RETURNS

Most Kickoff Returns
5 by Willie Shelby vs. Notre Dame,
1975 Sugar

4 by Robert McKinney vs.
Nebraska, 1972 Orange

4 by Willie Shelby vs. Penn State,
1975 Sugar

Longest Kickoff Return
62 by Lou Ikner vs. Penn State,
1979 Sugar

61 by Joey Jones vs. Texas, 1982
Cotton

34 by Joe Carter vs. SMU, 1983
Sun

FIELD GOALS

Most Attempts
5 by Tim Davis vs. Ole Miss, 1964
Sugar

3 by Philip Doyle vs. Army, 1988
Sun

3 by Peter Kim vs. Baylor, 1981
Cotton

Most Made
4 by Tim Davis vs. Ole Miss, 1964
Sugar

3 by Philip Doyle vs. Army, 1988
Sun

3 by Peter Kim vs. Baylor, 1981
Cotton

Longest Field Goal
51 by Philip Doyle vs. Michigan,
1988 Hall of Fame

50 by Bill Davis vs. Texas, 1973
Cotton

48 by Van Tiffin vs. Southern Cal,
1985 Aloha

48 by Tim Davis vs. Ole Miss,
1964 Sugar

46 by Tim Davis vs. Ole Miss,
1964 Sugar

45 by Philip Doyle vs. Miami,
1990 Sugar

42 by Peter Kim vs. Baylor, 1981
Cotton

40 by Tim Davis vs. Nebraska,
1967 Sugar

INTERCEPTIONS

Most Interceptions
3 by Jeremiah Castille vs. Illinois,
1982 Liberty

2 by Kermit Kendrick vs.
Washington, 1986 Sun

2 by Steve Wade vs. Texas, 1983
Cotton

Most Interception Yards
49 by Charles Gardner vs.
Louisville, 1991 Fiesta

49 by Mark McMillan vs.
Colorado, 1991 Blockbuster

44 by Barry Krauss vs. UCLA,
1976 Liberty

42 by Steve Wade vs. Texas, 1972
Cotton

38 by Donnie Sutton vs. Missouri,
1968 Gator

Longest Interception Return
75 by Hugh Morrow (TD) vs.
Duke, 1945 Sugar

60 by Buster Hill (TD) vs.
Syracuse, 1953 Orange

44 by Barry Krauss vs. UCLA,
1976 Liberty

PUNTING

Most Punts
10 by Woody Umphrey (388 yards)
vs. Penn State, 1979 Sugar

9 by Chris Mohr (412 yards) vs.
Washington, 1986 Sun

8 by Tank Williamson (322 yards)
vs. Penn State, 1979 Sugar

8 by Bill Smith (306 yards) vs.
Miami, 1990 Sugar

Most Yards
412 by Chris Mohr (9 punts) vs.
Washington, 1986 Sun

388 by Woody Umphrey (10 punts)
vs. Penn State, 1979 Sugar
322 by Tank Williamson (8 punts)
vs. Louisville, 1991 Fiesta
306 by Bill Smith (8 punts) vs.
Miami, 1990 Sugar

Best Average
45.7 by Chris Mohr (9 for 412) vs.
Washington, 1986 Sun
45.5 by Chris Mohr (4 for 182) vs.
Army, 1988 Sun
43.5 by Greg Gantt (7 for 303) vs.
Nebraska, 1972 Orange
43.4 by Buddy French (5 for 217)
vs. Texas, 1965 Orange
42.7 by Malcolm Simmons (4 for
171) vs. Texas, 1982 Cotton
42.7 by Bart Starr (7 for 299) vs.
Rice, 1954 Cotton

PUNT RETURNS

Most Returns
6 by David Palmer vs. Colorado,
1991 Blockbuster
5 by Willie Shelby vs. Notre Dame,
1975 Sugar
4 by Willie Shelby vs. Penn State,
1975 Sugar
4 by Robert McKinney vs.
Nebraska, 1972 Orange

Most Yards
74 by David Palmer vs. Colorado,
1991 Blockbuster
65 by Lou Ikner vs. Penn State,
1979 Sugar
51 by Tony Nathan vs. Ohio State,
1978 Sugar
50 by Major Ogilvie vs. Arkansas,
1980 Sugar

Longest Punt Return
80 by Cecil Ingram (TD) vs. Syracuse, 1953 Orange
72 by Jimmie Nelson (TD) vs.
Texas A&M, 1942 Cotton
62 by Lou Ikner vs. Penn State,
1979 Sugar

How the "Crimson Tide" Got Its Name

In early newspaper accounts of Alabama football the team was listed simply as the "varsity" or the "Crimson White" after the school colors. First nickname to become popular and to be used by the headline writers of the era was the "Thin Red Line." This cognomen was first employed during the coaching regime of J. W. H. Pollard, between 1906 and 1909. Dr. Pollard, now living in Groveland, Mass., credits Hugh Roberts, former sports editor of the Birmingham *Age-Herald,* as the originator of the name. "Crimson Tide" supplanted the "Thin Red Line" as Alabama's nickname either during the 1917 or 1919 season. It was used in a student paper headline in November 1919, but Birmingham papers used the term earlier. Zipp Newman, sports editor of the Birmingham *News,* probably popularized the name more than any other writer.

Al Browning is a native of Brewton, Alabama, and a graduate of the University of Alabama. In 1973 he began a sports writing career at The Tuscaloosa News, *from which he resigned in 1982 to become the personal assistant to Paul "Bear" Bryant, a position he held until Coach Bryant's death in January 1983. A former sports editor, he is now managing partner of Five Points Productions in Birmingham, Alabama.*